INTRINSIC SUSTAINABLE DEVELOPMENT

Epistemes, Science, Business and Sustainability

INTRINSIC SUSTAINABLE DEVELOPMENT

Epistemes, Science, Business and Sustainability

Frank Birkin

Sheffield University, UK

Thomas Polesie

Gothenburg University, Sweden

World Scientific

NEW JERSEY · LONDON · SINGAPORE · BEIJING · SHANGHAI · HONG KONG · TAIPEI · CHENNAI

Published by

World Scientific Publishing Co. Pte. Ltd.

5 Toh Tuck Link, Singapore 596224

USA office: 27 Warren Street, Suite 401-402, Hackensack, NJ 07601

UK office: 57 Shelton Street, Covent Garden, London WC2H 9HE

British Library Cataloguing-in-Publication Data
A catalogue record for this book is available from the British Library.

INTRINSIC SUSTAINABLE DEVELOPMENT
Epistemes, Science, Business and Sustainability

ISBN-13 978-981-4365-00-0
ISBN-10 981-4365-00-9

Typeset by Stallion Press
Email: enquiries@stallionpress.com

Printed in Singapore.

Contents

vi   *Contents*

PART II: Modern Times   **111**

Chapter 5   Passive Nature   **113**

Chapter 6   Modern Knowledge   **131**

Chapter 7   Square-Peg Business   **161**

PART III: Primal Knowledge   **195**

Chapter 8   Breaking Free   **197**

Contents   vii

viii   *Contents*

Preface

This book started as a treatise about new and more sustainable forms of business. It first attempted this from inside the business world itself — as so many other books have done before. What is so very different about this book is that it reverses the approach; we stepped outside the business world, outside the social world, and into a world of realities now described by science. We finished with a book that looks at business, at our institutions and at ourselves from a world that is emerging around us as we write.

The new world that we describe has massive consequences for how we conduct business, the forms that our social institutions take and for ourselves, living quietly or noisily through day-to-day lives. This new world is a world of knowledge and it changes everything in the human sphere from global development policy down to our attitudes to nature, to other people and to our own selves.

Technically the book uses an analysis of epistemes, those unacknowledged ways in which we order knowledge. Michel Foucault became famous for his analyses of epistemes.

Our role as authors has not been to bring about or create a change of episteme but has been to observe, interpret and report. Foucault regarded himself as a kind of archeologist who unearthed past epistemes in European culture to reveal their ancient forms and consequences; we do the same kind of thing, but we have unearthed something Foucault could not have found. We have unearthed a sequel to the Modern episteme which did not exist during Foucault's lifetime.

This book is written within the emerging episteme. It is does not use a Modern form of analysis: it is more like a novel. It describes things which have happened sequentially and holistically because the emerging order of knowledge is historically dependent upon past events with all their uncertainties, complexities and diversities.

The result is a set of ideas with the potential to affect everyone. It is a book for anyone with an intellectual curiosity and a desire to help resolve the big problems that afflict our planet.

This book does not have all the answers. A new episteme sets a new agenda, a new ordering of knowledge and thought — just what this means in practice is something for us all to decide.

We invite readers to consider the fresh view of an ancient simplicity that this book provides; and then to apply this vision imaginatively, creatively and practically to our institutions and lives, for the betterment of all.

Summary of Contents

The book has twelve chapters arranged in four parts as follows.

Part I – Approach The four chapters of part I introduce the book's key ideas that weave through subsequent chapters. Some of these key ideas relate to our relations with nature, change and openness in societies, ancient China, science, innovation, business and entrepreneurs.

Part II – Modern Times It is in this part that the origins of the Modern episteme are examined both by using Foucault's method and by developing our own studies. Part II is not only of historical interest; the Modern episteme is still with us and we need to be aware of it so that we may follow its eclipse and recognize change as it happens.

Part III – Primal Knowledge This part presents evidence for the emerging episteme which we have called "Primal". Other part III chapters review the consequences of the Primal episteme for an informed and *wise* person as well as for *intrinsically* sustainable business.

Part IV – Consequences The single chapter of this part considers more consequences of a new episteme, in particular for those who support such a change and those who do not.

Finally, it is important to stress that a change of episteme is not prescriptive. It may be unavoidable, but it is also liberating - for those who know what is going on.

Acknowledgments

This book has benefitted from the assistance of a great many people from all quarters of the world and of life. We are indebted to them all.

In particular we would like to thank Ann Birkin who has always subscribed to the emerging episteme whether she knew it or not. We also thank Liu Zhen, Olga Wernemyr and Mike Norman for lending just a little of themselves to characters in this book.

PART I

APPROACH

CHAPTER 1 — JUST BUSINESS

Attitudes

Fifty years ago, a child ran with amazement along the canal tow-paths in Middleport at the heart of the Potteries in the UK. At that time, there were still working-canals and in the eyes of that child, the bargees who came to deliver flints and kaolin to the ceramic industry were larger than life figures from another world. In contrast to the dull smoke-black, back-to-back houses squeezed in between the old, numerous and high-walled ceramic factories or "pot-banks", the bargees had decorated their barges and buckets, poles, plant pots, dishes, mugs and anything else at hand with extravagant floral designs, brief sayings or just blocks, bands and flourishes of the most vivid contrasting colours. Too small and shy to communicate with these demigods riding their stately "water-home-businesses", the boy could only watch with wonder as the sun-tanned bargees travelled out through industrial horizons of slag-heaps, firms, steel mills, noise, smoke and fire into the world unknown. The boy had no access to a working knowledge of nature that had supported mankind, and all other species, throughout many millennia. Instead his lot would depend on what he could learn from the society and culture into which he had been born. In his case on the skills, knowledge, aptitudes and dedication he could bring to making "pots" or mining, i.e., serving business in man-made processes.

A hundred years before that particular boy had been born, it was known that Potteries people were not healthy. In 1842, James Till was 43 years old and in poor health, as were many of the small, undernourished, pale, grimy "pot-bank" workers of the time. James had worked in the ceramic industry all his life. He reported to the Children's Employment Commission (Part II, 1842) just how he had managed to survive that long: "I have been a dipper 26 years... The

3

4   *Intrinsic Sustainable Development*

liquid used is not bad now as it used to be; there is, however, a great deal of lead used as well as arsenic. It has often affected me, but not to the excess that it has some men. I live very regularly; I keep myself regular, never giving way to intemperance, as some men. I ascribe nothing to myself in this respect, but to a higher source. The way in which it attacks us is first in the bowels and stomach. I take care to take medicine occasionally; I suffer now from some affection of the liver; if it was not induced by dipping; it is certainly aggravated by it..." Victorian society and its institutions had effectively condemned James to a life of sickness and early death.

But the boy by the canal was lucky. His society had provided him with the opportunity to obtain a university education and to keep his health. For whilst the plight of James Till and of his thousands of unknown colleagues had been addressed by many and significant improvements to working conditions and housing in Stoke-on-Trent, life expectancy in the Potteries remained low by national UK standards in the 1950's with infant mortality and premature deaths from heart disease and lung cancer at stubbornly high-levels at the close of the twentieth century.

The child grew up, acquired knowledge of this and that, but always remembered and thought about his past. What the older boy had experienced in his earliest years remained to inform his understanding and influence his interpretations. During his school years, he could feel empathy for those who suffered and this led to anger. At the same time, he felt disgust for those who caused suffering, but such moments became increasingly rare. There were also times when he imagined that there were no good people who could benefit from creating or supporting the kind of social institutions that inflicted such hardship on others, that anyone not somehow belittled, limited or reduced in a suffering world was guilty of at least negligence if not compliance if they did not actively work to stop such activities. Only in later life when he came to take stock of his own complicity did he come to appreciate that the world was far too complicated for such judgemental simplicity.

When the older boy left the Potteries, he travelled the world going far beyond any horizons that the bargees are likely to have known. He spent much time in East Africa, where the world had begun for mankind. There he noted the hardships of tribal life as well as its colour and vigour. He still remembers the Masaai with bright "barge" reds and yellows in their extravagant bead-work decorations and the tight unyielding grip of an elderly Masaai woman dark-brown, gaunt and desperate among the red brick-hard mud and cattle-skeletons of a water-hole during a draught. He gained a little sense of what the truly wild was like in its dangers, its meaning and value for people, the determination of life to make something, even celebrations, out of the bare minimum of resources and, through his reading and observations, some knowledge of the astonishing complexity of relations that maintains life in an intricate and uncertain balance on our planet.

The boy has now grown old. More recently he has been to China. He notes the warmth of the Chinese people and their large number of social links, their personal relations going from the extended family into distant "guanxi" bonds; the number of such links enjoyed by each Chinese person seems to be rivalled only by the variety of their foods. Primary colours, bright reds and yellows, persist in China as does a deep-seated sense of beauty and order or "harmony" which is the defining concept of ancient China, as old as China itself, and is instantiated in the structures of the Forbidden Palace in Beijing.

The older boy has also acquired a technical education, an accountant's view of the world. He is pleased to note that the Chinese rate of economic growth is close to a miracle since it has vastly improved the lives of many people so that in 2003 the per capita annual Gross Domestic Product (GDP) in China exceeded $US1,000 for the first time. China's GDP is now 4 times larger than that of 1980. It has lifted more than 250 million Chinese out of poverty, i.e., almost more than four times the population of the UK or just over 80% of the population of the USA have been lifted out of poverty in just over 20 years. This is what business can do.

6   *Intrinsic Sustainable Development*

This is indeed something to applaud. This is worthy of the bright colours of the bargees, of the Masaai and of the Chinese themselves; a celebration of life and human ingenuity and of social institutions that work so very effectively to help the most needy. It is a powerful message of hope for all the world's poor (In 2005, 36% of the total population of the Least Developed Countries lived on less than $1 a day whilst 76% existed on less than $2 a day (UNCTAD, 2008)). The future for mankind's poor looked brighter.

But the suffering of the poor in Africa and China is real and immediate for the older boy who remembers the world of his childhood. It was as if the Chinese had recreated in just a few years the harsh, inhuman, disabling conditions of industry in Victorian England. China has lost 7–20% of its GDP per year to pollution and other environmental damage in the last 20 years with 10 billion Euros being lost in 1992 alone. Of 412 test sites on China's seven main rivers in 2004, 58% of them were monitored to be too dirty for human consumption; of the 20 most polluted cities in the world, 16 are Chinese; and an estimated 30% of China's cropland is suffering from acidification at an estimated cost of $US13 billion (Nierenberg, 2006, p. 7).

Many Chinese suffered and a smaller number benefitted. This was also true of Africa and of the world in general. But the older boy now identified himself as one of the world's beneficiaries. He had security, enough food, clothes and many other goods and he had the free time to enjoy himself on vacation. But the ongoing suffering of others was something he had not wanted.

Nor do many of the other global "beneficiaries" want suffering to continue. They do what they can to prevent it, but the suffering continues. Sometimes without knowing it, they make the situation worse. Sometimes they make more problems than they solve. Sometimes it seems as if they can do nothing right. The older boy worried about doing the right thing for many years; there are many people who promote their "solutions" in technology, economics and social systems and the older boy considered these. But at the end of the day, technology, economics and social systems had created the world in which we live; these could not in themselves provide the answers he sought. The older boy could not get away from the simple understanding of the child running along the canal bank. The world in which he had to live was made by people, and it had to be how they related to the world that gave life and meaning to what they did; it had to do with attitude.

Origins

One of the first memories that the older boy can recall is of the child standing beside his mother waiting for a bus home. It must have been in the early 1950's and they had stood outside the Leopard Hotel in Burslem, one of the five Pottery towns of Stoke-on-Trent and once a pioneering, major manufacturing centre during the early days of the great British industrial revolution that has transformed the world.

The Leopard Hotel has been in continuous use as a public house since at least 1765. This fact is established by Josiah Wedgwood, founder of the Wedgwood ceramic company, a pioneer of the industrial revolution. Josiah's correspondence reveals that he dined at the Leopard Hotel in March 1765 with James Brindley, the master canal-builder. The two were planning the construction of a new canal to connect the Potteries to the Rivers Trent and Mersey. This was needed since the Potteries of Stoke-on-Trent desperately needed a better means of carrying their fragile ware to market other than the trains of mules then in use. In 1766, Josiah Wedgwood cut the first sod for the construction of the canal and Brindley carried it away in a wheelbarrow.

Wedgwood was born in Burslem the Potteries town that sits on a hill overlooking Middleport. As a boy, he had had a bout of small-pox that left him with a weakened knee. This misfortune was to be the making of a great industrialist for the weak knee meant that he could not work the foot-peddle of the "potter's wheel" and hence he had to abandon the usual apprenticeship and turn his attention to designing rather than making ware. He was very good at his new job and in 1759 he established the Josiah Wedgwood Company which still existed within the Waterford Crystal Group to celebrate a 250th anniversary in 2009.

8   *Intrinsic Sustainable Development*

Josiah Wedgwood (1730–1795) could have been called an "entrepreneur" in his day; the term having been coined by Richard Cantillon (1680–1734), the Irish economics theorist. Josiah was a dedicated perfectionist, experimenting for example with over three thousand samples to develop the "Poland Blue" glaze. He was also notably irascible during tours of his factory when his personal "quality control" generated much emotional heat as defective ware was smashed on the shop floor. But Josiah's unflinching obsession with glaze established Wedgwood as a market leader and that level of quality endures in the culture of the firm to this day. But the man's focus and determination had effects beyond the creation of fine table-ware.

Josiah was a great industrialist, important scientist, humanitarian, opportunist and "lunatick". His factory in Stoke-on-Trent sold wares to Queen Charlotte of England. He was one the handful of Englishmen who could be said to be founders of the Industrial Revolution that changed the world. As a scientist, his studies of better ways of assessing kiln temperature with a pyrometer, his new invention, earned him membership of the prestigious Royal Society in 1783.

But it was Josiah the humanitarian who responded to William Fox's 1791 anti-slavery pamphlet, *An address to the People of Great Britain on the propriety of abstaining from West India sugar and rum*. Josiah suggested that the appeal of the pamphlet could be further enhanced with the advertisement on the title page being replaced by the emblem of the Society for the Abolition of Slavery. Josiah had a wood-cut made of this emblem and produced it as a jasper-ware cameo in his pottery factory. This emblem contains the world famous design of a kneeling man in chains above the slogan "Am I not a man and a brother?" He mass produced these cameos which also served as the seal for the Society for the Abolition of the Slave Trade and had them widely distributed. In 1788, a consignment of Wedgewood's cameos was shipped to Benjamin Franklin in Philadelphia. They were there worn as bracelets and hair ornaments, and inlaid with gold as ornaments for snuff boxes as the anti-slavery movement became fashionable.

Josiah's opportunism was the basis for a major break-through for the fledgling Wedgwood Company when they became the first firm in eighteenth century England to copy the exquisite Chinese tea-services which used a fine mix of bone china typically decorated with blue and white designs. Josiah took from the ancient legacy of Chinese ceramic masters. New kiln-firing skills in China had brought about a ceramic age in the Han dynasty (206 B.C.–220 A.D.) to make the production of fine-glaze ware commonplace and the Tang dynasty (616–906 A.D.) introduced blue and white wares but by the end of the Yuan dynasty (1280–1367) and the beginning of the Ming dynasty (1368–1643) these wares were generally of a poor quality, possibly due to a shortage of cobalt. It was during Yung Lo's reign (1403–1424), that Chinese techniques improved and their wares attained the famous refined white-body and rich blue decoration. Wedgwood reproduced these ancient Chinese skills and his own UK industry flourished; royalties were not paid.

As an active member of the Lunar Society, an informal learned society of prominent English industrialists and natural philosophers, Josiah earned the nickname "lunatick". Their meetings were held in Birmingham on nights when a full moon would make journeys home easier and safer on dark roads lacking street lighting. As exceptional thinkers looking to the future, their nickname's pun on "lunatics" did not escape their attention!

Josiah had been a huge force for good, but he also helped create the world into which the child running along the canal side had been born; a world that had caused so much human suffering. Josiah could have done much better in another society with different attitudes, values and institutions.

It is the case that Wedgwood had lived during a pivotal moment in history (perhaps we all live so?), and he had enjoyed more than his share of luck but his life-line also reveals his enormous personal capacity for knowledge, genuine human concern and egregious vision. This man did accumulate great personal wealth, but it would be incorrect to think that money had been his prime motivation; his many diverse achievements reveal that much. Josiah's exceptional

"Human Momentum" had been as complex as it had been powerful, but it could have been very different.

Within the shadow cast by Josiah's work we find the suffering of people such as James Till and a degraded environment, the same degradation was experienced over a century later by the child by the canal. Josiah's great legacy, the furthering of the Industrial Revolution, has changed the world and many millions of people enjoy its prosperity. But the shadow cast by the work of Josiah and his associates has grown to encompass China and the rest of the world.

Karl Marx (1818–1883) is of course famous for casting light within this shadow. He made use of that selfsame 1863 publication of the Children Employment Commission in his case against Capitalism; notably reporting a Stoke-on-Trent doctor's comments that each successive generation of pottery workers is dwarfed and less robust than the previous.

Less systematically, but more dramatically, John Ruskin that greatest of all Victorian Englishmen had this to say about the shadow of the industrial revolution:

> "Gentlemen of England, if ever you would have your country breathe the pure air of heaven again, and receive again a soul into her body instead of a rotting carcase, blown up in the belly with carbonic acid (and *great* that way), you must think, and feel, for your England, as well as fight for her: you must teach her that all the true greatness she ever had, she won while her fields were green, and her faces ruddy; and that greatness is still possible for Englishmen, even though the ground be not hollow under their feet, nor the sky black over their heads."
>
> *The Crown of Wild Olive, lecture III, 123-4 (1866)*

The work of reformers such as Marx and Ruskin and countless millions of others has helped to take much of the suffering away from many people. But we do not want to develop a future world in which reformers are required; no more than we should plan for an unhealthy or litigious world for the advancement of doctors and lawyers. We should plan to have a world that can celebrate without reservation and with confidence and heartfelt meaning just as the bargees,

Masaai and ancient Chinese tried to do. To do that we need to better understand where we are coming from, to better understand our origins.

Survival

For our own modern times, evolution provides the sweeping basis for scientific explanations of origins and survival. Evolution as a concept is found at many levels from the individual to the collective and the conceptual. In biology, evolution is value free; it does not necessarily mean improvements. But when applied specifically to mankind, evolution does often imply some kind of improvement, but this is merely a reflection of the hubris of a self-aware species.

For many members of our own species, *Homo sapiens*, their evolution and survival is of the conceptual kind. This means that it is not a new physical form of *Homo sapiens* that is anticipated or fostered for survival but it is the form of the concepts that *Homo sapiens* holds to be true, or rather *truer*. Some members of *Homo sapiens* put forward arguments that the world needs more people like Josiah Wedgwood, more entrepreneurs, to create more businesses and extend the developed world so that we may generate enough wealth to rid the world of poverty and establish robust, efficient production facilities and markets for the benefit of all peoples of the world; thereby reducing suffering. This has to be the case because many influential members of *Homo sapiens* no longer depend directly on nature and her resources for their survival but upon intermediary, socially-constructed institutions. From here on, such institutions are referred to as business.

Business may seem sometimes to have its own, independent evolutionary and survival processes, but it is actually the case that it is no more and no less a concept held to be true by members of the species *Homo sapiens*. Consequently businesses are governed by the knowledge, values and attitudes of these members, by people.

Josiah Wedgwood, the entrepreneur, is identified here as a good example of an individual with an attitude appropriate for business evolution and survival. To achieve what he did could not have been easy. Victorian society did not readily support entrepreneurs. Victorian entrepreneurs may have had the world at their feet but they and Victorian society had to establish the institutional infrastructure and rewards for entrepreneurial activities. Their initiatives endure to this day.

Wealth measured in monetary terms and free markets are examples of the kind of institutions thought to be appropriate for entrepreneurs. Indeed the "freedom" in free markets is nothing less than the recognition that entrepreneurs should be allowed to do what they want, within legal and moral boundaries, to gain monetary wealth. At a more specific level of analysis, the limited company is another example of an institution suitable for entrepreneurs for this creates a conceptual entity that reworks different classes of monetary wealth to make them increase in size. It is a prime occupation of the legal system to formalise these concepts and institutions so that they may acquire a more than ephemeral intellectual and social identity.

Monetary wealth is sufficiently removed from the real world to stand alone as a regal, universalising concept overseeing business and for which all resources, benefits and values are mere subjects in attendance. Money is king in the business world and as such it rules all that business people handle, use, value and know. "Commodification" has been identified as a process by which all things are converted into commodities for market transactions and this is inevitable given the monetary lens through which modern business people necessarily see the world. All that is known and imagined by modern business people may be summoned to attend the court of King Money to be dressed in those numbers so familiar to the monarch. Money, like a king's seal, can stamp its mark on all that we know.

Free markets are argued by some to be the *sine qua non* of flourishing trade and business activities. Proponents of free markets argue that by removing government interventions in markets and thereby encouraging untrammelled market activity particularly between nations, competition will force individual businesses to improve their performance so that ultimately only fit and strong companies survive. In the USA for example, government subsidies paid to protect farmers for rice, milk, sugar, cotton, peanuts and tobacco production are argued to work against free markets and hence against free-market business operations and therefore against the long-term survival interests of Americans as consumers, producers, taxpayers, and citizens.

But as they stand, the concepts of monetary wealth, free markets and their legal substantiations are heartless constructions of a business. They are mere shells, hollow entities, empty containers without function, aspiration or emotion. They do give form and substance to the major part of any business entity, but they are not alive. The source of life for a business entity is an institution existing at the micro-level of analysis, within individual businesses themselves; it is the Return on Capital Employed (ROCE).

The ROCE is the beating heart of a company. In technical terms, it is a simple accounting equation that is familiar to us all. The "return" is the benefit or gain we obtain for making use of resources, the "capital employed". When we put £100 into a savings account, this is the capital employed. When at the end of 12 months, the bank or building society pays £6.5, or 6.5% p.a., interest on our investment, this is the "return". This is the intrinsic process that generates a business living "pulse".

But since a business is a mere concept, ROCE would be an impractical, intellectual exercise if it did not capture the aspirations and emotions of those holders of the business concepts. It is the case that ROCE does capture the hearts of people and it can do so modestly for such as granny's savings in a building society, or with much hard work such as trawler-men with their mortgages, and very grandly for global companies such as Microsoft or venture capitalists in nanotechnology and e-commerce.

Free markets do provide a means of enhancing the capability of a company to satisfy customers and money is the universal medium for measurement in business, but ultimately it is a company's ROCE that provides a basis for its survival. Those companies that do not make efficient use of resources in meeting customer needs give way to those that generate better returns for their investments, that do meet customer needs more efficiently, that do have positive monetary flows; in other words to those companies that better fit the specifications of the business institutional world.

It is not unreasonable to imagine that the concept of success attributable to better-fitting companies, and hence "survival of the fittest", would appeal to successful entrepreneurs such as Josiah Wedgwood. There is something of the personal dedication, the constant awareness of the need to improve, the pressing desire to lead in the market place and the nagging need to make constant efficient use of resources that is captured in these words. It also helps to defend entrepreneurial methods against critics. Wealth, power and success *per se* attract criticism from the less successful and having an explanation that reaches beyond human envy to provide a deep-seated justification for entrepreneurial activity is also perhaps a necessary social institution, a legitimation mechanism, and "survival of the fittest" does just that. There is also the powerful possibility that "survival of the fittest" in business might just reflect something recognised as real in the wider world, something of Charles Darwin's evolutionary theory.

Like it or not, something of the concept "survival of the fittest" has embedded itself inside popular understanding of businesses in free market economies as well as in the mechanisms of evolution. Thereby the expression as used in business becomes much more than an optional concept about which we may have a decision to make and implement for example to get rid of it. By seeking an association with the natural world, the business concept of "survival of the fittest" can move to the background, become hidden, taken for granted, an unspoken but necessary condition that is well known to be widespread, robust and enduring in both human and natural worlds.

The expression "survival of the fittest" was used by Charles Darwin, but it was not his idea. A British philosopher, Herbert Spencer (1820–1903), first thought it. Spencer was a sub-editor on the free-trade journal *The Economist* when he published his book *Social Statics, or The Conditions essential to Happiness specified, and the First of them Developed*. This is a book about free markets but, as you may appreciate from the book's title, Spencer also wanted to say something more universal about the human condition. It was perhaps inevitable that his work would include evolution, an emerging theory in his time and one in which Spencer's personal life was deeply embedded.

Spencer was born in Derby and in later life he served as secretary to the Derby Philosophical Society, a scientific society which had been founded in the 1790's by Charles Darwin's grandfather, Erasmus Darwin. The intellectual inheritance bequeathed to Victorian England by Erasmus was considerable and is worth considering as an example of both the wide-scope and population-smallness of the Victorian intellectual world. Erasmus Darwin was a co-founder of the "Lunar Society" that Josiah Wedgwood was to eventually attend; in the book *Zoönomia, the Organic Laws of Life* (1818), Erasmus put down early ideas on evolution that were to be more fully developed by his famous grandson; the Lichfield Botanical Society was formed by Erasmus to translate the works of the Swedish botanist Linnaeus from Latin into English; and Erasmus's poetry was admired by both Wordsworth and Coleridge, outstanding poets of their generation, for the links that it made with science. In the poem *The Temple of Nature* (1803), Erasmus traces the progression of life from micro-organisms to civilized society and it originally had the title *The Origin of Society*. It is interesting to note how many links we could make, how many such "contingencies" interconnect and flow together to make the histories we may observe and the futures we foresee.

To return to Spencer, his linking of insights into free markets with evolutionary theory is to be anticipated among the Victorian thoughtful. But it is nonetheless instructive to note that that some people still think that Spencer first used the expression "survival of the fittest" in direct response to Darwin's evolutionary theory and then applied it to the credentials of free markets in *Social Statics*. It is instructive, because this mistake illustrates something a little more than a wishful association of ideas in someone's imprecise historic analysis; that is the desire of free market theorists to establish a universal foundation for their ideas in this case by association with the publication of Charles Darwin's exceptionally successful idea. Unfortunately Spencer's *Social Statics* was published in 1851, eight years before the publication of Darwin's *On the Origin of Species*.

16   *Intrinsic Sustainable Development*

Okay you may judge, the dates are out but Spencer is after all correct in his thinking and should be applauded for coining "survival of the fittest" before Darwin. But this attempt to link free markets, "survival of the fittest" and Darwin's evolutionary theory simply illustrates a little more of an underlying, prescriptive and dangerous, side of Human Momentum: a deep-seated tendency to solipsism, with a consequential foreclosure of knowledge. For our use of the word "solipsism", it is necessary that you suspend any individualistic judgement that you might have made about "self" and put to the test an extended, more biological and evolutionary understanding of "self" as human self, *Homo sapiens* self, or at least allow the consideration that "No man is an island, entire of itself" (from John Donne's (1572–1631) *Devotions Upon Emergent Occasions, Meditation XVII*).

Spencer actually made use of use Lamarck's (1744–1829) evolutionary theory, not that of Darwin. This theory of evolution had "individual effort" as the driving force. During lifetimes, according to Lamarck's theory, individual efforts of organisms developed some characteristics and made others redundant; this is a form of adaptive change during life that gets internalised in individuals and then passed on to offspring. This understanding of the heritability of acquired characteristics, this "soft inheritance", was once widely accepted. Spencer essentially applied Lamarck's theory to society and argued that man becomes adapted to a social condition only by living in that condition and then that these acquired adaptations are passed on through children. Hence within Spencer's arguments, the efforts of a creative entrepreneur like Josiah Wedgwood contribute not only to the creation of Josiah's own social conditions but they are also the cause of his own individual adaptive evolution which is then inherited by his offspring. Josiah's efforts would have been for Spencer a text-book example of the processes of evolution that recreate the best the human race has to offer. Conversely, those pot-bank workers who diminished in size generation by generation exemplify the fate of the less able, the less fortunate doomed by ineluctable biological evolutionary processes to pass on degenerative characteristics to their offspring.

But Josiah of course is not alone in his efforts. There was and is a significant group of people, a class, who work as Josiah did, the entrepreneurs who create and direct that most influential of applied human activities, business. If we can see their efforts as Spencer did, then the lives of entrepreneurs and the social institutions which they create and with and within which they continually interact, such as free markets, monetary measures and ROCE mechanisms, become more than accepted conventions or norms: they become the meaning and form of life as evolution in action. These are very useful arguments for establishing a "superior" social class — an elite.

This then is a directed form of evolution; evolution with a purpose, teleology in action. For Spencer, this evolutionary mechanism had a clear and single purpose and that would culminate in "the perfect man in the perfect society" which came close to a conceptual realisation in Fukuyama's 1992 book *The End of History and the Last Man* which argues *inter alia* that future democracies will contain markets of some sort in a final form of human government; and that history stops when this perfection is attained.

However this kind of understanding puts the cart before the horse. In the understanding to be developed within this book, this kind of approach takes one opportunistic analytical slice from the many possible in understanding a highly complex reality and proclaims bluntly or with sophisticated arguments something like "this is the one and only true slice". This is merely an example of the simplistic, self-indulgence that over weans the small self. It is an aspect of the same tendency that goes beyond assertion to ontology in the "selfish-man" being inconsiderate of others, the selfish-corporation looking after its own profit and nothing else and the more deeply thoughtful, yet simplistically universalising, superficially objective and generous but none the less internally self-reducing and mean tendency to identify and unify with the idea, philosophy, system or faith that both expands one's understanding of the self and yet plants it firmly, in a small-scale version, exclusively and irreducibly on, around or within the world and even the known universe. This latter remark is perhaps better expressed by William James below when, incidentally, he is disparaging Spencer's application of evolutionary theory:

> "The plain truth is that the 'philosophy of evolution' (as distinguished from our special information about particular cases of change) is a metaphysical creed and nothing

Intrinsic Sustainable Development

else. It is a mood of contemplation, an emotional attitude,
rather than a system of thought — a mood which is as old
as the world, and which no refutation of any one incar-
nation of it (such as the Spencerian philosophy) will ever
dispel; the mood of fatalistic pantheism, with its intuition
of One and All, which was and is, and ever shall be, and
from whose womb each single thing proceeds. Far be it
from us to speak slightingly here of so hoary and mighty
a way of looking at the world as this. What we at present
call scientific discoveries had nothing to do with bringing
it to birth, nor can one easily conceive that they should
ever give it its *quietus*. ... A critic, however, who cannot disprove the truth of the metaphysical creed, can at
least raise his voice in protest against its disguising itself
in "scientific" plumes... the Spencerian "philosophy" of
social and intellectual progress is an obsolete anachronism,
reverting to a pre-Darwinian type of thought just as the
Spencerian philosophy of "Force," effacing all previous distinctions between actual and potential energy, momentum,
work, force, mass, etc., which physicists have with so much
agony achieved, carries us back to a pre-Galilean age."

William James (in Jacoby 2008, pp. 75–76)

The above passage by James is quoted here in its entirety just as
it is used in Jacoby's arguments about the influence of pseudoscience
on today's American culture. Jacoby concludes this part of her study
of American anti-rationalism and anti-intellectualism with the identification of two causes: "The first is the belief of a significant minor-
ity of Americans that intellectualism and secular higher learning are
implacable enemies of their faith. The second is the toxin of pseudoscience, which Americans on both the left and the right continue
to imbibe as a means of rendering their social theories impervious to
evidence-based challenges." (*ibid.*, p. 81).

Our intended meaning of the word "solipsism" accommodates
both James' and Jacoby's accusations. We will shift attention to the
attitude, mindset and psychology of the kind of individual who may
be accused of such charges. For we argue that it is the construction
of a particular kind of individual self, solipsist, no matter how "collective" this individual construction may or may not be, that is the

underlying cause of the closure of minds to evidence and fact observed by both authors above. If we were to be more sympathetic, solipsism is motivated by the human need to find simple, certain answers to big questions when confronted with the bewildering complexity that is just now getting to be better known as actual reality, or even existence.

We will provide one more example of what we intend to embrace with the word "solipsism". At the start of the third millennium in the Christian era, there is very strong evidence from all quarters that aspects of Human Momentum, especially those made manifest in business, have something very wrong with their understanding. Consequentially related sets of problematic issues affect all aspects of actual business activity from cleaning toilets to the food we eat, the way we travel, house, clothe ourselves, shop, communicate, entertain, reward each other and, for many, find meaning in our lives. This wrong understanding is popularly known by its antithesis, sustainable development.

In the past, societies struggled with nature to survive. Now the challenge is very different. We have to overcome the Human Momentum misunderstandings which direct the practical applications of our knowledge and determine how we use and relate to the world. The needs of sustainable development also require us, the world's people, to think again about what kind of businesses we want. It is no longer sufficient for a business to be economically robust, to provide a satisfactory ROCE measured by money in free markets: it now needs to be socially, environmentally and ecologically robust as well. Furthermore since society, ecosystems and indeed the Universe itself are larger than any entrepreneur or business corporation, "survival of the fittest" has to lose its Spencerian and Lamarckian self-supremacist meaning and businesses and business people have to become more adept at "fitting in", i.e., being the "the best at fitting in" for better or worse, as Darwin explained, in order to become more robust.

This implies significant change to the way business and business people operate. Such significant change has been put on the agenda. World leaders who met at the World Summit on Sustainable Development in Johannesburg in 2002 agreed to launch a "Ten Year

Framework of Programs on Sustainable Consumption and Production (SCP)" to bring about fundamental changes in the way societies produce and consume. In February 2005, a meeting of 250 scientists in Oslo recognised that this Ten Year Framework of Programmes had a significant expectation gap: "Efforts to develop consumption systems that are markedly more efficient and effective are still largely unknown. To date there have been few practical steps toward realizing their implementation" (Oslo Declaration 2005). This is known as the Oslo Declaration on Sustainable Consumption and it was sent to members of the European Commission with the intention of changing European research priorities.

Eight years after the launch of the SCP in May 2010, the United Nations Commission on Sustainable Development included the following words in a press release made in New York:

> "There was once the hope of an unending process of improvement in the lives and livelihoods of people. Today, fears are being expressed of a race between development and disaster.
>
> Economic growth has transformed the world beyond recognition, but its task is far from complete. Despite two hundred years of miraculous improvements in human well-being, two billion people are still mired in poverty, lack access to safe water, sanitation, or health services. Eleven million children die every year because of malnutrition and avoidable diseases.
>
> Economic growth always provided an easy answer, but the world needs to go beyond easy answers. We are learning that economic growth cannot go on for ever on a finite planet. We cannot continue to extract materials nor dump our wastes endlessly. It all adds up, and sooner or later will hit the planetary boundaries. Indeed, we some planetary boundaries have already been crossed and others have moved closer." (UNCSD, 2010)

Just Business

The 2010 press release quoted above from the United Nations Commission on Sustainable Development points towards a new relationship between how we provide for ourselves, our business and economics, and the natural world. If we were to ask "Is this kind of change possible?", we would be asking the wrong kind of question.

Such a question would arise in an attitude that sees purpose, and consequential culmination, in history. In this book, we will follow the scientific evidence that indicates that we should not overwork history in this way and that we should acknowledge the important role of contingencies. As the late great evolutionist at Harvard University, Stephen Jay Gould (1941–2002), claimed when seeking support for the expression "Just History": "A historical explanation does not rest on direct deductions from laws of nature, but on an unpredictable sequence of antecedent states, where any major change in any step of the sequence would have altered the final result." (Gould, 1991, p. 283).

It is the case that the perception of "Just History" is not new. The historian Michael Cook claims to write his histories in a similar spirit to that of the ancient Roman poet Lucretius which Cook describes as follows: "What happened in our world was in the last resort a matter of the behaviour of atoms — 'many atoms jumbled in many ways' that 'come together and try all combinations'. For Lucretius there was thus no teleology to history. Human culture and society were the product of evolution, not of the purposive interventions of gods." (Cook, 2004, pp. 354–355).

And if we do not overwork history, we will be less likely to overwork the future. If we do not see ourselves as players in some inevitable story, then we can open our minds to the fact that things could have been — and can be — very different. In this book, we argue that both "Just History" and "Just Future" are required to perceive, develop, implement and operate "Just Business" which we propose as a way of providing for our physical and psychological selves that is open and receptive to the best knowledge we now possess about how the world and its inhabitants work.

We live in a risky world. Geophysical events such as earthquakes, tsunamis and volcanic eruptions are caused by processes that mankind can neither control nor influence. They will cause major disasters if they have sufficient strength and happen to impact on centres of human population. Technology and planning can only help to mitigate any future disasters that geophysical events may cause.

Disasters caused by weather storms, tornados, floods, landslides, droughts, forest fires and extremes of temperatures may also be mitigated, but these are very different from geophysical events because we can influence their causes. The frequency and severity of meteorological, hydrological and climatological events are predicted to increase with climate change (IPCC, 2007).

It will never be possible to eliminate all disasters and hazards. Risk taking is, always has been and always will be a necessary part of human advancement. But there is a huge difference between risks caused by negligence and error and those caused by human intent. Climate change, increasing biodiversity loss, freshwater losses, increasing hazardous waste — including nuclear — emissions, and the degradation of the marine environment are now knowingly caused by mankind and all make Earth a less safe place for all of life (UNEP, 2010). The consequences of these man-made risks will cause direct hardship and deaths particularly among the world's vulnerable poor, but will also cause social and political instability with additional risks of conflict and terrorism, cost increases, economic losses, epidemics and resource shortages amongst which food and fresh water supplies are likely to be the most pressing. Whilst we do not have the power to threaten planet Earth, we do have the power to bring about the extinction of *Homo sapiens*; De Villiers (2010) makes this point in *Natural Disasters, Manmade Catastrophes, and the Future of Human Survival.*

Willing disasters would not be acceptable to any sane person ... but it appears that we cannot stop ourselves doing just this. Why are we doing so? The German philosopher Friedrich Wilhelm Nietzsche (1844–1900) predicted this situation and devoted his life trying to change things; more specifically, Nietzsche devoted his life to trying change attitudes.

The expression "Just Business" has of course other meanings in addition to that of the dominance of contingent causal relations. It can also mean "only" or "simply" business which is the kind of meaning used with a shrug of the shoulders when confronted with an event of unclear but business-related origin. This is a lazy use of the expression.

"Just Business" can also point to a broad gamut of human aspirations for a more equitable world. This use calls to mind Thomas Aquinas' "Just Price" that ruled in the Mediaeval European market place to ensure fairness so that, for example, a poor and starving person had to pay a lower price for bread than a rich merchant. On analysis however, this seemingly simple usage of "Just Business" becomes entangled with the meanings of hard words such as justice, truth, deserving, humanity and of course many well-meaning economic assertions.

If Josiah Wedgewood were to be born in 2011, the world would greatly appreciate his generous measure of Human Momentum blazing new trails for us to follow; but such new trails would now have to meander around new ways of doing business — new more sustainable ways of doing business. To do this, he would certainly need the full support of his other "lunatick" associates in science and industry as well as that of some of his family members. Josiah's grand-daughter Emma married Charles Darwin in 1839 in Saint Peter's Church, Maer Staffordshire.

Before and immediately after the Norman invasion of the British Isles in 1066, Maer village was under the control of the freeman Wulfgeat. According to the Doomsday Book (*c.* 1086), King William I's inventory of his recently acquired assets, his capital employed, Maer had one hide paying geld, land for two ploughs which was and is waste, woodland half a league long and forty perches wide and two acres of meadow. By 1281 there was a manor house at Maer and the present hall was built *c.* 1680. This manor house was once home to Charles Darwin who whilst in residence studied the estate's earthworms. It was also the home of Josiah Wedgwood II, son of the famous potter, from 1807 to 1843.

Maer Church, built before the manor house, occupies preferential higher ground overlooking the manor house that lies closer to the mere. Church and house are separated by a quite tree-lined lane where the older boy, once running along a canal bank, liked to ride his mountain bike. All this is Just History.

24   *Intrinsic Sustainable Development*

"When we think of the world's future, we always mean the destination it will reach if it keeps going in the direction we can see it going in now; it does not occur to us that its path is not a straight line but a curve, constantly changing direction."

Ludwig Wittgenstein, "Culture and Value" (p. 3e., 1977)

CHAPTER 2 — NATURAL MOMENTUM

Relations

One third of a century ago, that child once running along the tow path had grown into a young man as he stood with his wife on the southernmost shores of Africa. They watched the sun set over the Southern Ocean. Spindrift in the dusk hung like a veil along the rocky shore, concealing, but just as with a woman, adding mystery, delicacy and reserves of beauty to the vision.

The rocks on which they stood were Ordovician, which lies within the Palaeozoic geological era making those rocks around 350 million years old. Pounding the rocks were huge crashing waves that had rolled through an enormous fetch-length perhaps from as far away as Antarctica for the wind that pressed on their faces was gentle and could not itself be the cause of such a big sea. In the rock pools at their feet crystal-clear, highly energised white water raced, swirled around foam and loose fronds of slimy brown weed and stirred the green algae. The intelligence of the coal-black mussels and lumpy barnacles was enough to keep them tightly closed during the uncertainties of low tide; in their tiny lives, the shell-fish creatures waited patiently with the confidence of aeons that the natural lunar cycle would soon have the deep-sea mass of water returned and then they could feed. No buildings, ships, people, planes or anything at all to do with mankind were in the sight of the couple.

Towards the middle of the continent, Nchanga Consolidated Copper Mines (NCCM) extracted copper from the ground that is Zambia. NCCM was formed in 1970 with 51% of the shares of the Anglo American Corporation in Zambia at the start of the creeping nationalisation of foreign-owned mines following the Mulungushi Reforms of April 1968. Copper circuits, wiring, currency, medical and agricultural applications, jewellery, statues (including the Statue of Liberty) and many other manufactured items create the demand for copper, the markets, the ROCEs and the cash flows that paid the salary of the young man and the airfares to Africa for him and his wife. His technical education and training had taught him about industrial material sourcing and supply, market-price valuations, costs and revenues and accounting statements; all the systems and abstract representations of our modern human-wealth generating processes. That sophisticated working human-world can now be no more neglected by mankind than breathing. But during that sunset on a South African shore, the couple acquired a mindfulness of something more essential, more fundamental, far older and greater in all respects than the business needs and capabilities of *Homo sapiens*; something upon which they and Just Business ultimately depend.

On that beach, they had acquired a little first-hand experience of the natural process by means of which they and their ancestors had been fashioned, supported and provided with the mental capacities to wonder, to know and to reason. Their experiences were to have an enduring impact upon them. They had found meaning and value in something located outside an economic market but still located nonetheless in exchanges, but these exchanges were those described by meteorology, oceanography, ecology, biology, physiology, psychology, electro-chemistry, particle physics, cosmology and many other studies of the material interactions that constitute the natural sciences, that constitute the world.

It would be very hard to find objective, evidence-based research that would support the claim that natural science in its purest forms is motivated simply by a fundamental human need to know more about whom we are and from where we came. The utility of the world and the data and information generated by natural science with its complex reciprocal relations with societal objectives and personal ambitions mean that any such simple motivation for natural science has to be inevitably modified. But during those moments on the shore, the young man and his wife did discover more about whom they were and where they came from. To do this, they did not call

to mind the few names they already knew of the huge array of material exchanges in which they were inescapably immersed, of which
they were constituted; nor in those fleeting moments, did they want
to know anything of the mental constructions in which mankind,
perhaps all intelligent life, create their own versions of reality, of
truth for them alone. They were happy to find and nurture the precious exchanges between themselves and the world as they were to be
found; in more immediate, more fundamentally simple, more open,
more enriching ways than conventional conceptual linkages and their
attendant constraints allow. They had found a little of those rare
emotions and feelings that are both subjective and objective; becoming manifest and sensed as parts of an individual body and mind but
not wholly part of, or originating in, an individual body and mind
because of the essential ongoing flowing exchanges or processes of the
natural world, the universe, which constitutes the dynamic, interactive, creative whole of which we individually are but small, self-aware
parts, capable nonetheless of knowing something, however miniscule,
about the whole.

Most of the photons that fell on the eyes of the couple were already
some eight minutes old, having taken that long to travel from the
reddening sun. The nitrogen and oxygen that entered their bodies,
their breath, was taken from cool, early spring, oceanic air brought to
them by the fresh, world-travelling wind. Their lungs absorbed and
used what the green plants had exhaled. They also breathed some 385
parts per million by volume of carbon dioxide but at that time they
did not know that these particular invisible molecules were becoming
more numerous, increasing by about 8% between 1958 and 1982, and
that this increase in something that is after all just a trace molecule
would be enough to seriously threaten the viability of all corners of
the human and other natural living world. Even there, in the extreme
remoteness and specious purity on the edge of Africa alongside the
Klasies River mouth, global business activities, especially the burning
of fossil fuels, crossed remote continents and oceans to reach them.

Back in 1976, the two young people had stayed on that shoreline
for the remains of the day; then they waited and watched alone in the
growing darkness. They waited for the night sky and those glimpses

further back into time. Some of the electro-magnetic messenger particles, the photons, that were made discernible falling on their eyes had been travelling in space for billions of years out of galaxies far beyond their own; and if they had had the eyes to see, they could have looked back into their own sense of time and have become consciously aware of particles falling on their bodies that had first been emitted from stars long before the ancient rocks upon which they stood had been formed. Mountains had had the time to rise and pass like clouds whilst the photons that fell on their eyes that night had been hurtling through space at 299,792,458 metres per second, the absolute speed of light.

Under that night sky, within the seeming quietude of their minds and bodies, something gentle stirred. The intergalactic photons registering on the photoreceptors at the back of their eyes, the cool charged electro-magnetic potentials of their breathed molecules and the myriad host of other exchange and balancing mechanisms were just ticking-over, idling gently as the mindfulness enforced by their chosen isolation from other distractions, controlled their inner-calm and permitted a submission to the sublime that by unconscious reflexive processes in turn affected their material selves. Signalling waves of electro-chemical activity suffused their neurophysiology circuits, passing on calming messages throughout their bodies, enabling an awareness of their flowing sleepless eternal nature with the firing of the more subtle neurons of their brains.

On reflection, looking back over so many decades, it is difficult to say just who those people were. We may know their names, ages and the holiday photos they took show just how different they looked. So young, but where did they start and end? If you had prodded them, they would have been well aware of their own bodies but at a fundamental level, for perhaps only a few moments, they were open, sensitive to material processes with distant origins in winds, oceans, vegetable cellular activity, stellar nuclear-fusion, distant galaxies, the entropic potential of cosmic order and the quirky worlds of sub-atomic particles. So at one, or at several, or possibly at an infinite number of levels of physical reality, they were standing on that starlit shore as incredible individual focussed centres of harmony within myriad waves of particle and electro-chemical interactions involving the messages of billions of electrons and photons from outside their bodies as well as the signals of their own 100 billion or so neurons, each with approximately 10,000 synaptic connections, that constitutes one of the most complex entities known to man, the human brain. Names, passports, birth certificates, jobs, incomes and homes say so little about who those two people were, and are.

Within themselves for a few too-brief moments, their conscious minds, some part of their cognitive processes, their awakened thoughts, were subdued, slow, absent and the rest of the cosmos was alive, buzzing and invasive. This account of their interactions is of course a reflective embellishment, a retrospective explanation, a memory coloured and substantiated by a lifetime's reading and exploration. Those people simply did not know — did not want to know — all of the above facts and explanations during their time of standing on that African shore. That was their unique time, their personal and immediate probing of reality. But the fact remains that their experiences were real, life changing, or rather life-focusing, because they have never stopped trying to make sense of what they felt and they look for it still in wild places, in mountains, on the frontiers of knowledge, in science, in art and in their relations to other people and to nature.

Much of this is nothing new. Many people have life-changing experiences; moments of awareness that the ways in which they have been regarding themselves and the world around them have been incomplete, perhaps wrong. What is new is that science now supports the experiences of that young couple. There is nothing factually incorrect in the preceding paragraphs and the response from the young man and his wife were imaginative, not fantastic; they are described in natural, not supernatural terms. It seems a strange, rare way of thinking about ourselves, but the ways in which we are constituted and embedded in the natural world are innumerable and alien to our everyday worlds; from our emotional lives to the food we eat, the sun that warms us, the electro-chemistry that maintains us to the clocks that mark the passing of our perceptions of time within personal corridors of space-time, and they are all stranger than anything

30   *Intrinsic Sustainable Development*

the human race has known before including all the monsters of fantasy and all the welcomed or feared interventions of one or another deity which frequently (perhaps necessarily) tend to be extensions of human daily lives in one way or another.

The scientific knowledge the human race now possesses tells us much about the real world that exists outside our everyday mental constructions. With this knowledge, science challenges enduring notions of whom and what we are; which, as well shall see, has already had a big impact upon business. But there is remaining potential in the world revealed by science for more significant and profound changes in our institutions, our businesses and ourselves. Science reveals us to be deeply and inescapably embedded in nature; just other animals driven by the sun and as inseparable from our physical planet, cultural ecology and emotional content as a pet goldfish is from a bowl of water. It is time to think deeply, creatively and freely about how we and our institutions, especially our forms of business, may flourish within this new scientific understanding, this new reality.

After all in spite of the conceptual closures of such disciplines as accounting, economics and law, businesses exist within the same particle-exchange universe as that young man and his wife. As a principle, this is perhaps not problematic, for science has already challenged everyday notions of what businesses are. It has taken our understanding of business performance well beyond the representations of accounting, economics, law and many of the more limiting forms of management. During the last thirty years or so, many aware business people have been learning how to represent and make sense of many more business "transactions" than traditional free-markets, profit and loss accounts, balance sheet statements, Return on Capital Employed calculations, management theories and other utilitarian or efficiency frameworks capture.

Business Relations

The 1970's was a decade during which many countries became officially aware of the appalling environmental damage that their businesses were causing. For example on the 1st of January 1970, the National Environmental Policy Act was signed in the USA and that created the Council on Environmental Quality that advised President Nixon about environmental issues. On the 22nd day of the same month, the president of General Motors, Edward Cole, promised pollution-free cars by 1980. Also in 1970, the world's first Earth Day was held on April 22nd and the US Environmental Protection Agency was established.

In Sweden between the 5th and the 16th June 1972, the first of a series of global environmental conferences, the Conference on the Human Environment, was held in Stockholm. This conference led to the formation of the United Nations Environment Programme (UNEP). At the end of 1972 on the 7th December, one of the most widely distributed photographs in history was taken by the crew of the Apollo 17 spacecraft. That photograph was taken at a distance of 29,000 kilometres from Earth. It is the very first time that mankind looked back at its home planet. That view of the planet was nicknamed the "Blue Marble". It alone is said to have introduced a new awareness of ourselves, our species on one small home planet within the vastness of empty of space. That new awareness of ourselves, *Homo sapiens*, in the universe is said to have been a significant factor for changing attitudes and furthering the cause of the worldwide environmental movement.

1974 was the year in which Chlorofluorocarbons (CFCs) were hypothesized to cause ozone-layer thinning. On the 10th July 1976, the chemical dioxin (2,3,7,8-tetrachlorodibenzo-p-dioxin) was accidentally released some 15 km to the north of Milan in Seveso, Italy, where it killed animals and exposed the local population to the highest known exposures to this organic pollutant. Even small concentrations of dioxins can be potent. They accumulate in food chains and build-up in fatty body tissues. Many threats to human health have been attributed to dioxins including: a cause of cancer; an inhibitor of reproduction and sexual development; a source of damage to the human immune system; a cause of a severe form of persistent acne; a threat to the enamel of children's teeth; a factor in central and peripheral nervous system pathology; a cause of thyroid disorders; one source of pelvic pain in women that is often associated with infertility; a cause of diabetes; and an influence on the numbers of male to female births so that more females are born than males.

Towards the end of the decade on 28th March 1979, the loss of coolant and partially melt-down at the Three Mile Island nuclear plant in Dauphin County, Pennsylvania USA, was a milestone event for the environmental reform of the nuclear power industry. Also in 1979, Earth First! was formed in the USA. In 2010, the website of the Leeds' UK Earth First! community informs us that they promote "the use of direct action to confront, stop and eventually reverse the forces that are responsible for the destruction of the Earth and its inhabitants".

It is not surprising that a raft of environmental acts, regulations and conventions were created in the 1970's. Indeed the major European Union law established to improve the safety of sites containing large quantities of dangerous substances, Council Directive 96/82/EC of 9 December 1996, is also known as the Seveso II Directive after the 1976 Seveso dioxin disaster.

Businesses were forced to respond: they had to become more environmentally friendly or close down. But businesses exist to solve our problems, so the other side of a constraint is a business opportunity. UK Trade and Investment (UKTI) is funded by the UK government to promote UK business activity and they valued the global market in environmental goods and services at $US515 bn in 2002. They expect this market to grow to $US688 bn by 2010 and to just under US$800 billion by 2015.

In response to increasing knowledge of environmental impacts and associated changes in attitudes, businesses have changed their processes and products. These changes impact everyday life with such as green petrol, CFC-free aerosols, plastic-bag distribution controls, organic foods, smoking bans, the eco-labelling of products and services, energy efficiency measures, carbon-emissions reduction, renewable-energies and so much more. Many more change should be anticipated. President Barack Obama for example has made the reduction of the CO_2 emissions that cause global warming a key green objective of his presidency. Global businesses and societies have been and are revising their understanding and attitudes regarding kinds of responsible businesses; but core changes in business theory and practice have yet to happen.

Changes in business processes and products will continue to arise as our technological capability grows and alters or increases its impact and as science identifies more and more of the human interventions in the complex dynamic particle-exchange processes. It is important to keep in mind that science is not creating anything materially new with these revelations. It is merely providing knowledge of relationships that have previously been unrecognised, forgotten or usurped by other concepts, words, technical languages, arguments, ambitions and understandings and attitudes to ourselves, our actions and our place in the world.

What we do with the new knowledge that science provides is up to us and to society. So far, the business response has been to try to absorb these freshly revealed relations within existing business systems and understanding, without fundamental change. Core objectives in accounting, economics, marketing and finance are the same now as they were over two hundred years ago with the exception of global financial markets whose transactions have become more specialised, more mechanised, more speculative and even more remote from everyday life.

Memories

Evidence survives from around 125,000 years ago to indicate that our ancestral mothers and fathers lived in caves near the Klasies River mouth in Tsitsikamma; close to where that young man and his wife had stood on the southernmost coast of South Africa. Apart from trendy 1970's clothes, all these people were essentially the same. They were members of the same animal species, *Homo sapiens*. The ancients had only crude ways of providing for themselves, of pursuing their business; but otherwise they could think our kinds of thoughts, perform our kinds of acts, suffer our kinds of anxieties and feel our kinds of emotions, pains and fears.

34   *Intrinsic Sustainable Development*

The evidence reveals that those truly ancient Klasies River people had dined on shellfish, antelope, seals, penguins and some unidentified plant foods, roasting them in hearths built for the purpose. They had lived in caves. The young man and his wife also ate shellfish, meat and vegetables and they loved BBQ's but they had lived only temporarily in a canvas tent at that location. They all had walked the same shore, witnessed similar spectacular sunsets through sensual spindrift, sensed awe and wondered where their next meal was coming from.

Fossil evidence suggests that other members of the *Homo* genus were around at the time of the truly ancients, but that those others, *Homo erectus* and *Homo ergaster* for example, primarily scavenged food from kills made by other animals that were better equipped for hunting. Those *Homo sapiens* mothers and fathers of the Klasies River caves knew how to hunt which implies that these people possessed higher levels of social organising and planning skills. Furthermore stone tools and flakes made from beach cobbles were recovered from the earliest levels of the site and are a testimony to the inchoate technical skills of *Homo sapiens*.

After a few days, the young man and his wife moved on to the magnificence of False Bay closer to Cape Town, then to their work in Kitwe in Zambia and eventually, some eighteen months later, to a little town called Alsager in Cheshire in the UK. Over the years, they were to change their hearth more permanently only five more times, but whenever time and money allowed, they loved to travel, to explore their world and applied business technology took them west and east many times. It may be the case that they inherited their restless feet from their really ancient mothers and fathers, for other evidence suggests that those Klasies River caves were never permanent residences, being occupied for only a few weeks and then their occupants would move along the coast to the next good hunter-gatherer stand.

It would be a relatively easy task to explain the behaviour of people alive today by referring to sweeping "family" characteristics; that is by enumerating attributes, values and behaviours which we have possibly inherited from our very distant ancestors. To make our case more substantial, we would wrap these attributes and claims in an argument: "Natural Momentum," we could say, "is a human birthright forged during the millennia of our evolution and residing, irreducible at the core of our being to provide meaning, influence, guidance and companionship in our lives. It is a formative presence, a set of emotions, intuitions, likes and dislikes, responses and aesthetics that are as hard-wired as any part of our material being just as much as having a head, two eyes, legs, arms, a heart, liver, kidney and so on."

In this way not only can we attribute the business of tourism to our specie's restless millennia of ancestral wanderings for better stands but there is really no limit to the process: love for other humans especially those closest to us can be derived from the small group and tribal bonding that was once indubitably essential to our survival; love of nature from the child-like, formative aeons that our species and its ancestors spent in the great outdoors gathering and scavenging when nature was the only provider; a likening for sweet and fatty foods from our bodies' physical need for them, together with their paucity in our early diets; a focus on immediate risk from aeons of enforced learning subsequent to regular survival encounters with predators such as lions, bears and snakes; uneasiness in the dark because this is when many predators chose to take advantage of us; an obsession with possessions from the status and security they once bestowed when few could make the relatively huge investments to obtain and carry them; and religious creation myths from a combination of the many loose-ends to primitive knowledge, a pressing need for emotional security in a dangerous and impartial world, and that hallmark of our species, the capacity for linking concepts and ideas together in abstract worlds of our own making.

You could, no doubt, think of other ways of explaining fundamental aspects of our behaviour, our psychologies, in evolutionary terms. Many of these explanations may indeed be true, i.e., they did evolve within us over immense periods of time for good survival reasons and they remain, persistent if buried deep sometimes, within our being. But how do you know that this is the case, that they are real evolution acquisitions that would persist no matter what opinions or ideas

Intrinsic Sustainable Development

we may eventually hold or whatever fresh experiences, needs and demands we may find? How do you know that your arguments are nothing more than just that; just elaborate, extended mental linkages between concepts and, usually, some facts that resonate with something more or less familiar to yourself or with that which you really want or need and which you then project onto the exterior world as an explanation of that world in a tailor-made reality which remains however obviously wholly of your own making with total disregard for the truly determinative influences of the benefits and comforts your fantasy world bestows on yourself and society? Your arguments can be made complex, intricate, supportable by grains of truth, hints of evidence and favoured memories to become convincing especially for those minds made less discerning by immediate personal motives and needs that really have to believe in any such things. Add to this well-worked, meaningful and fully rational content, a mode of delivery that is earnest, sincere, honest and responsible in the manner of the best orators and sales persons, then it becomes exceedingly difficult for lay-people and experts alike to make distinctions. Indeed, if such arguments do provide significant benefits for *Homo sapiens*, then, we could argue, does not this simple fact of utility bestow some kind of actual reality on the fantastic reality that we personally have made and maintain?

After all, the history of discarded and live religions reveals the human appetite for self-constructed sophistry to be so voracious and diverse that it is indeed likely to be something hard-wired into our survival by aeons of evolution! Maybe our psyche cannot function properly with too many loose ends around the big questions of who are we, what are we doing here, where is here and what is death? We need answers. Maybe there is a drive for wholeness, for completion within us, perhaps within nature, which works against partial solutions? Evolution is replete with chicken and egg situations where an explanation of one part cannot be completed without reference to other parts, perhaps even to some elusive whole: an explanation of the egg requires knowledge of the chicken and knowledge of the chicken is not only knowledge of breeding cycles and eggs but also of nests, feathers, pecking-orders and life-cycles and hence of

Chapter 2 — Natural Momentum   **37**

temperatures, climates, carbon-cycles, food availability, predators, seasons, weather, clouds, solar-power, solar systems, stellar furnaces, black holes, the cosmos....

The world is more complex than any one simple idea or set of ideas that we can hold in our minds at any one time; an observation supported by Whitehead, the mathematician and process philosopher: "My demand is, that the ultimate arbitrariness of matter of fact from which our formulations start should disclose the same general principles of reality, which we dimly discern as stretching away into regions beyond our explicit powers of discernment." (Whitehead, 1927, p. 115). But that young man on the African shore, his wife and billions of other people needed and need some simple answers so they can relax, sleep at nights and feel comfortable in their lives. But we need to be very careful that the simple answers we choose do not prohibit or inhibit our exploration of the complex real world. Real reality has a habit of catching up with and overtaking even the best, most elaborate, most rational and most durable of our delusions; as unsustainable development shows.

It would therefore be a mistake to strongly assert some sweeping nature-force, a "Natural Momentum", as one such simple answer, as an organising principle around which we construct our societies and our lives: but that mistake would be minute, insignificant and relatively benign in comparison with the mistake of ignoring or excluding "Natural Momentum" altogether. For both errors are errors of closure, of placing too much emphasis on instrumental knowledge, understanding and reason that serves our perceptions of our immediate needs and purposes. Errors of closure are major contributors to solipsism, that eclectic reduction of knowledge to privilege the self which severs our connections with that greater world of complex, interconnected and changing reality. But there is a need for simple, communicable answers; social and personal cohesion is dependent upon as much.

The authors of this book have a suspicion that the simple answer that defines who we are, what we do and how we might do it together necessarily and relatively easily becomes manifest in action, unless we are captives, slaves or otherwise forced to act against our will such

38   *Intrinsic Sustainable Development*

as by inappropriate social systems or beliefs; this is the inner principle and objective of freedom. But simple answers quickly become more complex because many of our actions are concerned with one or another aspect of providing for our real and perceived physical and psychologically needs and as such they cause actions and then the simple answer has the additional reflexive task of accommodating the consequences of these actions, many of which will be necessarily unforeseen. This is saying no more than there is another chicken and egg situation here, whereby our simple answer, needs and actions formatively influence each other. So alongside Natural Momentum in the simple answer, there needs to be for self-aware mankind some accommodation of a process whereby we both act and then learn from the consequences of our actions; that is an inclusion of a self-aware reflexive element within what we identified in chapter one above as Human Momentum.

The authors of this book remain open to the idea that Human Momentum may indeed be revealed to be no more than a species-specific application of Natural Momentum. Evolutionary psychology is an emerging science that has something to say about this possibility. However we suggest that it is logically inevitable that mankind works with this splitting of the world, this dualism that recognises both Natural and Human Momenta for whether we are indistinguishable parts of nature or not, there is something that does in one sense indisputably separate us from other animals; that is the unavoidable fact that we get to know the world by using human eyes, minds, hearts and ideas. Chimpanzees, crocodiles, may-flies and aerobic bacteria, for example, do not do that; they are present in the world by means of their own very different senses, needs and capabilities.

So even if we find union with other animals within Natural Momentum and the revelations of evolutionary science, we do so on very species-specific terms. Conversely at the very moment at which our simple answer separates us from other animals by recognising the uniqueness of *Homo sapiens*'s presence in the world, it also unites by finding commonality in the universal differences between species: i.e. our unique appreciation of the world is no more different in its uniqueness than that of any other species.

The Best of Times

> "It was the best of times, it was the worst of times."
>
> *Charles Dickens, "Tale of Two Cities" (1859)*

In chapter one, we introduced the expression "Just Business" and this expression may now be more accurately defined as the tasks our species undertakes to meet its subjective perceptions of actual and perceived material and psychological needs, which in turn are modified by reflexive learning about the consequences of our actions. "Just Business" becomes manifest as a subset of relationships within scientific studies of a particle-exchange universe. If you can postpone judgement on many serious, sweeping and significant assumptions, it is much simpler to remember that "Just Business" is grounded in our best knowledge of reality.

We want this definition of "Just Business" to also incorporate both that "simply" or "only", shrug-of-the-shoulders interpretation as well as meaning a more "just" form of business. So we want an everyday, taken for granted, as common as shelling-peas or taking a bus, meaning of "Just Business" to bring about a more just world. This is the subject of this book and our approach to working at this task is to challenge our knowledge of reality.

Scientific studies tell us what is known of reality, but not what reality *means* for mankind. The meaning of reality is used by *Homo sapiens* to construct images and interpretations of its individuals and societies and to guide the development of an overall, detailed under-standing. History helps us to appreciate different human realities and, hence, the changing potentials of our futures.

For example, Jared Diamond (2006) argues in his book *Collapse: how societies choose to fail or survive* that environmental and social degradation proceed hand in hand when societies fail and that we should learn from this association: "...it is not a question open for debate whether the collapses of past societies have modern parallels and offer any lessons to us. That question is settled, because such collapses have been happening recently, and others appear to be imminent. Instead, the real question is how many more countries will undergo them." (*ibid.*, p. 517).

For the greater part of our history, we hunted wild animals and foraged for berries, roots and other wild foods. This way of providing for ourselves would have been easy in good seasons and locations, but at other times in other places it must have been relentless hardwork driven by the spectre of starvation. At times, some seeds, nuts and fruits that would have been taken back to camp would have been dropped on bare ground. On returning to the camps months or years later, higher concentrations of grains, vegetables, fruits and nuts would sometimes have been found. Our more observant ancestors could have experimented by dropping extra fruits, vegetables, seeds and nuts at camp and waiting to see what happened next....

What happened next was that agriculture was "invented" around ten thousand years ago. You might expect that such agriculture would have been comprehensively and rapidly adopted by our ancestors. Imagine a hunter-gatherer family coming upon orchards, domestic animals and fields of grain. They would not have needed, you may think, too much convincing of the benefits of settling down and forming their own social groups that could live alongside and support each other in agricultural enterprises. However, a 1960's study of the !Kung Bushmen living in the Kalahari Desert provides some reasons as to why not everyone would have been eager to make this change.

!Kung women rested and slept 10.5 hours a day to consume about 473 kcalories (473,000 calories). Another eight hours a day of light activities would have consumed a further 800 kcalories and obtaining food involved walking for an average 1.2 hours from their temporary campsite to sources of Mongongo nuts using 270 kcal. Collecting the nuts for 3 hours, requiring a estimated 675 kcalories and walking back to camp with a full load of nuts another 462 kcalories. This adds up to a daily intake of 2,680 calories (Pimental 2007, pp. 49–50) which is higher than the average daily needs in developed societies of about 2,000 kcalories for woman and 2,500 kcalories for a man.

In a typical working day, a 12.5 kg load of Mongongo nuts was brought back to camp. Once shelled, this load of nuts provided 1.75 kg of nut meat or 10,500 kcalories. The 2,680 kcalories expended to obtain 10,500 kcalories of nut energy results in an energy input to output ratio of 1:3.9 which may reduce to as low as 1:3 as the distance walked between camps and sources of nuts increases. A typical !Kung woman went to fetch nuts 2.2 days a week on average within a range of 1.2 to 3.2 days. So in an average week the Bush-woman obtained around 23,100 kcalories of nut energy and consumed 14,296 kcalories for her own needs. This provided an 8,804 kcalories or 38% average surplus which helped feed the one third of their population not collecting food, the children and elderly. This energy surplus also was sufficient to fuel essential activities such as gathering firewood, moving camp, constructing shelters and making clothing. But the !Kung placed a high value on their leisure time. They spent many of their 4.8 average not-collecting days per week dancing and socialising.

When asked why they had not adopted the agricultural practices of neighbouring tribes, an !Kung bushman could and did reply: "Why should we, when there are so many Mongongo nuts in the world?" Other remnants of hunter-gatherer societies in the world also enjoy similar energy ratios which enables Marshall Sahlins (1968 and 2003) to argue that present "developed" societies posit man as a slave to closing the gap between unlimited wants and insufficient means and furthermore that this situation is a tragedy of modern times.

It seems quite possible then that hunter-gatherer groups have, and probably frequently had even in the distant past, much leisure time on their hands. Hence the question arises: "Why did we leave this energy efficient form of existence?" It seems to contradict a law of nature if mankind expends more energy to achieve given outcomes when less would suffice. Furthermore there seems to be many other disadvantages that wait for those who abandon the hunter-gatherer lifestyle for agricultural society. In his essay *The Worst Mistake in the History of the Human Race*, Diamond (1987) provides evidence of the health problems that came with agriculture some of which is reproduced below.

- Paleopathologists have learned from ancient skeletons found in Greece and Turkey that the average height of hunger-gatherers towards the end of the Ice Age was 5′ 9″ for men and 5′ 5″ for women and that these heights had dropped to 5′ 3″ for men and 5′ for women by 3000 BC following the adoption of agricultural practices. Modern Greeks and Turks have still not regained the average height of their distant ancestors.

- From approximately 800 Indian skeletal remains found in burial mounds in the Illinois and Ohio river valleys of the U.S.A., researchers identified deleterious health changes in Indian populations that occurred around 1150 AD when their societies changed from hunter-gathering to intensive maize farming including:

  - a nearly 50% increase in enamel defects indicative of malnutrition,
  - a fourfold increase in iron-deficiency anaemia,
  - a three-fold rise in bone lesions reflecting infectious disease in general,
  - an increase in degenerative conditions of the spine probably reflecting a lot of hard physical labour, and
  - a reduction in average life-expectancy at birth from about twenty-six to nineteen years.

In *The Worst Mistake in the History of the Human Race* (1987) Diamond provides three reasons why the adoption of agriculture was so bad for us:

(i) A shift from a varied hunter-gatherer diet (Mongongo nuts being of course only one example of the many diverse foods to be found in Nature) to one dependent upon a single or small number of the starchy crops typical of those first farmers;

(ii) Dependence on a limited number of crops which entailed a high risk of a poor or totally destroyed harvest; and

(iii) The need of agricultural practices for people settling in increasingly larger social groups which become breeding grounds for a wide range of parasites and infectious diseases.

Diamond's reasons remain relevant today since a mere three plants, wheat, rice, and corn, provide almost half of the total calories consumed by mankind whilst nine others account for the other half; drought is a widely recognized cause or contributor to recent famine disasters and, as noted in chapter one, it seems likely that climate change will make this far worse; and finally, from a microbiotic perspective, our global society historically and presently serves well the needs of plague, measles, typhus, syphilis, smallpox, leprosy, malaria, tuberculosis, new strains of flu, HIV/AIDS and many more socially communicable diseases.

From a macrobiotic perspective, the cause of our predicament is likely to be more easily discernable. Let us suppose for a moment that our planet has indeed been visited by the flying saucers of an advanced civilisation lying somewhere deep within the Milky Way. We can give them the title of Visiting Intra-Galactic Anthropologists (VIGAs). They would have seen many living simian species including our ancestral forms living in natural environments alongside other Hominidae, ancestral humans and other large apes, from about 12 million years ago. The human line became differentiated from other apes, gorillas, chimpanzees and bonobos, in the subsequent Homininae group that includes *Toumaï*, the 7 million year old pre-human skull found in Chad in 2001 by Michel Brunet, and *Lucy*, the young Australopithecus fossil and previous "grandmother of the human race" found in Ethiopia in 1974 but actually being a mere 3.2 million years old Homininae.

The VIGAs would no doubt have excitedly filled their notebooks and multimedia recorders as Homininae started using stone tools around what we call the start of the Palaeolithic, or Old Stone Age, about 2.6 million years ago (i.e. very recently in the last 0.068% of the history of life on Earth that started about 3.8 billion years BP). The use of stone tools was the first example of cultural accumulation exhibited by our ancestors and this started a whole new chapter in our history. But even so, the VIGAs' records would show that for the first 2.55 million years of their visiting the "cultured" human ancestors or about 98% of their visiting time from 2.6 million years BP, our ancestors were not significantly different from other descendants of great apes that could also use simple stone tools.

In time, the VIGAs would have been able to note the evolutionary differentiation of the Homo genus which includes *Homo habilis* and *erectus* and then the VIGAs would eventually have had to break camp in Africa to keep up with developments and move to what

44   *Intrinsic Sustainable Development*

was to become the small Georgian town of Dmanisi, where in the year 2000 AD a large number of 1.8 million year old Homo fossils were found. These constitute evidence of what is possibly our earliest exodus from Africa. The appearance of *Homo sapiens* some 200,000 years ago is obviously very significant for ourselves, but perhaps not so for the VIGAs for whom we would have been at that time just another member of the Homo genus.

But "suddenly", around 50,000 years BP, our species began to show signs of accelerated cultural development. This was made evident in ceremonial burials of the dead, clothing made from animal hides, the use of traps and co-ordinated hunting parties, and creative cave paintings. The VIGAs themselves may well have identified this point in time as one of our species' Great Leaps Forward just as our own anthropologists were to do thousands of years later. Indeed such was the rate of cultural acceleration that a mere 20,000 years had to pass before *Homo sapiens* commenced recording its own history. Another 20,000 years after that, about 10,000 years BP at the start of the New Stone Age, another Great Leap Forward occurred, when we "invented" agriculture and many of our ancestors changed life-styles from hunter-gatherers to agriculturalists, settled down, accumulated possessions and, more importantly, technological and cultural knowledge.

In Palestine, archaeological evidence exists that some 10,000 years BP a largely sedentary population left behind sickles, mortars and clay-lined storage pits to suggest that they had harvested wild grasses. But relatively quickly after that, those wild seeds dropped around camp would have been deliberately planted for convenience and then genetically engineered, unwittingly, as those plants were selected that were the easiest to harvest. But there was a problem with wild wheat and barley that shatters as it ripens so that seeds fall to the ground. As Cook (2004, p. 32) notes: "In domesticated forms, by contrast, mutations in one or two genes are enough to solve the problem to mutual satisfaction." These changes, the major technological breakthrough that produced domesticated einkorn wheat, was such a great success that the ancient Palestinians had thrived. Their population increased so much that by about 8,000 BP they were sufficiently civilised and numerous to create the world's first man-made ecological disaster by burning too much timber for manufacturing lime for plastering their houses which was to set a trend: "down to the present day farming has contributed greatly to the erosion of the Near Eastern Landscape" (*ibid.*, p. 25).

So next year, 2012, if our patient visitors decided to make first-contact and we were able to ask them what they thought about *Homo sapiens*, how do you think they would answer? Would the visitors play to our conceits and praise the advanced civilisation that we flaunt or would they consult their records and provide a more objective assessment? We think they would be objective for after all they could hardly be expected to ignore 98% of their notes (Their own time-investment in research would hardly let them do this, especially if they have got to justify their results to value-for-money research-fund providers back home!). So anything they had to say about whom humans are and about how we relate to other people and to the natural world would necessarily be significantly influenced by our Stone Age and older ancestors. Those aeons spent as hunter-gatherers living in small groups in close proximity within the natural world during which time the sum of billions of interactive material exchanges within and without their selves worked on the constitution of our ancestors, just as they do on us, and fashioned them as successful and enduring occupants of specific ecological niches that culminated today in the fundamentals of how we feel, value, socialise, sense and respond to the world, to the unavoidable sense of the passing of time and to that defining mark of our species, the capacity for abstract thought. The VIGAs would be able to do that with confidence since they would have the historical evidence. We cannot do so, since we do not sufficient evidence; not yet.

With their objective, broad perspective and evidence, it is likely that the VIGAs would judge that our very recent departures from ecological niches and our attempts to live more independently of nature are likely to be problematic, since we possessed neither the knowledge nor experience nor understanding to appreciate the richness and importance of our constitutive interactions with nature.

They may indeed have plotted many recent, but ephemeral, experiments in civilisation along a grand sentient-Earth learning-curve as *Homo sapiens* struggled to re-conceive of itself again and again as its fledgling conceptual autonomy confronted, considered and changed before the demands and opportunities both of social institutions and of nature. It would be reassuring if the VIGAs had recorded significant advances in our knowledge in the last few hundred years and perhaps, if we are very lucky, they might identify some slim chance that we might just be able to see the world for what it is and ourselves for what we are and that we might be able to overcome our terrible, self-imposed, fearful limitations. Or they might conclude that this 2% of our species' time spent in civilised living since the first Great Leap Forward (some 50,000 years or about 0.0014% of the time that has elapsed since life began on this planet) is simply far too short a period to have had any discernible impact on what we know about who we are and what we have to do to limit or avoid disaster.

It is also reasonable that the VIGAs would think that our species' very recent rapid and enormous population growth is a very significant constraint on our ability to reflect as well as to act. Population growth when the climate improved after the last glacial period was both a significant consequence of, and a major driver for, promulgating that Great Mistake.

Approximately 2,000 years ago, there were some 300 million people living on this planet. More than 1,600 years were to elapse before this number doubled to 600 million. In 1750 our total numbers were estimated as 791 million, but this figure took just 150 years to double to 1.7 billion by 1900. One hundred years after that at the start of the third millennium AD, an estimated global human population of over 6.1 billion people means that we have experienced almost a 3.6 times increase in population in about 100 years. The *2008 Revision* from the Population Division of the United Nations Department of Economic and Social Affairs expects that we will have added a further 0.9 billion to our number by early 2012 and that if present trajectories persist we will surpass 9 billion people by 2050.

But it is not likely that population growth will be the only constraint on humanity recognised by the VIGAs; they are likely to identify an aspect of our social institutions as another. Some of our institutions are probably genuinely good for all of mankind and they cannot be otherwise (you might expect to find at least one or two); some cannot do other than serve the interests of particular, frequently not numerous, kinds of people to the detriment of others, such as slavery; however most social institutions are somewhere in between, being intrinsically neither forces for good nor bad and wavering in their consequences between overall benefit and overall cost such as business, economics, accountancy and free-markets. It is this last group of institutions, the ones lacking clear and universal consequences one way or another, that represents the majority in a particle exchange universe, and it cannot be otherwise. No single focussed collective of actions is likely to produce results judged to be beneficial all of the time when there are so many dynamically and creatively changing, interdependent interactions taking place at any one time; the issue here is that many people appear to believe that this is not so.

Those people who benefit from a particular institution of whatever kind will necessarily support it - someone has to. For example, settled agricultural practices and their consequential villages, towns and, then, cities gave rise to more disease and lower quality foods with higher risks of famine for most people, but not for all people. Some people benefitted greatly from the stored supplies of food created by field harvests, orchards and herds and with the right institutional support, such food stores can be easily taken away from those who produced them: "Only in a farming population could a healthy, non-producing élite set itself above the disease-ridden masses". (Diamond, 1987, p. 66). Hence social inequality was another force, in addition to population growth, behind the transition to agricultural societies.

However social inequality is ancient. It predates settled agricultural communities. A 22,000 year old Palaeolithic burial site in Russia contains the remains of two children who were indeed privileged in life for their clothing is elaborated with over ten thousand sewn-in beads which would have taken many thousands of hours to make.

(Cook, 2004, p. 51). If we assume the production time for the bead work to be 2.5 thousand hours then the work would have occupied a !Kung lady over two years to complete (i.e., working 8 hours a day for 2.8 days per week which accounts her 4.8 average free days per week less the 2 days a week for dancing, socialising and moving camp etc.).

Evidence that social élites enjoyed better diets and health than the toiling masses may be found in their skeletal remains; but it is a point that hardly needs proving. Up to the present day, this societal issue with prehistoric roots has not been well managed. In 2008 the World Health Commission on a Social Determinants of Health concluded that: "Inequalities are killing people on a 'grand scale'" (CSDH 2008).

This is solipsism in action; small-self assertions throughout *Homo sapiens'* time and space. But it does not stop with killing people; it is killing animals and killing nature on about as grand a scale as we can contemplate and everybody, victims and winners, will eventually loose.

Excessive population growth in the undeveloped world can, to the sophisticated, modern urban mind, seem hopelessly problematic; a result of the cumulative actions of the individual small-self ignorantly pursuing its own interests regardless of greater issues and consequences. On the other hand, excesses of inequality can also appear hopelessly problematic, the result of the cumulative actions of the individual small-self ignorantly pursuing its own interests regardless of greater issues and consequences.

The activities of the small-self are so widespread that it must be very likely that they are a part of Natural Momentum, a consequence of the agenda-setting actions of the "selfish gene" (Dawkins, 1999). It may appear that *Homo sapiens* and what we identified as Human Momentum in chapter one may well be integral parts of Natural Momentum; but this is too imprecise an argument to make. Individuals in nature can also work for a larger notion of self, a self with a Big "S", an extended-self. This kind of *S*elf perpetuates beyond the life of the *s*elf. There are many examples in nature of this and some in mankind; it is the stuff of everyday heroes.

Small-self actions are neither sophisticated nor progressive; they are vulgar and regressive. The extended-self grows with experience and as we discover more to appreciate, to value and to love; eventually we may come to understand, as Wittgenstein did, that we do not need to distinguish between aesthetics and ethics. We are always free to choose which kind of self we want in our lives.

> "I can tell you, it is not less sensation we want, but more. The ennobling difference between one man and another, between one animal and another, is precisely in this, that one feels more than another. . . . we are only human in so far as we are sensitive, and our honour is precisely in proportion to our passion."
>
> *Of Kings' Treasuries by John Ruskin (1865)*

CHAPTER 3 — ACCOUNTING CONSTRUCTIONS

As with so many conferences, the principal value of the European Accounting Congress in Antwerp lay in the opportunities created by unforeseen contacts made with like-minded people. For this is where the older boy met a large, gentle and sagacious Swedish Professor of Accounting who appropriately possessed a luxuriant Grey Beard. Their next meeting was to be within a half year, during a city-break in Sweden.

The ferry from Harwich, the MS Princess of Scandinavia, steered carefully between the flat, bare outcrops of granite islands that broke with a threatening, understated drama through the calm mists that lay thick that morning on the surface of the Kattegat to form the archipelago of Gothenburg. The older boy was on starboard deck vacantly watching the slow progress. Closer to port and in an intensifying cold, the ship slowed to five knots to follow a ragged passage through cracked sea-ice and slush to eventually dock on the north bank of the Göta Älv.

Day 1 — Representations

Grey Beard was looking very comfortable, sitting opposite the older boy at lunch in Gothenburg's Feskekörka, their "Fish Church" which is actually a bustling fish market. In the small restaurant on the mezzanine floor overlooking merchants, customers and the assembled dead sea-life, there was much reassurance to be taken from the vigour and continuity of an industry that is one of the city's oldest.

The fish-church-market could well have derived its name from the Swedish devout appreciation of food from the sea, but there is more to it than that. It was built in the style of a Gothic church by Victor von Gegerfelt in 1874 during the Victorian Gothic revival which created the Houses of Parliament as well as the Albert Memorial in London. But with the foundations of Gegerfelt's church dug deep within history, it is also a tribute to the *Geats*, an ancient Scandinavian tribe (taken to be the same as the *Goths* by some historians).

Beowulf, who cites the legendary Geats-Swedish conflict, referred to them as *Gēatas* whilst Jordanes, a Roman bureaucrat in the 6th century AD, called them Geats and noted that they were "bold, and quick to engage in war". The name "City of Gothenburg" means "in defence of the Geats" for it protected access to seas west and east and hence the Geats' prime fishing grounds and lucrative trade routes.

That lunchtime looking over the many hands swapping krona for fish, Grey Beard was himself fishing for comments as he returned to their conversation having finished his meal. "Gothenburg has an extensive trading history," he began, "including our own East India Company. The port is still Scandinavia's largest and it was once a world leading ship builder." He paused for thought and a sip of mineral water. "None of this would have been possible without the representations of money and the means of consistently representing these representations throughout complicated sequences of exchanges."

"Money and trade are real," Grey Beard asserted just as might be expected for a Handelshögskolan professor deeply immersed in the accounting and business of this south west corner of Sweden, "it is our history, who we are and who we will become."

The older boy gazed into his own small glass of Falcon and wondered if he had made a mistake in coming to Gothenburg. At the conference and in a few post-conference emails, he and Grey Beard had eagerly absorbed and developed the older boy's thoughts about environmental accounting and sustainable business. Even the particle-exchange universe, natural and human momenta, resource-flow accounting and free-market fantasies had been mentioned and apparently accepted as foundational. But now Grey Beard seemed to be in retreat, asserting traditional, business-as-usual views.

"Vikings made and sold beer like yours, as well as the boats and ships that made this town," Grey Beard said with a final flourish

Chapter 3 — Accounting Constructions   **53**

and then silence fell between them whilst they paid the cashier and made to leave.

Stepping outside the Feskekörka, they stopped aside the Dutch canal. In stimulating, very cold air, Grey Beard said something that opened another kind of door, partially in deference to his guest, but also to his own reflections: "Money has a kind of reality but perhaps not the most real one".

They walked briskly up the hill to the Business School on Vasagaten, where the older boy went straight to his seminar on environmental accounting. The participants were undergraduates. They listened attentively and in closing remarks they told the older boy that they liked his ideas. One of them said: "This is close to the soul of Swedes."

Later, drinking very strong coffee in an academic's personal office overcrowded with articles, books, bric-a-brac and small sculptures in wood and stone, the older boy told Grey Beard what the student had said. Grey Beard eased into the comfort of a large sofa and began talking once more; he could talk a lot. "My house", he explained, "is at the edge of Gothenburg in a clearing surrounded by trees, where deer wander. We Swedes have not left the forests. We love nature. There is so much of it here."

The rest of the afternoon was a preamble, a skirting around and exploration of issues, led for the most part by Grey Beard for the older boy was tired after his voyage, beer, lunch and seminar so he listened and enjoyed the sense of an adventure about to start. Hours later, as they walked in the darkening Swedish winter's late afternoon where distant city and natural outlines were ill-defined, both past and present could mingle in a shared unfamiliarity and hence the older boy, whilst content, could see no more than vague uncertainties along the path and in the future intellectual direction to which Grey Beard seemed to be heading.

Grey Beard gave an impromptu, rambling lecture, the main points of which now follow. Trees and iron-ore had made Swedes rich. Now we have trees. One day, Grey Beard had been told, we will run our cars and buses on trees. Once upon a time, Swedes were very good at accounting with sticks. It is not that long ago. We could not afford

54   *Intrinsic Sustainable Development*

paper and we had so many trees. Stick accounting was clever. Simple notches could record numbers of seals caught. The counting stick, the *Karvstock*, was still in use in the eighteen hundreds. It served also for management records. Tax-gatherers liked the wooden records since they were so durable. Two-sided sticks could show a man's personal mark and an opposite mark was made when the day's work was done. Octagonal-tallies tracked output units in a flour mill and a sixteen-sided tally once served as mine output records.

The karvstock became very sophisticated. For trade across Scandinavia, all three parties to a transaction, the consignor, carrier and consignee, were recorded in triple-tally, a stick split three parallel ways. For illiterate smiths working with money, sticks recorded the currencies in which they worked, the silver dalers and copper öres. The daler was named after the German Thaler just as the dollar. In 1777, the Riksdaler Accounting System started in Sweden. A riksdaler was worth 48 skilling which in turn were worth two öre.

Tallies were universal in the old world. A wooden tally was intricate, accurate and durable; precise as a receipt when, at settlement, creditors handed over the matching split stick. In mediaeval Italy, sticks recorded goods and money transactions. In a coffee shop in the old town, Grey Beard said of himself and the older boy, two professors of accounting: "We would have been out of work in those days with stick accounting. The Karvstock limited accounting representation. Business was simpler. Even in the monasteries of your English island, a tally-man counted milk with a knife and stick."

The two academics now had a fresh and pertinent observation to consider. Just how did they get their jobs? Marks on paper had come to replace notches in wood. The simplicity once enforced on accounting representations was thus removed by the low cost, convenience and much greater information-handling capacity of the new media. Paper had reached Europe in the twelfth century, approximately one millennium after its invention in China. When paper became cheap and common enough, histories, geographies, philosophies, scientific studies and suppositions, stories, edicts and all the large and small words, ideas, arguments, visions and records of

Chapter 3 — Accounting Constructions   **55**

performance, accounting records, that constitute our modern world would henceforth flourish as marks on paper.

The impact of paper was much greater than that of electronic media. The accumulation and dissemination of human culture was transformed. Knowledge and hence imagination and reason became much more of a common currency with the introduction of paper. Accounting was transformed by paper. It was to change during the next few centuries from crude representations in wood to systematically ordered sets of complex marks and relationships on paper that would eventually come to trace their own origins as an independent function with an evolutionary history and hence, within its own parameters, a form of life.

The older boy, still alert to environmental accounting from his afternoon seminar, argued that these steps to an independent kind of accounting were problematic; that they were steps taken in a wrong direction, the root cause of many problems including unsustainable development.

"I must give you a book," said Grey Beard to the older boy, "it is timely. It is an accounting history published to celebrate Pacioli's 500th birthday."

They talked over a cup of coffee to consider Swedish manipulations of Balance Sheets "snapshots" and Profit & Loss interpretations. They began with the very basics of accounting. Just as with tallies they agreed that marks on paper represented something real and simple in the world, materials, people and their time, machines, buildings, land, goods, energy sources and all those things you could bump into, a business's tangible assets.

Like undergraduates, they probed the basics of accounting. The infrastructure, the buildings, land, machines, plant, equipment, computers, furniture and vehicles *used* to make or provide the goods and services, are the Fixed or Long-Term Assets for they do not change their form on a day-to-day basis; especially they do not readily convert into money.

Those items that do change on a day-to-day basis and readily convert into money are *used up* by a business and are called the Current or Short-Term Assets. Current assets such as cash or bank balances turn into purchases of materials, component parts and energy. Sometimes these may rest awhile in one form or another, but that is not desirable. Current assets must be worked hard to generate Revenue and thus a satisfactory Return on Capital Employed (ROCE), that beating heart of a company. Current assets must be worked to increase their value so that they can ultimately be sold for more than their purchase costs, to generate profit. Workers are current assets; they too have to serve the ROCE.

The older boy saw the opportunity and pounced. "I think you have it there," he said casually, "Accounting has been stretched too far. The karvstock kept accounting in its place as a simple record. Now accounting has got so elaborate and inclusive it has gone beyond simple correspondence. It is used on another level, a level in which it creates a reality of its own. People, cultures, the living world are all subsumed by accounting. We are slaves to accounting's representations. It has over-reached itself. It has gone too far into its own world, forgotten too much of the wider reality. That is why we have unsustainable development."

Grey Beard did not hesitate. "Precisely so," he said, "we know all of that in Sweden. We have our own ways of accounting. We describe a business with a triangle with money, people and time at each of the corners. In this way we can show the context, the creativity, the constraints and opportunities and specificities. It shows so much more than traditional accounting. It is a much richer picture with real people in real places. It joins things up. I'll show you examples in my office."

"That's good," said the older boy, "for reality is joined up. But do your triangles go far enough? Do they contain enough joined-up reality?"

The older boy recalled the contents of his environmental accounting seminar. He had wanted to turn the cash representations of traditional accounting into physical measures. For all of the functions within a business or industrial entity, the older boy wanted to measure performance with physical properties, with kilos, joules, watts, sacks, cans, heads, lengths, weights, volumes, temperatures, acres,

Chapter 3 — Accounting Constructions   57

and floors and so on to give a representation of business success or failure in a physical or mass-balance account. Then we would see the real efficient business picture in energy and material just as with the !Kung example (which he had emailed to Grey Beard some months earlier).

Since Grey Beard did not reply, the older boy carried on with his thesis. "Nothing exists in the world at a single level of analysis," he explained, "interdependent levels of existence stack one within another, but we forget that. Quantum particle exchanges, interacting material physics and chemistry, creative and urgent and flamboyant life, interconnected ecologies, and complex consciousness all work together, are subsumed, forgotten, rehashed and put to a limited kind of work in the commonsense, day-to-day human world of lived business experience, observations, visions, desires, plans and policies. This is why our ways are unsustainable."

Grey Beard intervened. He thought that these ideas were too abstract, remote, too removed from business to have any chance of making an impact. The older boy pointed out that may be the case but remember that business activities do intervene in the world at many levels, whether we recognise these levels or not.

"We are all Capitalists now," Grey Beard retorted softly, "whether we recognise it or not. Like it or not, we are all Capitalists now."

"There is pattern, unity, simplicity and control in accounting," conceded the older boy. "For those who can see it, reality is transformed by accounting and there is beauty there. Even so, this is no habitat for human beings."

They stopped talking. It had gone dark outside over the cobbled street. As if to punctuate the end of their day's thoughts, Grey Beard said: "I was born in Alingsås and I will be buried there". They then said good afternoon and see you bright and early tomorrow and they went their different ways.

The older boy dodged trams, bicycles and cars to find a safe crossing through Kungsparken, down Magasingatan and Östra Hamngatan to cut through Nordstan on his way back to the Scandic Crown Hotel just behind central railway station. Along the shopping streets, the darkness had been driven out with Christmas lights, flickering pavement oil-lamps, and illuminated advent stocks in innumerable rows and broken, chaotic patterns rising in office-block windows to the 10th floor and more.

It was bright inside Nordstan and Åhléns, H&M, Twilfit, Hemtex and the other few hundred stores, boutiques, cafés, restaurants and bars within Sweden's largest shopping centre were all very busy. This was a market place but it was about more than money and accounting statements.

In the centre of the mall, twenty young and blonde Swedish girls stood on a raised dais. People crowded around them, floodlights picked off the girls individually and rock music played loudly. It was a beauty contest.

The older boy found a seat at a café on a terrace overlooking the contest. He drank a glass of Schnapps and ate a biscuit. He thought of his journey from England, but also of a journey long before, a journey from Africa. Memories of spindrift and dry, overwhelming heat were as warming as the Schnapps. He was considering how the Swedish workers would cope, what would they gain and loose, in the stores, cafés and bars making marks on sticks in lieu of cash, credit cards, tills and complicated accounting statements. He then thought of comparing Nordstan to a termite hill within which all inhabitants were busy converting the world to what they recognized as good, or to what they liked or deemed necessary. Marks on sticks would limit transactions and hence the size of Nordstan just as much as the mandibles of termites limited the size of their own mounds. But he could not really see a human world without sophisticated accounting to record its performances, to keep it together, to delineate ways forward. Maybe you just had to accept traditional accounting if you want cars, homes, wardrobes, security and the kind of social status that directs collective energies to more constructive behaviour. But just as he concluded that accounting's reality is perhaps big and adaptable enough to accommodate the kind of life most of us want to lead, he had to think that it would be a life lived alone.

After thirty minutes, he left Nordstan heading for his hotel and he crossed that dark open space around the railway station where only

a few lonely and distant street lights broke the gloom and where rat-
tling, warm yellow-glowing trams packed with commuters trundled-
by oblivious to the wind that raced without constraint from the icy
Göta Älv through the city towards distant homes in the suburbs. His
thoughts were still replete with Swedes in forests, their souls, shopping in Nordstan, beauty contests and habitats for human beings
when he reached his room. He was asleep within five minutes.

DAY 2 — Order

Grey Beard and the older boy met at ten the next morning in the
academic's office in Gothenburg Handelshögskolan and left the building immediately. They crossed the tram lines, walked through the
open green space of Hagakyrken and within five minutes they were
back on the cobbled streets of Haga Nygata deep within Haga district, a remnant of the old wooden town of Gothenburg.

In such a historic place, some of their first words that passed
through the morning mists were finding routes back into history.
They felt a better knowledge of origins would help them to better
know a way forward. In particular, Sweden already had a reputation
for being one of the most sustainable countries in the worlds and this
begged the question "why so?"

They found nothing in the history of Gothenburg that answered
this question. From what they knew of the Geats, the Vikings and the
several Swedish wars, such as those that followed the succession of
King Gustaf in the seventeenth century, there was nothing that struck
them as being sustainable or as laying seeds for future sustainability.
They considered cultural diversity for it came to them how insu-
lar individual national histories can be. Immigrants to Gothenburg
had played prominent roles in the making of the city: the Dutch had
brought their skills at building on marshes and had created a notably
spacious city, threaded by canals; many Scots settled in Gothenburg
some of whom were influential in its development such as Chalmers
who founded a university; and the rise in the city's wealth in the eighteenth century had come from fishing and trade but was increased
by the inauguration in 1731 of the Svenska Ostindiska Company by

60   *Intrinsic Sustainable Development*

the Scotsman Colin Campbell to rival the Dutch and British East India Companies and it sent expeditions to Guangzhou in China to trade in spices, porcelain and tea. There was no story to be read in Gothenburg's distant history that was any different from many other European cities which are now presumably less sustainable.

More recently, in the early nineteenth century, Sweden depended on agricultural wealth. It was then one of the poorest countries in Europe. At the start of the twentieth century, Sweden's large reserves of iron ore and timber fuelled a rapid industrialization making Gothenburg a world leading shipbuilder in the 1970's.

They entered Jacobs Café on Haga where the old boy purchased two coffees. "This is a very appropriate café for our digging up of the past," he said, "so reminiscent of old Sweden. Maybe Swedes are more sustainable because they have a living awareness of their own history, of who they are, where they came from?"

"It's a German style café," said Grey Beard flatly, "a little Swedish adaption maybe, but mainly German Art Nouveau, Jugendstil, another import."

They sat at their table by the window and thought and studied the world passing by. At length, the older boy spoke again: "But that little question 'why so?' for sustainable development. There must be a Swedish answer for that. You do it so well, a wealthy and equitable society, plenty of nature and wilderness."

"Economics must relate somehow to any answer," Grey Beard said, "Sustainable development comes at a price, a trade-off, but I am not sure we can formulate the answer in economic terms or even political-economic terms."

"Not even in yours, a successful socialist country? You have social equity with no slums, no real poverty."

"We pay high taxes. We redistribute the wealth and we have a mixed economy, socialist and capitalist. I study so many companies here in Gothenburg, all privately owned. This mix works for us, but that is not enough. Something else is at work for sustainable development."

"And that is?"

"Something quite simple. Something so simple, we cannot see it. We take it for granted. It has to be this way, because sustainable development will change everything."

They sat quietly, finishing their coffees and then left Jacob's Café to return to the Handelshögskolan. "We must do what we can with what we know best," said Grey Beard coming out of Haga. "We are accountants. Accountants say this and that has happened in the past and people listen and plan, invest and make things happen in the future because of the tales that accountants tell. Accounting brings order to the world and promises control in the future. Maybe that is where we should start looking?"

"In accounting?"

"In order! In the order we bring to the world. Sustainable development ultimately depends on the kind of order we bring to the world. We can make a start with accounting."

The older boy thought about this as they walked beside the canal past the Feskekörka. He did not like this idea. The world was far bigger than accounting; people were far bigger than accounting; accounting was just counting and money. If you try and understand sustainable development with accounting, you will necessarily exclude so much. It was a dead end. He put all of these points to Grey Beard.

"Exactly!" said Grey Beard, "Exactly. Exactly. We limit things. We extract just a few aspects. But we can make the reports clear. As such they may be useful --- as elements of a bigger picture."

They walked on hoping for clarity if not inspiration. Eventually back in the Handelshögskolan, it was very busy. Students were moving in large numbers out of lecture theatres at the close of the hour. Academic staff balancing books and papers and cups of coffee flitted in and out of doorways along the corridor that led towards Grey Beard's office. Casual words were exchanged in Swedish. The older boy could understand what they were saying not because he knew Swedish but because he knew these kinds of people in this kind of scenario. It was easy to distinguish pleasantries from serious comment with gestures, smiles, grimaces, activity and context in a universal facial and body language. The offices were very warm. Strong coffee was brewing somewhere.

"Many years ago," said Grey Beard once in the quiet of his own end-of-corridor office, "I defended my thesis on continuity and change in business accounting. I wanted to know then what is it that brings order that lasts? Is order enforced or enticed? What is it that never stays the same, yet is never different?"

"We are getting too good at knowing too much about how the human world works," said the older boy impatiently, because he believed that an accounting-based approach to sustainable development was far too narrow a focus. It was going to take them up a dead end.

"You need to understand accounting as some kind of orderly science and art," said Grey Beard. "It is an in-between."

"No, it is not like that! Accounting was never an objective science. You are confusing reality with representation. Nor is accounting an art, for it has no aesthetic content. This kind of confusion might well be the root cause of unsustainable development. Accounting is just a convention, a socially accepted way of ordering money in industry and business."

"And this orderly accounting way comes from where?" asked Grey Beard.

"Efficiency!" said the older boy impatiently. "We want to use resources efficiently and keep track of money. Accounting fits the bill to do just this. Efficiency dictates order. It is economic in origin."

"Spoken as a true believer," said Grey Beard flatly. "It seems we have much work to do."

Grey Beard took a book from his desk and handed it to the older boy. "I mentioned this yesterday. It's about Pacioli. He discovered order for accounting."

The older boy read the sleeve of the book, *Accounting History: some British Contributions* (Parker and Yamey, 1994): "This volume brings together published work by the major British scholars in the field. It is a contribution to accounting scholarship on the 500th anniversary of Luca Pacioli's 1494 *Summa de Arithmetica.*"

"In Luca's world," Grey Beard began, "accounting was an extension of the art of mathematics." During the next hour or so, Grey Beard talked about Pacioli and order in accounting. The older boy listened. Luca Pacioli had been born into a poor family in Tuscany around 1445. As a young man, Luca worked for a local businessman, but found that he had two strong motivations in his life: a love of mathematics and a desire to travel. Luca quit his job, joined with an itinerant artist who took him to the great cities of Italy including Rome where he met Pope Paul II.

In Renaissance Italy, Grey Beard explained, the European world, was God's world. We can barely imagine it nowadays, but the world at that time was something given by God and the way you got to know that world was to read it like a book, a huge, multidimensional, interactive, multimedia simulation of a book. There was no difference at all between written words and marks on the Earth. Everything that existed was to be read and interpreted as if part of one great book. Signs on a page, letters and words, were exactly the same as birds that flew, running streams, a man's life, or a merchant's transaction.

If you wanted to acquire knowledge in Renaissance Europe then you unearthed and deciphered the signs of God's mind as written into those "books". It is not surprising that a meeting with the Pope, God's spokesperson on Earth, changed Luca's life. Near to his 27th birthday in 1472, Luca took the vows of Franciscan Minor.

Grey Beard stressed just how a different way of ordering knowledge had changed what was known not just about one or two isolated religious or artistic specialities but about everything. If you change the foundation of the way in which you order knowledge then, logically, all that you know changes. The best of scientists understand this, Grey Beard explained. Science is nothing if it is not about keeping an open mind.

Both Grey Beard and the older boy immediately recognised the significance of such a change in the way that we order knowledge. If a different way of ordering knowledge of the world once held sway at some time in the past, why cannot a different way of ordering knowledge apply at some time in the future? Why should we think that the way we now order knowledge is the only way? Some other way may be much more appropriate especially now that for the first time in human history the world is largely explored and full of people. For all of human history mankind has had the option of moving on, finding new places to lay a hearth, start a colony or conquer and subject people to take what is wanted. We simply cannot do that anymore.

To anchor the older boy's understanding of a historically different way of ordering knowledge, Grey Beard suggested that he searched on his office computer for the history of the plant St John's wort, *Hypericum perforatum*. The older boy searched the World Wide Web for information and read that St John's wort is a perennial plant with extensive, creeping rhizomes. Its stems are erect, branched in the upper section, and can grow to 1 m. in height. It has opposing, stalk-less, narrow, oblong, yellow-green leaves which are 12 mm long or slightly larger with transparent dots throughout the tissue and occasionally with a few black dots on the lower surface. Its flowers appear in broad cymes at the ends of the upper branches, grow up to 2.5 cm across, have five petals and are bright yellow with conspicuous black dots. The sepals are pointed, with glandular dots in the tissue. There are many stamens which are united at the base into three bundles.

St John's wort has a complex life-cycle that includes a mature plant-cycle with vegetative and sexual reproduction. It thrives in areas with either a winter- or summer-dominant rainfall pattern; however, distribution is restricted by temperatures too low for seed germination or seedling survival and altitudes greater than 1500 m, rainfall less than 500 mm, and a daily mean January temperature greater than 24 degrees centigrade are considered limiting thresholds. Depending on environmental and climatic conditions, and rosette age, St John's wort will alter growth form and habit to promote survival. Summer rains are particularly effective in allowing the plant to grow vegetatively, following defoliation by insects or grazing.

St John's wort is known to have curative properties. The Cochrane Collaboration at http://www.cochrane.org/, reports of St John's wort that: "The available evidence suggests that the hypericum extracts tested in trials (a) are superior to placebo in patients with major depression; (b) are similarly effective as standard antidepressants; and (c) have fewer side effects than standard antidepressants. There are two issues which complicate the interpretation of our findings: (1) While the influence of precision on study results in placebo-controlled trials is less pronounced in this updated version of our review compared to the previous version, results from more precise trials still show smaller effects over placebo than less precise trials. (2) Results from German-language countries are considerably more favorable for hypericum than trials from other countries." (Linde *et al.* 2008).

"So much information about one little plant," observed the older boy, "so what?"

"This is modern knowledge about the plant," replied Grey Beard. "It describes a plant as something independent, growing alone in the world with this or that dimension, shape, size, colour, form etc. It links the plant into man's world only for its usefulness to man, for its utility. It was once so very different."

"For modern knowledgeable people," Grey Beard continued, "St John's wort is a small flowering plant with medicinal properties. It has long been known for its healing properties. Perforated St John's wort was used to heal the wounds of Crusading Knights.

But the plant once signified much more than that. Its leaves have transparent spots that are oil glands and which were taken by our ancestors to be a sign for skin, a belief which was reinforced by the plant's ability to heal. Also when you crush its flowers or seeds, a reddish-purple liquid oozes out just as if it were bleeding."

Grey Beard searched his shelves. He located a pressed flower in a book, a specimen of St John's wort. "I give this to my students with this talk," he said, "it helps them understand what I am saying if they can look at the flower. This plant is at its best in June and it was once gathered during the pagan celebrations held on Midsummer Day. Its healing powers, yellow stamens, bright golden flowers and skinness showed the pagans that this plant had something of the regenerative power of the sun. When Christianity came along, the pagan evidence on hand for the mystical power of the plant was too strong to be dismissed. The Christians argued that St John's wort's bright-yellow possession of sunlight was sufficient proof of the presence of the supernatural, after all everyone knew that spirits of darkness hated light. It became well known that Satan had no power over anyone who carried a talisman of St. John's wort."

"I'm sorry," said the older boy, "but this is all superstition. Is this really relevant to the needs of sustainable development?"

"You people from the island kingdom are so impatient. Let me finish. When the pagan's Midsummer Day celebrations were taken over by early Christians in the name of St John the Baptist, St John's wort was still gathered to be hung over door or window or worn or consumed to keep darkness and the devil at bay. To prove the point, early Christians could squeeze the plant to show the red blood of St John oozing out of his beheaded body."

"Discredited superstitions," said the older boy.

"Maybe now but not then. That was their knowledge, their reality. It was how they knew the world and themselves. If their way of ordering knowledge has become extinct, why not ours now or in the future?"

"Maybe," said the older boy, "but what about accounting? Accounting is not about superstition."

"But it was once more than we know. Luca Pacioli became a mathematician at the University of Perugia where he stayed for six years. He wrote a mathematical treatise, the *Summa de Arithmetica, Geometria, Proportioni et Proportionalita*. In the *Summa,* he described double-entry bookkeeping, or the Venetian method as it was then called. Luca's system was state-of-the-art. It revolutionized trade and business. It made Luca a celebrity and earned him the title of 'Father of Accounting'."

"Surely this is an example of how reason overcame superstition and helped establish the modern world?"

"Yes. Of how one way of ordering knowledge of the world replaced another. But there was more to Luca. He was invited to teach mathematics at the Court of Duke Sforza in Milan where Leonardo da Vinci studied. Luca and Leonardo worked together for seven years and the artist illustrated Pacioli's next publication *De Divina Proportione*. It was Luca who gave Leonardo greater knowledge of perspective and proportionality. It was the father of accounting who helped create *The Last Supper* in the Santa Maria de Gracia cloister in Milan."

"So he had good connections. It was Leonardo who was the genius not Luca."

"Don't be so mean. Luca had his share of genius, even as an accountant. Luca rediscovered the Golden Ratio from the ancient Greeks. In a famous lecture on 'Proportion and Proportionality', Luca revealed the universal importance of this mathematical ratio to religion, medicine, law, architecture, grammar, printing, sculpture, music and all the liberal arts. It was like a harmonic mean, universal, interdisciplinary."

"If accounting had developed differently," the older boy conjectured, "it might have retained more harmony and proportion and interdisciplinarity."

"Accounting could have been very different."

"But it isn't. It is specialised, narrowly conceived within strict boundaries, protected and reinvented every few years by the accounting profession to keep their salaries high. This is what we have to deal with, not a romantic notion of what accounting could have been."

"Ah!" said Grey Beard, "look at the time. We need to introduce more harmony into our own lives. I am hungry. We have talked enough for one day. Let us go and eat. There is a Japanese restaurant in Viktoriagatan. One of my favourites."

DAY 3 — Knowledge

Grey Beard arrived at the Scandic Crown Hotel on Polhemsplatsen at eight the next morning to take breakfast with the older boy. It was their last day together and they both felt that much work had to be done.

When the meal was finished, Grey Beard gave the older boy a copy of *The Order of Things* by Michel Foucault (1970). "It's spare," Grey Beard said, "my bookseller sends me many books each month. I read them all. Take this one, put it in your baggage, read it on your ferry home. It will be good for you."

The older boy went to his room to clean his teeth and leave the book. He put on a sweater for there was heavy snow falling and swirling outside his window.

Back in the lobby, a small formally-dressed crowd had gathered around the reception desk. Grey Beard had a second cup of coffee. "Let us not rush," he said, "Look at that weather. We can put out our ideas right here. All these business people have somewhere to go. It will be quiet soon."

As it was, the hotel lounge area was empty by nine twenty. Grey Beard had them move to more comfortable seats near the grand piano. The older boy said: "Last night I was thinking about St John's Wort. It is a good example. I can see how mediaeval people had a very different way of knowing the world. Their way looks very primitive, naïve and wishful to us. They had had the whole world turning around themselves and their beliefs. I guess it is natural to try and explain everything from what you know."

"It would be hard to do so from what you do not know!" Grey Beard observed, "Episteme. The word today is episteme. It is from the Greek. It means to know."

"The plant and mediaeval thought is interesting," inquired the older boy, "but are we not losing sight of sustainable development? Seeing mediaeval knowledge as something different from our own does not help us to become more sustainable."

"It does if sustainable development knowledge is something very different from our own."

"Well that might be the case but you and I cannot do anything about that. We are definitely not in the business of creating a new order of knowledge."

"Nobody ever was. No single person creates a new order of knowledge. That we certainly cannot do, but we might help identify a new order. We can call the new order of knowledge an episteme, as Foucault did."

The older boy asked: "A new episteme for sustainable development?"

"No not really. A new episteme not *for* anything. An episteme is not planned or worked out *for* anything. It just happens. It would be good if it were sustainable."

The older boy hesitated and looked at his watch. He felt that Grey Beard was missing the point with these arguments. He had previously encountered the work of the Frenchman Michel Foucault and had on that occasion decided to leave it well alone. Foucault and the other post-modern, deconstructionists seemed to his rational scientific eyes to be just so much French intellectual pomposity. The older boy wanted something simpler, more real.

"It is real," asserted Grey Beard as if he had read his mind. "An episteme is a real thing."

The older boy took off his sweater for the interior of the hotel was warm. "It looks like hot air to me," he rejoined.

"No, it is not so. An episteme shows how people order their knowledge, how they construct reality. It defines what and how they get to know their world and themselves. It influences what they value, how they make meaning. It determines who they are."

The discussion then slipped into something earnest and intense. Grey Beard explained how Foucault described the transition from the Renaissance mind to what Foucault had called the Classical episteme. The Renaissance Period in Europe lasted to the 16th century. It was an age that based knowledge on signs and resemblances. Those people placed the written word in first position when it came to knowing the world so they approached everything as if it had been placed in the world as part of a bigger purpose, God's purpose. They looked for, found, unearthed and deciphered signs and clues in everything, so that hidden truths, buried purpose, may be revealed for all to witness.

Their knowledge was ordered by the resemblances they could find between things such as St John's wort's skin, sun-light and bleeding. They made up meaning by embedding the signs they found into their body of knowledge; by, as it were, bringing hidden resemblances and similitudes into the light and creating associations. They made no distinction between the meaning they found in words in their ancient books and the meaning they found in all other things on, in and above the Earth. In this way they could weave together text and evidence into coherent wholes. For Renaissance minds, to *know* was equivalent to *interpret* and it was an all-inclusive act. Nothing in time present, past or future or in space outer or inner lay outside their knowledge. Holistic, whole, holy and health necessarily merged into one for them.

"Time to walk," said Grey Beard when he finished his little lecture at about eleven forty five. "We need some fresh and cold Swedish air." The older boy put on his sweater and coat and the two men left the hotel together.

The outside air was bitingly cold on their faces. They took a left turn outside the hotel and crossed roads, cycle ways, tramlines and a canal which was overcome by means of a narrow ledge fixed to the top of a lock gate that dropped precariously into the snow and ice that lay across the water. On the opposite bank they trod carefully in the snow for slippery cobble stones had been used in the towpath. They passed through an old wrought iron gate into a formal garden layout.

"These are our gardens," Grey Beard announced, "Trädgårdsföreningens park. Not at its best at this time of year."

Path and flower beds were barely distinguishable in the snow which was not yet so deep as to prevent walking. They walked by the conservatory. It was locked, but condensation from the moist interior air coated the glass rendering it opaque and making it look invitingly warm.

"We will not be revealing the inner signs of the glass house today," Grey Beard joked. "Let us move on."

They talked as they walked in the falling snow between trees and hillocks in that dull winter's morning. Whoever had laid the path was not concerned about going anywhere in particular. It was a path to be enjoyed for the journey alone. It was very beautiful in the snow.

"There are many special plants here," said Grey Beard, "it is a scientific kind of garden as well as an ornamental one."

Eventually they exited the garden into Södra Vägen which they followed as far as the junction with Vasagaten and they took that road as they headed towards Grey Beard's office once more. Vasagaten was austere, cold, windy and lined by many plain walls so the two men did not enjoy this part of the walk so that when they came to Kungsportsavenyn they changed direction and headed to Götaplatsen with its statue of Poseidon.

Grey Beard pointed to the large statue and said: "He looks really cold today with no clothes on. You know when they put him there in 1931 he caused much embarrassment. We were embarrassed by his nakedness. I think that is not how you island people think of Swedes."

When a bookshop with a coffee bar came into view with steam rising from its window, they swiftly moved inside. They purchased drinks and settled into deep brown-leather chairs overlooked by ranks of books.

"You have Foucault now in your room," Grey Beard said, "he will be very useful."

The older boy hesitated. "I am not so sure. Sustainable development needs people to be aware that they are living on a small planet and to act accordingly. It's simple really, a matter of education."

"I agree. It is simple but what if the education is inaccurate? What if the education is a big part of the problem? What if we educate people the wrong way? Maybe something in our knowledge is so far away from sustainable development that we will never be able to educate to avoid big problems with what we now have."

"But if that is the case what can we do? We are not educators or philosophers, we are accountants. We should stick to what we know. Do what we can in our own small field of expertise."

"Our field is big enough. Maybe small fields of expertise are part of the problem," Grey Beard said as he took a notepad out of his briefcase. "I worked last night. I translated my Foucault notes into English. Here they are. Let us take a look at them."

72   *Intrinsic Sustainable Development*

Foucault's Classical Episteme (1650 – 1800)

- Rationalism
  - Replaces exegesis
  - *Rational Order* is to the Classical age as *Interpretation* was to the Renaissance
- The primacy of the text has gone
  - Things and words become separated from each other
  - Words no longer bear the marks of things
- Renaissance epistemology proceeded by linking signs with their resemblances to better know the depth and meaning of the God-given totality of existence
  - *It drew things together*
- Rational Classical epistemology starts with the same God-given totality of existence but proceeds by *discriminating*
    - What has become important is no longer resemblances but *identities* and *differences*
- Descartes denounces "Renaissance resemblance" as a confused knowledge mixture that must from now on be analysed in terms of *identity, difference, measurement* and *order*
  - All knowledge is now obtained by the *comparison* of two or more things with each other
  - There exists only two forms of comparison
    - 1. Measurement of continuous or discontinuous sizes
    - 2. Order by recognition going from simplest to next simplest and on to the most complex
- *Mathesis* is now the universal science of measurement and order
  - The route to all knowledge of simple relations that can be represented by algebra
- *Taxinomia* for knowledge of complex relations represented by systems of signs
- Magic is no longer of use
  - The erudition that once read nature and books alike as part of a single text has been relegated to the same category as its own chimeras

Chapter 3 — Accounting Constructions   **73**

"You see," said Grey Beard, "how Foucault distinguishes the two epistemes. He says they are so different that a person inside one cannot know the other. You can only look back to another episteme as an alien world, seen at a distance through the lens of your own knowledge. You never really enter such a world as its residents would have done."

"You think we really can make a new episteme for sustainable development? One that is so different from our own that right now we cannot really see it?"

"No. We cannot make a new episteme. Nobody *does* that. We just provide a description of the episteme."

"We can only make clear what is already there, but not recognised."

"That's it," replied Grey Beard and he rose to obtain second cups of coffee.

During the following hour, the two academics went through the notes on Foucault's Classical episteme. They saw that whilst the primacy of the written text had gone, words remained important. They became the medium of thought, the very representation of thought. To know something became equivalent to speak or know language correctly. The ordering of language had become the control for the ordering of knowledge; the order of the Classical episteme was structured within a general grammar.

As the Renaissance episteme accepted that everything in the world was like a word or a sign there to be interpreted and revealed within God's greater intent, the Classical episteme used a God-given rational order first found in general grammar, the given way of ordering words and meaning, and then applied it to everything else.

Both the Renaissance and the Classical episteme started with a whole, complete world. Their ways to knowledge were ways to separate the given whole-known-world into constituent parts. For the Renaissance episteme, the whole world had been a text and parts were identified by their resemblances to one another and to the whole which was revealed when their inner mystery, their real meaning was made clear. St John's wort took its place in the ordering of knowledge when the symbolism of its skin, sunlight and blood was made clear, unearthed, brought into the light.

When classical minds began to measure things systematically, to look for the obvious, measureable ways in which things differed one from another then the ways of the Renaissance began to look arcane, mysterious, childishly naïve. The way of ordering knowledge in the Classical episteme was to be much simpler, more transparent and more reliable. Minds in the Classical episteme took everything they knew at face value with no hidden depths or meaning to be revealed. It was laid out for all to see as if on table top. Then they got to know what was on the table top by systematically identifying differences, separating out the parts.

"I think the Classical episteme describes accounting very well," Grey Beard argued. "Accountants take all the costs and revenues of a business and lay them out for all to see on a balance sheet and profit and loss table. Nothing is hidden or laden with mystery. The costs and revenues are made known by identifying the ways in which they differ so the total costs and total revenues are broken down by finer analysis into material costs, costs, overhead costs, sales income and into more and more finer classifications as in the Classical episteme."

The older boy picked up the argument: "Accounting is a good example. It starts with its own totality of existence, the total costs and revenues for a period of time, and separates them not by how they resemble one another but by measurements of identity and difference. It was Descartes wasn't it? He thought that mathematics could be used as the foundation for all knowledge so by measuring things, you got to know them, this was Classical knowledge. But where did this order come from? You can measure and note differences but you would end up with an undifferentiated list of separate items without order."

"There are two answers to that question my young friend," said Grey Beard to the older boy. "You can build up an order just by comparing the measurements you have made and the differences you have noted. One thing is bigger, fatter, wider, denser, harder than another and so on. You can further build on this way of ordering by also recording the simplicity and complexity of things. Once known by measurement, simple things build up into more complex things which are the also known. It is all done within a mathesis, a universal science of measurement and order. It was once accepted as the route to all knowledge."

"That is simple," said the older boy, "but Foucault makes it harder. I woke early this morning and looked through *The Order of Things*. He has a diagram of the table of knowledge in the Classical episteme. It is far more complicated than you make out."

"It is as simple as I said," said Grey Beard, "but the minds that created the Classical episteme were steeped in metaphysics, in the ultimate nature of reality."

"This is what I mean," said the older boy, "we are definitely out of our league with metaphysics. Accountants do not do metaphysics."

"Your island kingdom is a very busy place. You want to rush everywhere as if you know where you are going. Take it easy, do not worry so. Accountants do metaphysics whether they know it or not."

Grey Beard settled back deep into the worn leather of his chair. "Take a deep breath and listen carefully. The Classical episteme was on one level very simple because they assumed an order that could be revealed by measurement. But they were clever men. They knew that what they were getting to know with their measuring was only what they saw, only the representation of order and not the order itself. The order itself was the real underlying order which they could not know and they got to know only representations of realities."

"This is dualistic," said the older boy. "This way of thinking splits existence into two, what we can know of existence and what exists."

"Exactly. As you might expect with such careful and thoughtful rationalists, the Classical episteme was very thorough in dealing with this dualism and how the two parts came together. If you take the sum total of everything that Classical minds were aware of in all of time and not distinguishing between fact and fancy between seal and sea-monster, then move away from these simple certainties and enter a grey or unformed area of knowledge. What do you have?"

"The mystery or God's work?"

"Well yes. But how do you think things were known or ordered in this grey area? Remember that the Classical episteme was formed immediately after the Renaissance episteme."

The older boy thought for a while, but could find no answer.

"Associations and resemblances just as with St John's wort and the Renaissance episteme," said Grey Beard with unconcealed enthusiasm. "The grey area of knowledge in the Classical episteme was an area that could not be fully known, but lingered at the edge of ordered knowledge and gave a foundation to that knowledge. This was the area of impressions, reminiscences, imagination, memory and all that involuntary background; a rudimentary order in which first steps were to be taken towards a conscious, known existence. This is the metaphysical strength of the Classical episteme. They could not know this underlying area of God-given order precisely with a well-ordered mathesis and taxinomia, but only vaguely, fleetingly with their imagination."

The older boy just listened and sipped his strong coffee. Grey Beard was getting into his stride with his explanation of Foucault.

"It is dualistic. It creates the world they fully, consciously knew, which is the world of nature. But it also creates a world they only partially knew, which is a world of the imagination. Both worlds contribute to the final, complete ordering of all knowledge to be realised in the fully conscious world, where the order is as clear as that of the order of their medium of knowledge, the ordering of words and language, the order of general grammar. They argued that these two worlds, that of nature and that of the imagination, had to come together, to unite, in a process of genesis."

"Just as with the Old Testament Genesis?" inquired the older boy.

"Quite possibly," replied Grey Beard as the older boy took and thumbed through the notes on Foucault.

"But what is this all about?" asked the older boy. "Foucault does not give many diagrams in the Order of Things which is just as well. This is so complicated." The older boy pointed to the notes and the four words *attributive, articulatory, designation* and *derivation.*

"Do not worry my friend," said Grey Beard, "these words describe the way things to be known come from the area of the vague imagination to that of measured nature. This is the Classical episteme's metaphysics in action. Foucault uses them to describe how the area of imagination becomes known and ordered." Grey Beard added to his notes as follows:

- *Genesis*
  - The *attributive* function relates to appreciative value and being in its original uniqueness and is performed by the verb in general grammar and value in the analysis of wealth.
  - The *articulatory* role relates to the multiple extensions of *attributive* function to all words with a nominal function --- i.e. to nouns --- in general grammar and to estimate values in the analysis of wealth which are defined and limited within the system constituted by all possible exchanges, where each value finds itself positioned and patterned by all the others.

- *Ordered Knowledge*
  - The function of *designation* now appears as an analysis of roots and of the elementary language of action in general grammar which corresponds to the origin theory of monetary prices.
  - The function of *derivation* is observed as words in their multiplicity acquiring adjacent meanings, changes in form and field of application, new sounds, new contents appearing as tropes and shifts of meaning in general grammar and the extended system of interdependent exchange prices in the theory of monetary prices.

"You see," continued Grey Beard, "for the classical way of thinking genesis is the function whereby things in the imagination become known in their uniqueness and multiplicity with attribution and articulation respectively. When known in Classical knowledge, these same things possessed other aspects in addition to their genesis. They had designation or their roots in general grammar and derivation or the way they changed and evolved in the scheme of general grammar."

"This is too hard to understand. I really do doubt its relevance to our sustainable development problems," objected the older boy. "I think this kind of obtuse intellectualism is somewhere very close to the core problem. It constrains minds, entangles them, locks them within themselves and closes them off to the wider world of feeling, emotion, experiences of other forms of life of nature's grandeur, of the particle-exchange universe. These kinds of intellectualism, whether as post-modernism or neo-classical economics theory, represent the same obstacles that we need to overcome if we are to become sustainable. We need new values, new ways of providing for ourselves, new sustainable lifestyles and that will not be achieved by intellectual dilly-dallying."

"And you think that how we know is less important than what we know?"

The two academics simultaneous reached for what remained of their coffees and emptied the cups. They both felt stiff and awkward. The older boy started to look around at the shelves of book but at first saw nothing in English. When he did spot an English title he felt relief. It was a paperback book about attitudes in Sweden to ecology and nature. He purchased the book and waved it at Grey Beard to make a point.

"After lunch," he said to Grey Beard, "I need to get a few presents. I'll go my own way if that's okay?"

Departing

The next day the older boy felt guilty at the way he had abandoned Grey Beard. But he thought it for the best. Foucault was hard work without sufficient clear benefits for sustainable development. The older boy thought he simply did not have the time to waste on Foucault.

On the MS Princess of Scandinavia, the older boy stood at the stern whilst the ship sailed down the Göta Älv and into the Gothenburg archipelago in hard, penetrating, bitterly cold but brilliant sunshine. Light from the low sun bounced off the calm sea and dazzled him.

Later as he relaxed in his cabin, he lifted from his bag the Foucault book that Grey Beard had given him. He took the book with him to the Admiral Bar, purchased a Falcon beer and sat alone at a table for two between a porthole and the casino.

He read *The Order of Things* partly because he judged Grey Beard to be more knowledgeable than himself and partly because of Grey Beard's parting words: "Take care. Thank you for visiting us here in Gothenburg and remember that accounting is far too important to be left to accountants."

CHAPTER 4 — OPEN SOCIETIES

Place of Departure

Ten years after his city break in Gothenburg, the older boy was on an early morning flight from Manchester to Schiphol airport en route to Beijing. He was dozing as the plane touched down.

In Schiphol airport with a few hours to wait, the older boy wandered among the shops along Holland Avenue. In the museum shop there was a small exhibition of posters promoting the publication of a book about the Baroque period of art in Europe. The poster showed work from various Baroque artists. Caravaggio's sexual inclinations were clear enough in the transformations of ordinary young men into full-lipped warrior saints or pouting cherubic angels. It was Caravaggio, the older boy read on the back cover of the book who inspired Peter Paul Rubens in northern Europe. In the poster displaying Rubens's *Rape of the Daughter's of Leucippus* the same sumptuous forms and other worldly human-transformations were clear again albeit the men were now manly and it was the women who were to be more than womanly.

The book stated that the Baroque period corresponded to a period of time between the years 1600 to 1750 when Europe was experiencing a transition between cultures. The older boy recalled that this period corresponded roughly with what Foucault had identified as the Classical episteme. On impulse, for there was no clear purpose in his mind, the older boy purchased a copy of the book. He sat down in a quiet corner of the airport lounge to read it.

He read that the Baroque period had arisen when the Roman Catholic Church and its followers reacted against revolutionary movements in Europe that had produced new forms of scientific knowledge and religion. By way of example the book reminded him that the new science of those distant days had inverted the relationship between the Sun and the Earth; Copernicus having shown that our planetary system was solar not telluric. That one immense fact had reverberated like an earthquake through informed social institutions and knowledgeable individuals across Europe.

In addition to such revelations from a re-emerging scientific method, a group of dissident Christians in northern Europe railed against what they claimed to be the systemic corruption of the Catholic Church, a corruption that extended as far as the Pope himself. Around the 31st October 1517, this dissent grew into a social revolution as Martin Luther nailed his *Ninety-five Theses* to the door of a church in Germany and launched the Protestant Reformation.

Faced with momentous changes such as these, the Catholic Church and European aristocracy did indeed know that the earth was moving. The Church responded with its own "counter-revolution", the counter-reformation that emerged eventually from the Council of Trent (1545–1563). The Church wanted to win back faltering hearts and minds to the Faith and they decided to do this by directly and clearly publicising their mission to the world and communicating the glory of man as revealed in ancient themes. This communication was to be accomplished by a new artistic movement, and that was eventually to become known as the Baroque.

Whilst the Catholic Church ostensibly wanted the Baroque to draw on and represent other-worldly aspirations in order to secure secular power, the aristocracy of the day would have settled for a secular purpose alone; but church and aristocracy in Europe were intertwined and the fall of one would take down the other. So the opulent wealth, flamboyance and high drama of Baroque art was used as a way to impress people and to legitimate aristocratic rights and power. Rubens was not be the only person awe struck by Caravaggio's work which indeed could have been brushed with the light of God. But Baroque art was not limited to painting; it created magnificent buildings across Europe. The deeply religious Italian sculpture Gian Lorenzo Bernini produced in marble what Caravaggio had done in oils and he earned himself a reputation as Michelangelo's successor. From Bernini's St Peter's Square in Rome to Sir Christopher Wren's

St Paul's Cathedral in London, Baroque art re-affirmed the wealth and power of God, of the Church and of European aristocracy.

The older boy was both fascinated and disappointed with what he read. He was fascinated because the Baroque might be related to Foucault's Classical episteme. It may be that the two correspond; that the Baroque's innate order was the same order that Foucault attributed to the Classical episteme. Or, more likely, they may be antitheses of each other with Foucault's description of the strictly rational Classical order facing up to the flamboyant irrationality of grand catholic myth. The older boy knew too little about the situation to decide one way or the other.

The source of his disappointment was his own naivety. He felt loss in the thought that the Baroque had not been sourced by pure artistic inspiration; disappointed that issues of wealth and power had empowered it. He skimmed through the rest of book catching key words and wondering if the book's analysis had not been written by a Dutch Protestant or latter-day Marxist. He did not want sectarian views; he had wanted to make contact with a reality uncontaminated by human purpose and his artistically vulgar mind had once imagined that the Baroque had done so.

He sat back in the rigid airport chair, glanced upwards and saw that the gate number for his flight had still not been displayed. He carried on reading to employ the nervous energy that he always experienced before a long flight. *Trompe-l'œil*, he read, had been developed in the Baroque and that it was the "use of extremely realistic imagery in order to create the optical illusion that the depicted objects appear in three dimensions, instead of actually being in a two-dimensional painting". Very well, he thought, this is a clear symbolic representation of hidden depths.

Foucault's Renaissance episteme, he recalled, had been based on exegesis, the revelation of hidden meaning in texts whilst the whole world itself was then read as text. When the Classical episteme came along, that process of revealing deep layers of meaning had been lost. Rationalism then ordered the visible world, products of imagination, time past and time future within a single, all-encompassing two-dimensional table. Magic, mystery, divinity and what we would call reality were folded over and over within this table; nothing was left out, but consequently there was no hidden depth to anything, no arcane meanings to be revealed, no hidden associations to be unearthed; nothing could lie outside the two-dimensions of the visible, rationally ordered Classical mind. So it may be the case that *Trompe-l'œil* was for the instigators of the Baroque a reconstitution of a lost third dimension; a surprise; another level of meaning; a thing that all we think we see as some one thing but which is not, and is but the representation of something other, something hidden by the artist and which may be revealed by those who are in on the secret and which may be revealed by them for all to see as being more deep within or outside the flat, two-dimensional representational space of an oil painting.

The book also informed the older boy that the Baroque made widespread use of metaphor and allegory. This he mused is the clear converse of the Classical episteme; metaphor and allegory is the underbelly of that age; the blatant opposition to rational measured precision, that algebraic mathesis and taxinomia of signs based on the diligent, systematic, tedious recording of identity and difference. The Baroque was beginning to look more and more like the antithesis of Classical rationalism: it had been a grounding for imaginative interpretation and exegesis in clear opposition to that of the rigors of an imposed rational order.

Similarly Foucault's Classical episteme provides a ready source of validation for the Baroque's use of *maraviglia*, that use of artifices in art, performances and literature to inspire wonder and astonishment. Presented merely in an entertainment, *maraviglia* could captivate and win hearts and minds over to the notion that there is more to the world than that revealed by reason. The older boy pondered over a description of *Deus ex Machina*, the Baroque theatrical device by means of which Gods descended, with stage mechanics, from the "heavens" to rescue a hero or a struggling plot in the most extreme, dangerous or even absurd manner. For the older boy, this was clearly an enactment of anti-rational mythology.

But in this moment of triumph, of an understanding achieved, the older boy felt a murmur of despair. Here was just another episteme, he was thinking. Maybe I could make these historic epistemic analogies up all day long, one after another, but what for purpose? These epistemes reflect nothing more than an elaborated point of view held in place by a trestle of shaky arguments and assumptions. The older boy sat back in his chair tired with the effort of thought. His eyes were sore with reading in the artificial light. For a while he just stared at other passengers and airport staff rushing both up and down Holland Boulevard. They all had somewhere to go, clear and simple destinations with duties, responsibilities, and commitments, and they went on their ways without twisting in spirals of debilitating self-reflective despair. This is what he had really wanted from Baroque art, something to lift himself out of himself with clear inspirational, pure artistic purpose. He felt motivational simplicity slip further from him as he discovered the Baroque's power and wealth motivations and its technical chicanery. He began to doubt whether simple, straightforward, open, honest societies were possible.

Things to Know

The gate number displayed for his flight, KL0897, was tagged "Wait in Lounge". He closed his eyes and thought about himself, his work, his positioning. Ten years previously, immediately after his city break in Gothenburg, the older boy had read Foucault's book *The Order of Things* but had remained unimpressed. He could not see the book's relevance to sustainable development in spite of Grey Beard's insistence. The older boy had consequently put Foucault aside and had instead applied himself to researching and publishing about corporate environmental management and accounting. With the help of European Union research funding, he had participated in the development of preventative environmental management systems designed to stop business environmental problems before they started and had investigated practical solutions for improving the sustainability of island tourism. Latterly however the simplicity and gains of environmental management and accounting had begun to seem inadequate in the face of escalating sustainable development problems. "We have now picked," he would say to himself, "the low-hanging fruit."

He needed new insight and direction for his work. When he could not find it, he tended to blame himself. In his darker moments trawling his memories and understanding, he sometimes came across a mythical image of Foucault. The archaeologist of knowledge was sitting on a rock, bald and talking incessantly, rhythmically to the point at which his voice sang; in front of the visitation, at Foucault's feet, was a fast flowing river that formed angry, inescapable whirlpools around the rock.

In his lighter moments, Foucault as Lorelei proved highly amusing and the older boy could now adorn the vision with golden trestles, red lips and cherubic cheeks just as Caravaggio had done with his favourite boys. With more profound associations however, the older boy would link mythical Foucault with the young Nietzsche and, hence, with Wagner, and within the whirlpools that the fast flowing river created at their feet were to be found people, or more accurately, notions of self-hood, of little and larger selves, of what we are, what we are doing, where we are going, of how we see ourselves, and all the centuries of stubborn artistic, philosophical and personal struggles that combine into the taken for granted attitudes and ready-to-hand knowledge with which we venture forth each and every day, and which eventually may dissipate suddenly, shockingly, or imperceptibly, slowly into thin air.

His gate number was now identified as D08. The older boy got up, went to D08, sat down and fished inside his briefcase to find a few things to do during the nine hour flight. He found a copy of his latest academic paper, his notes on Foucault and the book about attitudes in Sweden to ecology and nature. This was the very same book that he had purchased in a coffee bar/book shop in Gothenburg so many years ago in the company of Grey Beard.

He held this book about attitudes in his hand, but did not open it. He felt as if there were too many things to know in the book; too many things that he was not ready for, that he simply could not handle. So instead he opened his latest academic paper, now in a final stage; it was a study of new business models for sustainable development in Nordic countries.

The paper started brightly with a *2002 GlobeScan Survey* (http://www. globescan.com/) of "sustainability experts" from around the world. The experts had been asked to rate a number of countries and regions according to how well they "are" or "are not" managing the transition to sustainable development: 52% rated Germany well; 25% of them thought that Great Britain and Canada were doing a good job; 20% rated Japan well; but France was judged to be handling the transition well by only 12% of the experts. The 210 participating experts came from a total of 36 countries in Europe, North America, the Asia/Pacific region, Africa, the Middle East, and Latin America and from five sectors: corporate, government, voluntary, institutional (e.g. academics), and service (e.g. consultants). The range end-members were the United States of America rated as performing the transition to sustainable development well by only 4% of the respondents; and Scandinavia rated as performing well by a massive 83% of respondents. So the older boy had undertaken a study tour of Scandinavian companies and cities asking why they had been rated so good at sustainable development.

What the older boy had wanted to discover were straightforward accounting and management techniques, approaches and goals that he could take and distribute to less sustainable parts of the world. In fact he had discovered something far more simple and far harder to communicate and emulate. He had discovered what the Scandinavians seemed to have known for a long. It was something endemic to them; taken for granted; too obvious for comment; too personally and socially embedded and accepted to become manifest in analysis or subject to any internal questioning; something too homely; too intuitively correct; too emotionally strong; too substantial and existentially real to change; and something much too valuable to lose.

The older boy had approached each company and city in his study with an undisclosed agenda other than it was about sustainable development. He had a list of semi-structured interview questions to use later in the interviews after his main question had been asked. But with no other preamble or discussion about the nature of his research, the older boy began each interview by reporting that 83%

of the experts in a global survey had rated Scandinavia as handling
the transition to sustainable development very well or well. He then
asked "Why?"

The answers he received were consistent. Answers did of course
vary in detail but each person interviewed whether male or female,
in business or not, said that two factors accounted for Scandinavia's
good sustainable development rating: (i) the concern Scandinavians
had for their fellow countrymen; and (ii) a Scandinavian love of
nature. Business accounting and management was not once mentioned in the answers given to the older boy's first question.

Eventually interviewee's had elaborated on their answers. However even for the business people who were interviewed, it was frequently the case than their sustainable business performance was
described as "growing" out of love of nature and their fellows. For
example, a senior management representative of Norsk Hydro ASA
(http://www.hydro.com/en/) linked the creation of their company's
culture to equitable Norwegian society. She explained that Norway
had many small farm-owners and the only equivalent they had to an
aristocracy was, in her terms, a "distributed bureaucracy" of clergy,
sheriffs and lawyers who had not inherited their positions and who
had lived lives close to those of ordinary people. The history of Norsk
Hydro, she explained, is inextricably intertwined with equitable Norwegian society. Their company's founder had started a factory in a
remote part of Norway and as the company grew, they had to build
houses, a hospital, shops and a school for their staff. Hence any history of Norsk Hydro the company has to refer to these "deep Hydro
values", to people and to nature. "Furthermore," she argued proudly,
"Hydro's way of operating sets a paradigm for other Norwegian companies which after all originated in the same society". Norsk Hydro,
his paper went on to explain, is a global leader for sustainable development within extractive industries.

UPM-Kymmene (http://www.upm.com/en/) had similar origins
but this time within the Finnish forests that remain its prime
resource. UPM is one of the world's leading forest-products manu-
facturers and producer of printing papers. They too claimed a deep-
seated social responsibility that was in place from the very start of

the company. UPM's values are "Openness, Trust and Initiative" and whilst they have a long-standing experience in sustainable forest management they have ambitions to take the initiative in an emerging "bio-economy" of bio- diesel, ethanol, chemicals and diversity.

In Denmark, the management philosophy of Novo Nordisk A/S (http:// www.novonordisk.com/) also takes them inexorably in the direction of sustainability but theirs is more focussed, created specifically within the company, and not inherited in detail from society. Novo's ambition is to defeat diabetes across the world. Their representative who spoke with the older boy told him that the company's board of directors would review the company's global position, their technology, science, production and marketing facilities, sales levels and financial markets positioning and then make strategic decisions about how best to act to achieve the company goal, to defeat diabetes. In this way, Novo's relationship with the realities of business, the profits, market shares, turnover and so on, that necessarily take the lead in businesses-for-the-sake-of-business kinds of business is inverted: business realities are the means by which Novo works towards attaining its goals of defeating diabetes. So business success for Novo may be essential, but it is not an end in itself. Ironically for Novo, this attitude has been a recipe for great business success, according to narrower business performance appraisal measures.

Novo's representative told the older boy that in Denmark there is neither a powerful elite nor an influential aristocracy. Denmark was described as having a "petite bourgeoisie" who ruled but who lived and worked in close proximity to ordinary people. It is this arrangement, the older boy was told, that underlies Danish sustainable development successes.

Outside Copenhagen, the older boy visited the Kalundborg Industrial Symbiosis (http://www.symbiosis.dk/). Company members within the symbiosis utilise each other's "waste" on a commercial basis so that the industrial complex as a whole minimises its environmental impact. There were seven companies in the symbiosis: Dong Energy Asnæs Power Station, the plasterboard factory Gyproc A/S, Novo Nordisk A/S, Novozymes A/S, the oil refinery Statoil A/S, the construction material recycling company RGS 90

A/S and the waste company Kara/Noveren I/S. The local town of Kalundborg takes waste heat from the symbiosis and enjoys other benefits. The whole symbiotic complex had been created, the older boy was informed, by the slimmest of chances: four golfing friends started to talk about environmental management in their four different companies in Kalundborg and one thing had led to another. . .

In Sweden, the older boy visited Grey Beard, not as an interviewee, but to gain access to one of Grey Beard's friends who lived in Lidköping Kommun, a city on the southern shore of Lake Vänern, not far from Gothenburg. This city, it proclaims for itself, "Focuses on the future". Grey Beard's friend explained how Lidköping Kommun had developed and implemented a democratic "vision" as a way of pursuing sustainable development. The project had started four years prior to the older boy's visit with a blank page and no more ideas than the requirements of Agenda 21 (1992) and the question "What do we need to do for sustainable development?" The visions of the people of Lidköping were then provided by the people themselves; they noted down their thoughts and sent them to the town hall. A group of volunteers from the Kommun sorted the thoughts into categories and best ideas were selected, translated into strategies by the Kommun's council and eventually recorded in a book that directed city decisions.

In the final section of his paper, the older boy reported that many interviewees had identified taxation as an important tool for implementing sustainable development. The Kalundborg spokesman was proud that social equity was maintained in Scandinavian countries by their tax systems. "In Denmark," he had said, "taxation means it's very hard to get rich, but also we have virtually no poor." Similarly, a representative of the city of Oslo reported the presence of an "equality ideal" among the people of Norway and he had said: "Taxation in Oslo focuses on maintaining this equality."

The older boy finished the final reading of his paper and put it away. He waited slumped in his chair with his eyes closed. It seemed to him that his paper had to do with the kind of knowledge that people might worry about on Monday mornings in offices and factories around the world but he had still had doubts about the relevance of Foucault.

People all around him gathered their belongings and made for the gate. There must have been an announcement but he had been too deep in his thoughts to notice. He shuffled forward and opened his passport at the photo page. "The glory and magnificence of the Baroque," his thoughts ran, "was so creative, so ebullient, so expressive, deeply religious, rich, regal, inspirational and inclusive but nonetheless reducible to the fears, insecurities, mean-spirited arguments and petty, small-self views of a class of people who had so much to lose if things were to change. Here certainly was a transition in the order of knowledge that people had worried about on Monday mornings in boudoirs, palaces, cloisters, stately-homes and chateaux across Europe. The events in Paris on the 14th July 1789 were proof enough that they had been right to have worried."

"May I see your passport please?" the pretty stewardess asked the older boy. She did not appear to be worried.

Flight KL0897: Towards an Economic Ecology

An in-flight meal had been served and its remains tidied away when the older boy tuned his headset into music channel number three and re-opened his briefcase. He felt that it was the appropriate time to open the book about Swedish attitudes to nature. There were several things on his mind.

Or rather several things *distracted* his mind. None of them were clear enough to be *on* his mind; they lurked in the shadows of his consciousness. He could not perceive them clearly, so they stayed in the background, stimulating his imagination and raising his hopes only temporarily. They quickly lost their shaky form and weak momentum under a moment's critical reflection. The individual regions of the distraction were clear enough to the older boy: that particle exchange universe, Scandinavian social equity and love of nature, sustainable business models, human momentum and the Baroque. The individual regions were not the problem; it was their synthesis into a coherent whole, the links between them, the continuity, that persistently eluded him.

He opened the book about Swedish attitudes to nature to get to better know one of his regional distractions and perhaps find a way to link it into his broader system of thought. A page of notes fell out of the book and slipped under the chair in front. Only by leaving his seat and with the co-operation of a fellow passenger could he retrieve the page. Back in his seat, he pulled down the tray and placed the page upon it. He leaned forward to study the page.

It contained notes that he had made long ago after working with Grey Beard in Gothenburg and first reading Foucault. It had been during one of his earlier attempts, he realised, at a synthesis. On flight KL0897, his earlier purpose came back to him as a refreshing surprise: "I had been trying to link Foucault to Swedish attitudes to nature. That's it! I had wanted to show how views of the world, attitudes, values and actions may all hinge on a change of episteme."

It had been a very early attempt at a synthesis. Like his subsequent efforts, it had failed, but his mind's distractions would not let it rest: "Maybe," he was thinking, "it will look different in the light of what I now know." He studied the page very closely indeed.

The Classical episteme belongs to another world. "It is a world I can never enter," he thought. Nonetheless Linnaeus's conception of nature and society sharing the same order was a clear enough systemic link that his mind's distractions would not allow him to blur.

The idea that our understanding of "evolution" did not have a precedent in the Classical episteme was also very interesting for the older boy. It meant that one basic, foundational idea, something that might be very close to our core understanding that directs our way of ordering knowledge in the Modern episteme is of our own making. The Modern episteme did not inherit the idea of biological evolution; it came to us, via Darwin, and redefined who we are, what we are doing and the world in which we live. This one simple idea had the power to change epistemes, to change worlds.

Evolution was an interesting idea, but not at all useful, he thought, for his present synthesising purpose; not anyway without more knowledge. In a similar, self-defamatory and critical vein, he dismissed his page of notes because they dealt only with the Classical episteme. "What good is the Classical episteme to us nowadays?" he was asking of himself.

Chapter 4 — Open Societies   **93**

Table 1.   The Older Boy's Notes on Foucault

<u>Foucault on Natural History in the Classical Episteme</u>

1. Biology did not exist in the 17th & 18th centuries since they were then concerned with the dividing up the visible structure of the living world and not with the intrinsic processes of life.

2. The Classical episteme got to know things in a measured, rational order that was analysed according to visible <u>identities</u> and <u>differences</u> of things. So an animal or plant is what is seen and measured and it no longer has hidden resemblances or associations to reveal as in the Renaissance episteme, e.g. St John's wort.

3. Adanson was of the opinion that one day it would be possible to treat natural history as a rigorous, mathematical science.

4. Adanson also remarked that nature is a confused mingling of beings that seem to have been brought together by chance. But for them the great mixture was the results of a chronological series of events (such as described in the Bible) and not events originating in the living species themselves (as in Darwin's evolutionary theory).   These events have a kind of evolution or historicity but this is due to great biblical cosmic changes; it was these changes that affected astronomic systems directly and gave rise to the visible taxonomy of species.

5. <u>Hence there cannot be an "evolutionism" in Classical thought</u> for time is conceived in terms of the great cosmic revolutions in which creatures live.

6. These "evolutions" are linked with revolutions in the whole solar system and were arranged by God in advance.

7. Linnaeus had conceived of the project of discovering in all the concrete domains of <u>nature and society</u> the same distributions and the same order.

He immediately answered his own question with the thought: "Because it allows us to see epistemic change in action, in all its theoretical and practical means and consequences." Fired with an enthusiasm that overcame the relaxing influence of the small bottle of red wine that he had taken with dinner as well as the dimming of the cabin lights, he read the book about Swedish attitudes to nature. When the cabin lights were raised to serve breakfast some five hours later, he was still reading.

"Linnaeus had no option," the older boy concluded as he finished his breakfast. Linnaeus, the Swedish naturalist, had not been *forced* to think according to the training, dictates or epistles of the Classical episteme; nor had there been some kind of conceptual "structure" or rutted track of thoughts from which Linnaeus could not escape. Linnaeus had been brilliantly alive, earnest, enthusiastic, self-determined; pushing hard to extend the boundaries of knowledge; leaping energetically over the flat, visible, rational territory of that whole totally inclusive table of the Classical episteme ordering of knowledge; opening new vistas; and enjoying new ways of integrating the scientific knowledge of the world. Linnaeus had no option but to *integrate* knowledge; it was impossible to think otherwise in the Classical episteme. For Linnaeus knowledge had been laid out flat, rationally and visible as if on a table, but it was also complete, coherent, whole, holistic and holy for it was in God's complete world and He had omitted nothing. "Linnaeus had had no option", the older boy concluded, "but to integrate knowledge for in the Classical episteme, it simply did not exist in parts."

Because of Linnaeus, the older boy made tentative steps towards appreciating what Foucault's epistemic analytical method might bring to sustainable development in our own times. In the Classical episteme, the world had been a coherent single knowable entity; in a change of episteme, that coming of the Modern, knowledge had lost its integrity. An obvious question now presented itself to the older boy: "Could a new episteme possess integrated forms of knowledge better suited to the needs of sustainable development?"

He could not answer this question because he had no idea what a new, other than Modern, episteme would look like. So he contented himself in the last hour of flight KL0897 with reflecting on things of importance he had gleaned from the book about Swedish attitudes to nature.

It appears that Linnaeus (1707–1778) is now known as the father of modern taxonomy and one of the fathers of modern ecology. He had been born in Småland in southern Sweden. By the time of his death, Linnaeus had been acknowledged throughout Europe as one of the most acclaimed scientists of his time:

- Jean-Jacques Rousseau once sent this message to Linnaeus: "Tell him I know no greater man on earth";
- Goethe wrote posthumously of Linnaeus: "With the exception of Shakespeare and Spinoza, I know no one among the no longer living who has influenced me more strongly"; and
- August Strindberg had written: "Linnaeus was in reality a poet who happened to become a naturalist".

Linnaeus had possessed a holistic attitude in which nature, God, the material, the social and the spiritual were intertwined. For Linnaeus, God worked through nature, forming individual organisms and regulating the relations among them. This divine order and purpose, which Linnaeus called the "economy of nature" (*Oeconomia Naturae*, 1749), underlay the appearance and functions of plants, animals and their interactions *in toto*.

With a prickling interest, the older boy had referred to the book's index to look up the "economy of nature" and read that it is derived from Linnaeus' idea of an animal economy which in turn had roots in something called "physicotheology" which was said to have an origin in antiquity. Ancient physicotheology was based on a harmony and equilibrium in nature and this led Linnaeus to develop ideas that lay the foundation for a Modern understanding of ecology. Linnaeus' early ecological ideas have been called "protoecology" and these ideas had not at first been well received in England; a country destined to be more interested in the industrial exploitation of nature rather than harmonious mutual development.

After Linnaeus' death, it had been up to two other Swedes, Per Kalm and Samuel Ödmann, to carry his work forward. In Kalm's travelogues there are many protoecological observations especially regarding man's impact on nature. He described how in America during the mid 18th century, whole forests were being cut down, species of birds driven to extinction, and drainage ditches were being dug so extensively that they were changing the climate. Kalm even went so far as to contrast the greed of European settlers with the American Indian's harmonious ways of living.

Kalm had regarded the farming methods of the American pioneers as worthless. They cut down forests for cultivation to take advantage of the black soil that had been building up over hundreds of years, but they soon exhausted these soils after a few harvests, so they had to abandon their fields and clear new ones, cutting down more trees. "With better knowledge of natural history," Kalm had written, "a more sustainable form of agriculture could have been achieved." Kalm continued: "Hardly could we in Sweden and Finland treat our valuable forests with more hostility than is happening here: they look only to immediate profits, and never even dream about the future." (Per Kalm in *A Depiction of America in 1748.*)

The older boy was fascinated to read about the reception given to Linnaeus and Kalm's work in some quarters of the then wider world. Linnaeus's nature philosophy had been characterized by words like "speculative", "outmoded" and "fantastic", and the ornithological historian Streseman had regarded Linnaeus' analogies between birds and mammals as "disastrous". But some people came to celebrate Linnaeus's work. The great geologist Charles Lyell is thought to have had one of the clearest grasps of Linnaeus's ideas regarding the economy of nature. Similarly Gilbert White, the author of the classic *The Natural History of Selborne* (1868), found inspiration in Linnaeus.

Charles Darwin too would have come across Linnaeus's work during his many meetings with Charles Lyell. In the 1840s, the publication of an English version of *Oeconomia Naturae* would have allowed Darwin to read Linnaeus in translation. It was during that period that the expressions "husbandry of nature" and "polity of nature" become more and more common in Darwin's manuscripts and letters.

Darwin's concepts of different species having "allotted places" or a "proper business" had origins in Linnaeus.

As he drank his second cup of breakfast coffee the older boy was to rethink the conclusion that Darwin was influenced by political economy as Spencer had argued; Darwin's ideas about evolution and an economy of nature stemmed from the views of earlier naturalists like Linnaeus and Lyell, who in turn are indebted to physicotheology with its roots in antiquity. It was not for example the economist Robert Malthus who had seeded Darwin with ideas about the "struggle for existence" and "population pressure", since both may be found within the Linnaean tradition in (i) Lyell's first treatise *Principia* (precociously named after Newton's great work), and (ii) Paley's physicotheological bestseller *Natural Theology* which was available in England well before Darwin read Malthus in 1838.

The older boy began wondering just how Linnaeus's inclusive, holistic approach had been transformed into the fragmented knowledge and rigid disciplinarian boundaries that divided Modern knowledge. He wondered how economics had become so independent, foundationally separated, and not some kind of integrated economic ecology. He then fell asleep, book in hand, for the first time on flight KL0897. He woke some ten minutes later to a cabin made brilliantly bright by powerful sunshine bursting through all its wide open portholes as the plane banked to reveal stunning views of the vast and empty Gobi desert some 34,000 feet below.

Beijing: Opening Societies

"Forget all your preconceptions" was the advice given in the UKTI booklet about making a first visit to China. The older boy found this to be good advice. He prided himself on his ability to keep an open mind and also on his knowledge of the world but during his first days in Beijing he found the city bigger, busier, more modern, cleaner, richer, friendlier, stranger and more enigmatic than anything he had anticipated.

He adjusted quickly to the superficial differences which, if taken street by street, precinct by precinct, were approachable on a human scale in spite of the great size of the city itself. His guide helped him to settle into a comfortable way of exploring that juxtaposed the strange and unexpected with familiarities. This was no more true than during his adventures with Chinese food for his guide mixed each day "safe" dishes with challenges involving unusual animals or parts of an animal: sea-squirts, duck's tongues, fish heads, pig's ears, chicken feet, eyes, and maggots. If he were to remain unaware of what he was eating, the food was generally acceptable or good, though he found tastes and textures varying in the same meal from bland and smooth to hot, spicy and impossible to eat such as roast duck's head. But there was always Starbucks which, in spite of his disappointment at finding another cultural transgression, he found reassuring and welcoming especially so because the menus were global-international and the staff spoke English.

In was in a Starbucks' café that after two days, he had nicknamed his guide "Queen's Chinglish", "QC" for short. His guide was Han which made her a member of the single largest ethnic group on the planet representing over 90% of the population of China and nearly 20% of total global population. The nickname came about for three reasons. First of all, there was the way she spoke English. She was very precise with her intonations of the English language, which she knew well enough after spending four years in the UK as a student; first on an English language course in Edinburgh, then taking an MBA and finally during the first year of her PhD programme. Furthermore her demeanour was on a scale that extended from the fussy and over-considerate when dealing with her foreign guest to a firm but unassumingly matter-of-fact way of taking control of any social situation that involved her fellow citizens. She was small, but she ruled her world with ease and charm. This itself suggested a queenly epithet for her.

The third reason was that she found so much with which to contend. She had received so many criticisms of China and Chinese policies whilst living abroad that she now possessed swift and well-honed responses such as: "for hundreds of years Tibet has been a part of China", and "I was in Tiananmen square as a little girl and I saw rebels killing people in the street with sticks and blows". To balance her inveterate support for China, her PhD studies on environmental and sustainable development issues provided her with many criticisms of Modern China. But even at her most argumentative, QC was not aggressively confrontational. She could skilfully, subtly win over her listeners as well as anyone who might be heard speaking in the Old Bailey.

Technically QC's English did need some polishing and the two people, the older boy and she, quickly slipped into a double-act of her initial mistake being corrected by him and then quickly followed by a courteous but formal apology with profuse thanks for drawing attention to and correcting the mistake. This sequence occurred no more so than in use of pronouns where "he", "she" and "we" were fully interchangeable for QC as were words for relatives such as "brother", "sister", "aunt" and "uncle" of whom QC had many such acquaintances far in excess of the biological limitations conveyed by even the loosest of English meanings. Then there were QC's random twists in English that were unpredictable and unexpected but always amusing. For example, on inviting the older boy to a small social gathering QC said that only her "friends and relevants" will be there, but it had been QC's request for an "Earl *Gary*" tea in Starbucks that had finally clinched the nickname.

The older boy was QC's PhD supervisor. She was studying sustainability in the Chinese tourism sector, which required comparing and contrasting constraints and opportunities for sustainable tourism development in China with those in Europe as well as a review in theory and practice of the relevant management and accounting tools and approaches that the global tourism industry had developed for this purpose. Their task in hand, the purpose of the older boy's visit, was to review her progress.

She told him that at the start of the second Christian millennia, the government of the People's Republic of China (PRC) had been achieving an economic miracle of 10% annual GDP growth but that the shadow of this economic miracle was killing China and the Chinese. She showed him a paper by Chan (2004) that reported that for China:

- One third of the country suffers from severe soil erosion;
- 75% of its lakes and about half of its rivers are polluted;

- 75% of its wastewater is discharged untreated;
- 60% of its people are drinking water that does not meet the World Health Organisation's minimum acceptable standard;
- 25% of Chinese die of respiratory diseases; and
- China is one of the world's largest contributors to global climate change.

"It so quickly happened," she said. "I was born in the Hutong in Beijing where the Zhou Dynasty build places for ordinary workers. It was always busy but not like this, no cars and buses, but many people and carts and bicycles and shouting. Chinese can be very noisy." QC paused.

"The streets were small and buildings low with many trees. I miss them. They have been so many replaced."

She continued with the progress of her study. The bad Chinese environmental performance had been "totally unacceptable" and had forced the PRC to change its thinking and policies. They had dug deep into ancient China and sought new applications of old ways as they planned to restore harmony. In 2006, they embedded "harmony" in their 11th Five-Year Plan.

In November 2007, the PRC had promised to invest 1.35% of the nation's GDP in environmental protection over the following three years: 640 billion yuan ($85.33 billion U.S.) on treating water pollution, 600 billion yuan ($80 billion U.S.) on cleaner air, 210 billion yuan ($28 billion U.S.) on solid waste disposal and much more. They also set themselves 7 goals which focused upon: air pollution control; fresh-water supply and waste-water disposal; solid and hazardous waste treatment; environmental monitoring and analysis systems; environmental consulting services; ecological and natural resources protection; and nuclear safety and radiation management. The success of the plan was to be measured with a series of targets including:

- A 10% reduction in total polluting emissions;
- 20% reduction in energy consumption per unit of GDP; and
- A 30% reduction in industrial water usage.

Later that evening, the older boy went through QC's work in his hotel room and corrected some grammatical errors as he tried to sense and understand the direction in which her thesis was heading. It was in those moments that he first wanted to know where Chinese harmonious development had come from, what it meant, and did it have the potential to synthesis his diverse distractions, the particle exchange universe, Scandinavian social equity and love of nature, sustainable business models, human momentum and, recently added, the Baroque and momentous societal change?

The following morning the idea that China, more ancient than Modern, might provide guidance, if not solutions, for his elusive personal quest took firm hold of the older boy's thoughts. He spent the morning studying the beliefs, history and development of China on the World Wide Web. From the legendary Xia Dynasty of some four thousand years ago up to the start of the twentieth century, China had endured with its own unique identity and approach. The Chinese of course were people, as ordinary and as exceptional as any you might find in London or Bradford, but that fact did nothing to confuse or dilute their very different trajectory. How had they viewed the world? What conclusion had they drawn and accepted about everyday life and death? What principles had guided their development? And in spite of himself, for he was still not at this stage at all reconciled to Foucault, "What kind of epistemes had they possessed in all their ages?"

It was bewildering and exciting to have so many new and strange ideas, facts and names and sequences of events. So much affecting so many people for such great lengths of time and he knew so very little about them. He began to feel that his knowledge of history, of himself and his own people was so parochial, arrogant and breathtakingly biased. The innumerable Chinese cities, rivers, mountains, beliefs, battles, loves, lives and deaths were so alien but familiar; so different yet so very human that the prospect of finding some essential, synthesising concepts seemed good. In his western mind, the older boy could see how he could stand at a distance from this great civilisation and observe its processes and functions more scientifically, free of some of his own prejudices and distorting memories. It would be his vast thought laboratory.

When he meet QC after lunch in a Starbucks two blocks from his hotel, he decided to enlist her help, unknowingly and obliquely of course, for he did not want to distract her from her own thesis, make it more complicated or include too much of his own thinking into her work so that she lost ownership. But it would be harmless, respectable and mutually rewarding, he judged, for them to follow the same intellectual path - at least for a day or two.

He quizzed QC about the origins of the Chinese concept of Harmonious Development. This was after all something central to her comparative study of sustainable tourism development in China and the West. She had answers ready.

QC said: "The concept of harmonious development was dominant for a long time in the history of China. In the ancient times, in the Book of Rites of the Zhou dynasty, the Li Ji, had limited hunting, logging and fishing to certain periods of the year. Master Kong, you will know him as Kong Fu-tzu or Confucius, had written this. There were many other great sages who said the same things: Mencius show the ancient Chinese people dangers of opening uncultivated land and tampering with the natures; Guan Zhong said that people who followed the rules of nature would be protected and helped by the nature while people who disobeyed would have punishment rewards; and Daoists believes nature inclines towards a harmonious development by its own ways, if we not apply being forced and constrained. Also look at this. . . " She wrote this Chinese script "天 人 合 一" in her notebook as she spoke: "It reveals ancient Chinese thinking. The first symbol is "tiān" which means the heaven, sky and nature. The second is "rén" meaning peoples, then comes there is "hé" meaning whole, together and uniting. Finally is "yī" for one, single alone. You say 'tiānrénhéyī' and it means all of heaven, nature and human all merge through continuous mixing and interacting, are one. We have known long time by Master Kong all nature is affected by human morality."

The older boy was far too intent on understanding what QC was saying to comment on how she was saying it. "Harmony," she continued, "ruled heaven and earth. The Ming dynasty built

Forbidden City in 1406 so emperor could better reproduce on earth heavenly source of harmony. The Hall of Supreme Harmony is where the Emperor held greatest ceremonies for it was there where all things in man, in nature, in universe were most harmonious and most peaceful."

They passed the afternoon in similar discussions. The next day the older boy had to visit Shanghai on University business. He would be back in Beijing in two days time, so he left QC with a task. He told her that harmonious development was important to her work, but also that she must be ready for critiques. The very thing that had held China together, some will say, was also the cause of her downfall. Harmonious development was a synthesising force, but it was so effective that it became a barrier that prevented Chinese people from progressing. The ancient Chinese had been so concerned about maintaining harmony between men and nature that they had not dared to investigate nature in fear of disturbing harmony. If they damaged the harmony they might not be able to fix it, so they dare not analyse nature, dare not look into her for her secrets. You need to support harmonious development with a study of Chinese attitudes to science. "Can you make a start on this these next couple of days please?"

QC was not taken aback. This was a kind of criticism she had already received and countered on many occasions. "Paper, printing, compass, gunpowder, hot-air balloons, football, seismographs and so many more inventions all come from China," she replied, "the Chinese actually discovered so many things, did so much of science."

"No," responded the older boy, "I do not doubt Chinese inventiveness. It is their **attitude** that I query. Did their notion of harmony make it difficult for them to conduct a systematic study of nature? Was there something in ancient Chinese religion, their view of the world that made procedural science difficult?" QC, for once, had no answers to these questions but she did promise to see what she could find out.

Science in Ancient China

Two days later the older boy and QC met again in the same Starbucks. "I have no answer," she told him, "because you asked the wrong question." She gave him her note book with two pages of immaculately written notes under the title "Attitudes to Science in Ancient China". QC's notes first summarised the main teachings of ancient China.

Confucianism, she had written, was founded by the philosopher Confucius (551–479 BC). He was most influential making the mould for Chinese civilization. He taught about human interpersonal relationships and he valued very highly logic. He did not care to talk about spiritual beings or even about life after death but that individual human beings can make a good society based on good government and harmonious human relations.

Lao-tzu (604–490 BC) and Chuang-tzu (369–286 BC) wrote about Daoism but it is a much older Chinese religion regarded as the folk religion of the Chinese people. Daoists believe in a heavenly universe of deities and cosmic process that come from the interactions of *yin* and *yang*. Yin is the feminine and denotes things that are negative, passive and concealing. Yang is masculine and for positivity, activity, dynamism, and the unconcealed.

Daoism maintains that the origin of the universe lies with the great ultimate, tai chi, which is also called *wu* or nothingness or non-being. The tai chi emblem, which consists of a circle with an s-shaped curve dividing it into two complementing black and white regions, shows the yin and yang as two cosmic forces wrapped in mutual inter-penetration each region containing the dot of its opposite. It is an empirical sign of the origin of the universe and its ongoing processes.

Neo-Confucian cosmologists in the Song Dynasty (960–1279 AD) used Daoist ideas and had the myriad things being created by evolutionary process of creation from the "great ultimate" through the dialectical interaction of the passive cosmic force, yin, and the active cosmic force, yang. The creating order is called the Dao, the Way, which governs nature, the Earth and human life and society. Hence the Dao should be the purpose of all activities from governmental to personal. The Dao is the most fundamental principle possible and it is the foundation of objective and natural cosmological law.

Yin and yang were the basis for classifications and explanations in traditional China; a systematic science for daily life, technology, medicine, and philosophy. The Daoists did not conceive of a separate spirit. They studied immortality but for whole person with body. This means that people and their bodies are dependent on their physical world, their environment and taking care of body health care. The Daoists had a great influence on ancient Chinese science.

Mo Zi (470 BC 391 BC) criticized Confucius. He believed in a personal God and spirits. He was like Christian and had mission to rescue people from suffering. He proclaimed that there is universal love. His followers are called Mohists and they needed science and technology to put their ideas into practice.

Mohists had an epistemology in which the human mind interprets impressions of objects presented to the senses. The Mohist great book, the *Mo Jing*, classifies knowledge. For example names are classified into three kinds: general, classifying, and private. Then the knowledge of correspondence occurs when a name corresponds to actuality. Knowledge of correspondence explains simple sentences such as "This is horse". With this kind of knowledge, names and actualities form pairs with each other.

The *Mo Jing* has statements about motion and moving spheres and Mohists consider forces and came close to discovering the principle of inertia. They had a primitive atomic theory in relation to their strengths of materials and Mohist physicists understood that light travels in straight lines. By using fixed light sources, screens with pinhole apertures, and possibly a camera obscura, they were able to study the formation of inverted images and the idea of the focal point.

"You see," said QC when the older boy had finished reading her notes, "ancient China had many scientific ideas. These are a few of them. I think ancient Chinese thought they had solved cosmological issues and knew about the processes of nature. They may be once complacent. But we also very practical. We prize highly sciences for engineering and practical inventions, not so much towards theories about nature. Teachers in the Han Dynasty wrote famous the *Nine Chapters Book* about mathematics to be used in all Chinese schools from the third century AD. What were they teaching in your schools at that time?"

"You have done well QC, as always," replied the older boy. "But I have not been idle myself. I have found you a friend. Joseph Needham was an Englishman who revealed how Chinese people had been pioneers in almost every conceivable field of science. He probably overstepped the evidence with some ideas for he made no allowance for the possibility of independent invention and parallel development elsewhere for his thesis was based on simple precedence. If China had it first then the rest of the world had acquired the knowledge by diffusion out of China and by no other means. Needham died in 1995 but he established a research institute in Cambridge to carry on his work. You should contact them."

"Thank you. I will."

"But even Needham was not convinced that the Chinese ever had anything like what we now regard as modern science. He thought that it may have been the religious and philosophical framework of Chinese intellectuals which made them unable to accept the ideas of laws of nature. To my mind, and extrapolating from what you have just said, I think the epistemology and cosmology of the ancient Chinese suggest that they had something similar to the epistemes that dominated Europe for a time to the end of the eighteenth century."

"I am sorry," interrupted QC, "I not know episteme."

"No, of course not," the older boy corrected himself with some embarrassment. "I'm just thinking aloud. You don't need to understand this. It's a complicated European thing. It is not a direction you need to go. But it is only a way of describing an epistemology just as you did for the Mohists."

To distract her, the older boy gave QC a quotation noted in his own book:

> "It was not that there was no order in nature for the Chinese, but rather that it was not an order ordained by a rational personal being, and hence there was no conviction that rational personal beings would be able to spell out in their lesser earthly languages the divine code of laws which he had decreed aforetime. The Daoists, indeed, would

have scorned such an idea as being too naïve for the subtlety and complexity of the universe as they intuited it."

(*Needham and Wang 1954, p. 581*).

"This is Needham's conclusion," said the older boy. "After what you have told me, I must say that I tend to agree with him."

QC did not hesitate with her reply. Her anger was controlled so she appeared cold, aloof, precise and indifferent: "I have been thinking for myself about what you say. I know a little of your culture too. I think your patron saint, St George, shows your attitude to nature very well. Nature is like a dangerous dragon beast for you, something to be beaten, overcome and destroyed. You do so because your religion has given you another place to go, a perfect heaven waiting for you when you have used up nature. We do not have anywhere else to go outside our bodies and nature so we love our dragon. We are a society that has an open heart for nature. Our sages and artist captured in brushstrokes each vibrant, living moment of nature's creativity. Ancient Chinese people could not abuse nature. They communed with her as a source of the highest spiritual satisfaction. They thought themselves a small balanced part of nature so they leave her alone no more than self abuse to your own body. They could not abuse nature and destroy her harmony for that would destroy their society, would destroy them."

Flight KL0898: Openness & Death

The older boy had greatly annoyed QC during that last day in Beijing. She had not liked what he had been saying about the limitations of the Chinese worldview and of Chinese science. In her own queenly, unassumingly-assertive manner, she had said things that stuck in the older boy's memory even the next day as she dropped him off at Beijing airport for Flight KL0898 to Schiphol.

"Openness" had stayed with him partly because it was so directly opposed to how he himself had previously regarded the Chinese. After Mao Zedong, China had been closed to the world but well before that, throughout Chinese civilization, the older boy had always suspected that the Mandarins, the Confucian bureaucrats, had stifled the Chinese people and curtailed their creativity with their ancient texts and edicts. But QC regarded ancient China as a dynamic unstable place in which revolutions had been frequent because of their notion of the spontaneous creativity of nature, of an order of the world beyond the rational understanding of men but nonetheless accessible, usable, applicable in morality, in the ways of conducting a life, lives, in accordance with a given way, a way of the world, a way of nature and man and heaven. Chinese society had been open to change not in a welcoming way – vested interests always form some resistance – but in the sense that it was a quixotic, equitable society. It was not and could never have been a social equality based on the *abilities* of men for they are not born equal in this regard. The Chinese had possessed *moral equity*; they had occupied a moral universe and their understanding of social equality had been based on moral knowledge, a moral equity in which everyman could be morally equal no matter what other abilities they did or did not possess. The right to rule China, the right to receive the mandate of heaven, was a moral right and in this sense China had been based on an open society, a far more open society than anything ever known in the west. Equality is the *sine qua non* of a free, open society and the Chinese had enjoyed such a moral equality which had been manifest in the emperor's mandate from heaven and in their **attitude** according to which heaven, earth, nature and man were one.

Death was something else that stuck in the older boy's mind on flight KL0898. He knew that QC was a very modern person but that she still had a large respect for ancestors. He did not know enough of her to judge if this respect warranted being called a cult. He had been inclined to add such respect to the easy Chinese eclecticism that had taken Confucianism, Daoism, the Legalists, the Mohist, Buddhism, the Jesuits, Christianity, Methodism, Marxism, and now neo-classical economic free-market theories and absorbed and modified them all in one great cosmic, pragmatic and harmonious Chinese melting pot. The Chinese ancestor cult was just one ingredient in this great pot; it was over three thousand years old and it would not disappear easily.

Death had also figured highly in that book about the Baroque. The older boy now took his fledging ideas about China and Chinese attitudes to death and ancestors and presented them to ideas about death gleaned from the European Baroque movement. Reminders that we shall die, "Memento Mori", had been common in Baroque art. Such mementoes took the form of skulls and bones or dancing skeletons depicted in painting, sculptures and literature. It was the means by which Europeans had relearned how to live with the presence of death once that completeness, that totality, that unity of cosmos, time, man, god, heaven, nature and daily life had been reformulated by the Classical episteme. The older boy recalled that in the rationally ordered table that is central to Foucault's description of the Classical episteme nothing had been omitted hence all matters of life and death were present in that table with equal weight and significance just as much as one hour spent that morning during his flight was equally one hour within eternity; but the Classical attitude to the totality of knowledge had been radically different from that of the Renaissance. Classical man was no longer an intrinsic member of that ancient European *Great Chain of Being*; he was now positioned outside knowledge, not within; he was now an observer, an external agent, looking down onto the Classical two-dimensional rationally-ordered table of all knowledge; he was no longer a participating, at home member of the universe conducting a heaven-sent, morally purposeful life alongside all other forms of life, and of death, but was now an abstracted, displaced, rationally, thinking mind. Classical man needed reminders of his own reality, the persistence, inescapable, and enduring qualities of death, and the Baroque provided that.

But Foucault knew more about death. In his description of the Modern episteme he had argued that death, or rather man's finitude, was central to, was the keystone of, Modern epistemological ordering; man's finitude created Modern knowledge of man and his world. That is why the Modern episteme is an anthropology. The older boy had not understood that point during his first reading of "The Order of Things" but now, on flight KL0898, something was trying to explain itself within his mind. He could almost feel the process, just as much as his distractions had prodded and shaped his consciousness. Death, the modern episteme and the older boy's distractions were beginning to gravitate towards their own ineluctable, dense, massive unification.

The older boy dozed, for the previous week had been a very busy and exciting time for him. He woke with the thought that it was a fear of death that was at the root of Modern man's alienation from himself and from nature. Was this the point that QC had wanted to make with her Chinese histories, her ancestors and gently forceful arguments? After all, when he had suggested they leave Starbucks and end their discussions (even though she had been approaching some summit with her arguments), she had said something that he had barely noticed at the time, for they were passing through the glass-plated doorway, feeling the fresh, cool outside-air. She had spoken quietly, powerfully from a well-controlled frustration. Her words now sprang bright and clear before his mind's eye: "Nature is dead in your culture, and so is you."

PART II

MODERN TIMES

CHAPTER 5 — PASSIVE NATURE

The older boy arrived home at the sensible time of four thirty in the afternoon. Over half of the fourteen hours of travelling time from Beijing had been "recovered" by the time differences between China and the UK.

He unpacked his bags. In his kitchen with his wife, they brewed a pot of Oolong tea using the small pot and two tiny cups that he had only two days previously received as a gift at a formal meeting with a Chinese government official. They watched fascinated as the long curly leaves unfurled in the steamy water. They threw the first wash away and managed to re-use the same leaves in four separate infusions before the drink became too weak. He went to bed at 9 pm having dropped asleep once or twice before their open wood fire in the living room of their cottage.

For the next day, and many more like them, he was busy with teaching and administration duties at Sheffield University. Christmas came and went, as did New Year and the first semester round of examinations and marking.

A Cold Start

Towards the end of January, the older boy had no duties at work prior to the start of the Spring semester. Very early one Tuesday morning, he sat before his computer and set about the task of creating a new academic paper.

It was during that morning that his work found a major new point of departure. The last words spoken by QC as they left that Starbucks in Beijing troubled him.

QC had told him that "Nature is dead in your culture and so is you". It had not been an easy statement to dismiss; on the level of

113

his immediate experience he was patently not dead, indeed his own Western culture was vibrantly alive. But during a period of deeper reflection on flight KL0898, the slaying of the dragon by St George as well as his own issues with raising awareness of nature within management and accounting were jostling for supremacy within his own melting pot of ideas and distractions. The particle exchange universe, Scandinavian social equity and love of nature, sustainable business models, human momentum and the Baroque had been augmented by Chinese harmonious development, however ancient, and the promise of episteme change. But the death of nature held for the older boy that morning the promise of a synthesis. Years ago the older boy had read and been impressed by Carolyn Merchant's book "The Death of Nature" (1983) and QC's was another voice pointing in the same direction albeit from a different culture; this was an important point for the older boy.

Dawn came and cast a weak, chilly morning light into the older boy's study. Outside, the same light lost little strength reflecting from snow and ice and it bathed plants, limestone walls and now incongruous garden furniture in a diffuse, shadow-less illumination. Deep in the dale, the sun itself would not be seen for several more weeks. On St. Valentine's Day, the sun would rise above the dale top and bring direct sunlight, with strong shadows, back into the older boy's garden.

The day that honours the Valentine Roman martyrs is associated with love between two people. The older boy could recall that there had been many Valentine martyrs in ancient Rome, all slaughtered because of their faith in their one Christian God. A specific St. Valentine had not been known until the middle ages, when he appeared in a wood-cut together with the legend that he was performing Christian marriages at a time when helping Christians was an offence punishable by death. St. Valentine, the story went, was beaten with clubs, stoned and beheaded.

The older boy went down to his kitchen to prepare a second cup of coffee. He waited whilst his oven timer measured out precisely four minutes for the brew. He was thinking that nature had died along with those Christian martyrs; the assertions of the one, the all powerful god and fantasies of another world more perfect and ideal than anything possible on earth, had taken men's minds away from the realities of life and death here on earth, had given people a way to hope for something incredibly better and had thereby, in a powerful way, killed nature.

The timer rang out impatiently. He rushed to turn it off lest it wakened his wife. Back at his desk he was determined to make a start on his new academic production. It was not easy and the very next day he deleted all his new work and settled down to make a fresh start. It was old hat, he was thinking, simply to rail against Christianity and how it had cast off nature, fought off nature, along with its multitudes of pagan gods. By eleven o'clock that same morning, and without the aid of Foucault, he had posed for himself an epistemic question: "What kind of knowledge would kill off nature?" He thumbed through Merchant's "Death of Nature" once more, but did not find an answer that satisfied him. Furthermore he wanted something more radical and more global than the Enlightenment seemed to offer; besides he had always felt that the Frankfurt school had overworked its evils. He was sure that there was sense, perhaps eventual wisdom, to be found in a rational and objective understanding; it would be a mistake to simply consider only the failings of the present day, the unsustainable business models and attitudes that threaten to cast out the baby with the bath water. Enlightenment rationalism and its scientific knowledge were, for the older boy, the only route to salvation for mankind; anything else was myth and fantasy and was as amenable and as false and as fleeting as a theme park. The older boy wanted something as profound and as ancient and as enduring as the Chinese concept of harmonious development and which in addition would pull together, consolidate and make sense of, his growing number of distractions.

He decided a change in venue was required. Since it was still only early afternoon, he took a train to Sheffield and visited the warm university library. He repeated that journey for the next three days and whilst he did not find anything of consuming interest about *dead* nature in all the assembled books and journals, he did find something illuminating about *passive* nature. The distinction between dead and passive nature was one of increased accuracy and reduced impact. It did not seem irredeemable. He read widely about passive nature and discovered that nature had not always been so in European thought. In at least one ancient part of Europe, nature had once been very active. There might just be something objective and significant here that could sway critical and rational minds. The working paper that the older boy prepared during the following weeks in January and February is reproduced below.

Working Paper: Passive Nature in European Thought

Presocratic philosophers (5–6 c. BC) in ancient Greece made the first attempts to explain the world by studying the world as they found it rather than by using mythical or religious explanations. They regarded the world as having its own creative, orderly and forceful powers; i.e. that nature is active.

They used the word "kosmos" to designate the totality of things which for them was intrinsically and elegantly ordered natural causative powers. The job they set for themselves was to identify and explain the causes of the internally-generated activities that they could observe. To do this, they made a distinction between the world of Nature and that of man, "phusis" and "techne" respectively.

Phusis is the root of modern word "physics" but for the Presocratic philosophers it meant that a natural entity grew and acted according to its own nature: "Nature is a principle and origin of growth" (Barnes, 1987, p. 20). On the other hand, to understand man-made objects, the techne world ranging from temples to vases and jewellery, they referred to something external to the objects themselves for a cause, to the hands and minds of men and women.

For Aristotle (384–322 BC), this recognition of two sources of creative power in the world did not impose a division on the world. For in Aristotle's mind, the man-made world was not something distinctly other than the natural world: it was just a matter of degree. He regarded the techne as an extension of the phusis so that nature was always the root cause of man's activities: crop farming from the natural growth of grasses; cooking from natural digestion; homes from shells, nests and burrows; and even the inquisitiveness of a scientist-philosopher was acknowledged to be a condition derived from the natural inclination to want to understand (Barnes 1987).

God's Agency

The ancient European world of active nature was brought to a close in AD 529 when the Emperor Justinian banned the teaching of pagan philosophy in the University of Athens. Europe was entering an age dominated by a Christian understanding of God, but the following centuries were not marked by the emergence of new, independent Christian philosophies but by a synthesis of ancient and new.

For whilst Rome itself had been profoundly shaken and weakened before and after its sacking in 410 AD by barbarians including Goths, the Roman Empire had continued in the East with the cities of Constantinople and Thessaloniki serving as new administrative and cultural centres. The locations of these two new centres to the northwest and northeast of the Aegean Sea respectively meant that ancient Greek influence would remain strong in at the emerging Christian world. In the 10th and 11th centuries AD, lingering ancient Greek influence was the source of a resurgence in science and arts that took place in the Eastern Roman Empire. St. Photius of Constantinople, for example, was one leader of this movement and his most famous book, "Myriobiblion", summarized ancient Greek works on theology, history, oratory, romance, philosophy, science, medicine, and lexicography. Early Christian theologians adapted the ancient Greek texts to suit their own Christian purposes; for example, Plato's "Timaeus" was turned into a philosophical explanation of the creation story to support the mythology of the Book of Genesis.

The works of Aristotle were also rediscovered by early Christian thinkers. It is not surprising for Aristotle's explanation of the causes of things is so useful that it remains influential to this day. He had argued that four kinds of causes are needed to explain anything:

(1) Material Causes according to which things are made such as wood, water or metal;
(2) Formal Causes which explain the ways things are arranged so that the formal cause of a jug for example would be a handle, a storage capacity and a pouring lip;
(3) Efficient or Moving Causes which are the primary sources of change that bring things into existence so that a moving cause for the jug would not be the hands of the potter who made the jug but would be the skills, knowledge and training that guided the potter's hands; and
(4) Final Causes which are the thing's purpose, aim or "telos" which for the jug would be to store and serve wine or milk.

Aristotle's four causes were universally applicable in both phusis and techne worlds. However, some philosophers thought that Aristotle had made a serious error by applying a final cause to phusis, the natural world. After all, they argued, the idea of an ultimate aim or purpose implies a mind such as that of the potter who wanted to make a useful jug. But Aristotle did not mean this at all. His final cause is an intrinsic property of the thing in question and as such it is to be found within the thing and not, like the potter's mind, on the outside. For a tree or a wild deer, the final cause would provide for Aristotle an explanation of the formation of the living entities as something *good* either for the existence or the flourishing of the tree or deer. Aristotle's final cause, or teleology, is based on the idea of natural design without a designer, a clear explanation of the formative role of active nature.

In effect, Aristotle had rejected Plato's idea that there was an external, higher reality of perfect form that was the cause of all the corrupt earthly things that we see around us. Plato's explanation of cause invoked a purposeful, perfect form with a source in a world external to that known on Earth and it is not difficult to appreciate that Christians would prefer Plato's explanation. After all, for Christians, the cause of all things is attributable to an all-powerful external agency, God. Hence Plato's, not Aristotle's, philosophical account of causation is an explanation far more amenable to a Christian reality.

Therefore in the Middle Ages, knowledge of the world did not refer ultimately to things in themselves, to their own intrinsic causal processes as per Aristotle, but to knowledge of an agency external to the lived world, to God and his universal creative presence in his world. This is the foundation for the ordering of knowledge in the Renaissance episteme as described by Foucault (1970), an ordering in which knowledge of worldly things was the same as knowledge of God's creations and interventions in the world. Such knowledge was to be gained by interpreting the whole world to uncover hidden meanings and associations just as if Nature were a book; indeed no distinction was made between knowledge acquired by "reading" nature and that by reading a book. Nature was the book of God.

In 12th century Europe, Aristotle was still respected; he was known as **The Philosopher**. His work was read and respected, but not as he had intended. His theory of causation for the phusis world had no place for the intervention of an external agent, no place for God, so it was unacceptable to Christian minds. For this reason nature had her active causal powers taken away from her and given to God. Nature was and can be a living holy presence for Christians if it is God's presence that is to be revealed in all things; but taking away nature's own causal powers in this way was a step taken towards the ultimate passivity of nature. The framework for science had been set by religion.

Rational Human Agency

In the 14th century, the enormity and horror of wars and plagues in Europe devastated populations and this forced the social order to change; it was to be the end of the Middle Ages. In Florence, a poet became the harbinger of change. Dante Alighieri (1265–1321), Italy's greatest poet and founder of Italian literature, wrote "Divina Commedia" which is a poetic masterpiece.

Dante's poem is a culmination of the medieval world view with its theme of the human soul's journey through life towards an ultimate meeting with God and, if approved, everlasting after-life. But there is much more to Dante's poem; it marks the dawn of a new age, of a new way of ordering knowledge, a new episteme. Divina Commedia contains accurate and engaging descriptions of human characters which are thought to have been based on real people in Dante's acquaintance. Dante weaves the poem's religious theme around a bitter denunciation of Florentine and Italian politics and he looks afresh at the qualities of the natural world: at a spherical Earth, at the movements of the sun, changing time zones, the changing direction of gravity in the centre of the Earth, and at the theoretical problem of winds arising in a hell that has no temperature differentials. Furthermore Cantos II and XV of Dante's poem discuss the experimental method in science with regard to the path of light falling on mirrors and consequential angles of incidence and reflection.

Dante grew out of two cultures. His mediaeval roots grew into something new that flourished with abundant nourishment from vigorous and emerging ways of thinking in northern Italy. In turn, these emerging cultures searched for what survived of ancient Greek and Roman civilisations. Northern Italians in the 14th century looked further back than the dictates in Church Latin and its entanglements with Christian ideals; they looked far back into antiquity notably, first of all, back to the Latin of Cicero (106–43 BC), the Roman statesman and philosopher. But as the 14th century progressed, northern Italian scholars began to look even further back in time into the language and literature of ancient Greece. Boccaccio was one such Italian scholar and he found in ancient Greece a world not dominated by the one Christian God. In the thoughts and institutions of ancient Greece, Boccaccio saw the importance of man, not God, and consequently he was to create strong secular, human themes in his written works. Boccaccio's masterpiece, the "Decameron", was written between 1347 and 1351 during a time of devastations caused by the Black Death. It is a book of novellas about a fictitious account of seven young women and three young men who had fled plague-ridden Florence to a nearby villa where for ten days they were said to have told bawdy stories of earthly erotic love to entertain themselves. In a crude way, humanity was beginning to find itself, in itself once more.

But Boccaccio was not alone in having such revolutionary ideas. In the 14th and subsequent centuries, painting, sculpture, architecture, and music were to flourish. Man was reinventing himself based on new interpretations of old knowledge. Florence was an early centre of these innovations: Dante, Petrarch, Brunelleschi, Boccaccio, Leonardo da Vinci, Poggio Bracciolini and Michelangelo were all closely associated with Florence and her territories; so too were Machiavelli and the banker, patron and despot Lorenzo de'Medici. Venice was a strong rival for Florence with works produced by Paolo Veronese, Titian and Tintoretto.

The revolution in thinking eventually spread beyond Italy to the north of Europe. The area we now call the Low Countries came close to equalling northern Italy in art and philosophy as well as economic power. Flemish painters and Jan van Eyck and Pieter Brueghel were the match of their Italian contemporaries whilst Erasmus of Rotterdam was one of the most important Latinist scholars of his age. By the 16th century, the cultural florescence that had started in northern Italy had transformed Europe. We now call those transformations a rebirth, a "Renaissance".

Whilst the Renaissance drew fresh insight from the ancient Greek world, strong and enduring Christian power meant that the European world remained firmly in God's hands: the source of causal power in nature was still external, nature still remained passive. Aristotle's influential, comprehensive and logical system of causation had been known throughout Mediaeval and

122   *Intrinsic Sustainable Development*

Renaissance times but the active nature causal powers of the Pre-socratic philosophers remained usurped by the Christian God.

However another twist in the understanding of the causes of things did emerge during the Renaissance; it was that of a God-given, rationally-ordered world. A fresh view of humankind known as "Humanism" had come along and had further inspired that Renaissance flourishing of artistic and intellectual talent. Followers of Humanism, "Humanists", were originally people who valued the arguments of the ancient Greeks and Romans in addition to those of the Christian clerics. For example, Eras-mus was a Dutch philosopher who was identified as a humanist because he was a student of both Christian theology and the ancient Roman and Greek worlds. In studies of ancient Greece, humanists found a basis for a scientific, orderly view of a world caused not by direct divine intervention, but by laws and princi-ples. In theory, the humanists were to argue, we can discover the rational foundation for these laws and principles. So humanists came to follow the 6th century BC advice of Thales of Miletus which was "know thyself"; they wanted the freedom of thought that Pericles (495–429 BC) had emphasised; and perhaps even to entertain the views of Xenophanes (circa 570–475 BC) who refused to recognize the power of gods.

With the passing of time, Renaissance Humanism became increasingly autonomous and changed in meaning to represent a kind of person possessing a rational approach to understanding and dealing with human affairs; an approach that significantly was without ultimate reliance on divine or supernatural interven-tions. In other words, humanity was beginning to stand alone on its own two feet, was flexing its own active nature, its own causal powers.

In this way, humanism came to stress not only human affairs as the proper focus for man's attention, but also the reasoning power of man as the way to gaining knowledge and, hence, power. God remained a significant presence in most individual lives, but it was now humanity itself and its own reasoning ability that was to acquire knowledge of the worlds of man, techne, and of nature, phusis. Individuals such as Montaigne would look to themselves and other people to fashion their own personal identities and to guide their own lives:

> "The finest lives are, in my opinion, those which conform to the common and human model in an orderly way, with no marvels and extravagances."
>
> *Montaigne (1993, p. 406).*

This form of Humanism still guides many attitudes, values, and institutions in today's world. But Humanists of the Renaissance did have one fundamental point of distinction from those of the present day. For the Renaissance Humanist, God had created a world that was perfect, complete, full and interdependent. All species that could exist, did exist and necessarily existed in order to complete the world. Everything had a place and everything depended upon things being there, in their proper place; removing one species from this perfect order would threaten the entire cosmic order; the world, ceasing to be full, would be incoherent.

This Renaissance need to maintain all species, had developed from the ancient Greek view that had been handed down once more by Aristotle and adapted by Mediaeval scholars. This form of conservation is known as the **Great Chain of Being** within which each and every creature or element of matter was linked to every other by means of a hierarchy of existence and being. At the top of the Chain, at the top of the hierarchy, was God. Beneath God in descending order, lay angels, devils, man, animals, plants and inanimate matter. This Great Chain is described below in a quotation from Macrobius, the 5th century AD Roman philosopher:

> "Since, from the Supreme God Mind arises, and from Mind, soul, and since this in turn creates all subsequent things and fills them with life, and since this single radiance illumines all and is reflected in each, as a single face might be reflected in many mirrors placed in a series; and since all things follow in continuous succession, degenerating in a sequence to the very bottom of the series, the attentive observer will discover a connection of parts, from the Supreme God down to the last dregs of things, mutually linked together and without a break."
>
> *Ambrosius Theodosius Macrobius (395-423 AD).*

As with the ancient Chinese understanding of cosmic Harmony and Dao, there was continuity, integration and interdependence within the European Great Chain of Being. Confidence in the completeness of God's world as represented in the Chain of Being was to underwrite what Foucault (1970) identified as the two-dimensional table of knowledge in the Classical episteme, where knowledge of all things was laid out for all to see.

The Great Chain of Being remained prominent in European thought up to the 18th century and was used by prominent people such as the philosopher John Locke, who used it in his influential "Essay Concerning Human Understanding" (1690), and the naturalist Bonnet (1720–93). In the 18th Century, the Swedish proto-ecologist Linnaeus re-worked the classifications of the Great Chain of Being by adding a couple of his own.

But that ancient integrity was to be destroyed by one of the philosophy's greatest names, René Descartes (1596–1650). Descartes introduced a division, a dualism, into the world; one which distinguished mind from matter.

René Descartes was the son of a French nobleman. He was an expert swordsman and an adventurer who spent his youth visiting courts and armies across Europe. He was a short man with a big nose and a large head and he was destined to become the father of modern philosophy. In 1619 as he crossed Bavaria during his life as a soldier, a bad winter forced him to stay in the small town of Neuburg-on-Danube. In a small room in his lodgings, a stove kept him warm as he listened to storms rage all around him. It was here that he was to have three dreams that changed his life. In his first dream, he dreamed that he was caught by a whirlwind that tried to push him over until he was forced to shelter in a college. He awoke terrified that an evil demon had put this dream into his head. His second dream was marked by a huge thunderclap after which he found himself in a room full of fire and sparks. This too worried him. But his third and last dream was calm for he had dreamed that he was in bed with several books at his side including an encyclopaedia and a book of poetry. He interpreted these dreams as a warning that he should give up soldiering and devote his life to philosophy. Specifically, he claimed that his last dream had given him a way to unify the whole of human knowledge: "If we could see how the sciences linked together, we would find them no harder to retain in our minds than the series of numbers".

Descartes' third dream was a major influence on his life, on Europe and on the world. He developed the dream into a method by means of which everything would be reduced to mathematics in order to build a single, unified body of knowledge. As part of his methodology, Descartes argued that he had to first demolish "everything" if he was ever going to establish a lasting foundation for the whole of scientific knowledge. Descartes accomplished this "demolishing" by doubting everything. True to his word Descartes doubted all knowledge; any knowledge could, after all, have been put in his head by that demon. But this famous "Cartesian Doubt" had one exception; he could not doubt that he was at that moment *thinking*. Consequently, whilst Descartes argued that his ideas about everything else could in fact be mistaken, he could not be mistaken about the fact that he was presently thinking. This one reliable fact is the source of his famous dictum "Cogito ergo sum", "I think therefore I am". From this small but seemingly unassailable foundational fact, Descartes believed that he could use reason and mathematics to build all knowledge of the world.

With this argument, Descartes introduced a new kind of passivity to bear down on the natural world. Descartes took rational thinking to the extreme. In the "Discours de la Methode" (1637), Descartes wrote: "I am a being whose whole essence or nature is to think, and whose being requires no place and depends on no material thing." This determined Descartes' view of himself in a very practical sense. He believed that the common use of language had misled people to adopt a mistaken identity; only mental statements such as "I'm happy" or "I'm thinking about lunch" said something about the real person. Anything said about your own body was a mistake; you are not really talking about yourself, just about a (passive) material body. For Descartes saying "I'm five foot ten inches tall" says something about my body not about myself. This fundamental split of mind and body strangely puts man outside his own body, and also outside nature. For Rene Descartes, man is not a part of nature.

But not being a part of nature was to be no obstacle for Descartes and his followers when acquiring knowledge of nature. Descartes was a major scientist. He wrote about the sun being at the centre of the solar system in "The World" (1629) but when he heard that Galileo in Italy had been arrested for the selfsame argument, Descartes wisely deferred publication of his own book. Descartes was the first person to publish the laws of reflection, that the angle of incidence is equal to the angle of reflection. To this day, every school child comes across his name in geometry when dealing with Cartesian coordinates, the "x" and "y" axes used in the graphical representations that link geometry with algebra.

But Descartes was not content with just representing or describing the world: he took the additional, immense step of explaining how the world works. Like many of his other ideas, his explanation of the workings of the world was to be very influential. He argued that the world is made of "corpuscles" or small particles of tiny and infinitely divisible matter that swirl around to create gravity and the world we can see. This vision of a physical world composed of inert particles of matter, "corpuscles", colliding and interacting was the foundation of a whole new "mechanical philosophy". Mechanical philosophy was widely employed in the second half of the 17th century by scientists such as Huygens, the Dutch astronomer and inventor of the pendulum clock; Gassendi, the French astronomer and atomist philosopher; Boyle, the English physicist famous for work on compressed gases and inventor of the compressed air pump; and Hooke, the English naturalist and physicist.

Mechanical philosophy also found practical expression in the 17th century's interest in creating small moving dolls or automata. This served to reinforce Descartes' belief in "mechanical" forms of life and to validate its basic tenets. Descartes himself once made a moving mechanical girl that made noises human enough for a ship's captain to suspect that Descartes' luggage contained a kidnap victim. But the idea of mechanistic explanations for living things went well beyond mechanical toys. A "mechanistic physiology" emerged and this was taken very seriously indeed: Borelli, a student of Galileo, explained aspects of muscle action in mechanical terms; Boyle successfully used a mechanistic colliding-particle theory to explain the behaviour of gases; Harvey applied mechanistic thinking to understand the circulation of the blood; and La Mettrie reached a pinnacle in mechanistic physiology with his treatise, *Man a Machine*: "Indeed, I am not mistaken, the human body is a clock, but immense and constructed with such ingenuity and skill..." (Capra, 1982, pp. 100–101).

In keeping with an understanding of the passive, particular structure of nature, Descartes had come to regard all of life, all living bodies including his own, as sophisticated machines. Famously, Descartes identified "res cogitans", a "thinking substance", which existed independently of anything physical. Res cogitans means something close to both mind and soul. According to Descartes, everything else in the universe possesses only the physical dimensions of width, breadth and height. His name for everything in existence other than res cogitans was "res extensa", an "extended thing" of passive matter.

Just how these two parts of the world, res cogitans and res extensa, joined together is not something that is made clear by Descartes. Descartes merely pointed out that the mind or soul occupies the pineal gland and it is here that the mind, res cogitans, and body, res extensa, interact; he left it at that. But these two parts of the world, thinking and extended things, are the cause of a famous and fundamental separation known as "Cartesian Dualism"; this has troubled philosophers for centuries.

But Cartesian Dualism, inert corpuscles and a mechanistic understanding is much more than a dusty philosophical museum exhibit. It is a view of a thoroughly inert world, a view of passive

128   *Intrinsic Sustainable Development*

nature which has neither its own intrinsic causal powers nor the breath of life breathed into it by an external God. Nature has become inert matter existing as extensions in space and time, nothing more. Living entities were for Descartes sophisticated machines. He dissected rabbits, fish and eels to show how these living machines worked. He came to regard screams of pain from the animals he dissected as being comparable to the mechanical noises you get when you dissemble a machine. For Descartes, such screams could not and did not denote suffering.

Descartes, by taking rationalism to an extreme, made great advances in knowledge and understanding and provided the foundation for calculative methods that were to be framework for science throughout the next two hundred years. He also gave a new slant to the idea that nature was passive by isolating mind, the mind of man and of God, from a machine-like inert nature that was, for all intents and purposes, dead matter.

The older boy paused in his writing. He was going to finish this working paper with the words: "Descartes and his followers went a long way to establish a unified, integrated system of knowledge that was governed by reductionist mathematical reasoning within which active nature had no relevance. His methods remain a huge influence in the world in which we live. Unsustainable development is a consequence of Descartes' method for it appears that traditional financial accountants and neo-classical economists still hold Descartes true to his words; they develop theories and practices based wholly on mathematical reasoning, within which nature has no role." But he could not do so.

The older boy judged that, at this stage, his knowledge of the way in which his own age had ordered its knowledge was grossly inadequate for identifying the causes of unsustainable development. Nonetheless, he felt intuitively that his conclusion was correct.

Passive nature was significant to past and present ages in Europe. The older boy also felt intuitively that some European people had been struggling for centuries to learn again what the ancient Greek

Chapter 5 — Passive Nature   **129**

Presocratic philosophers had known, that nature is intrinsically active and changeable. But he knew very well that feelings and intuitions carry little weight in an age dominated by evidence and reason. If he was to complete his project, to find a way of integrating his distractions and validating his feelings, he would have to get to know much more about how his own age ordered its knowledge.

"The hills are shadows, and they flow
From form to form, and nothing stands;
They melt like mist, the solid lands,
Like clouds they shape themselves and go."

From "In Memoriam", stanza CXXIII, by Alfred, Lord Tennyson (1809–1892).

CHAPTER 6 — MODERN KNOWLEDGE

The Mystery of Reality

Like an apparition that emits no photons, but is nevertheless "seen" by the mind's eye, the idea that nature is dead haunted the older boy's thoughts. It came and went at unexpected moments. So familiar was he in all that he had learned and experienced with an active living nature that formed and reformed rocks, mountains, oceans, living creatures, weathers, planets and galaxies that the idea of a dead nature was unreachable except in a ghostly, insubstantial presence.

The older boy had, at that time, no argument to take him from his feeling, his sense of the world, to the knowledge, social structures, institutions and attitudes that govern him and, increasingly, the whole human world. So he worked for a while at a more fundamental level, that of imagination and mystery.

His work and struggle was a personal journey. He looked to where other similar personal journeys had taken place. The mysteries of Eastern religions were effective and by reading Capra (1991) he could appreciate a sense of how some of them, such as Hinduism, could be based on an intuitive understanding of the particle exchange universe or, specifically as in the case of Daoism, active nature. But these were not new ideas. They had already been considered by western thinkers; Hegel for example saw close parallels between the interacting, inevitability and creativity of opposites in his dialectics, the foundation for Marx's version of materialism, and yin-yang cosmology. But Christian mysticism contained far more influential revelations for him since they were closer to his spiritual upbringing and it sought the same kind of intellectual and human liberation that he required of his own work; a freedom for an extended living being and not just the freedom to pursue some other form of limited rationality.

For example, the Methodist poet, Reverend R.S. Thomas, claimed to be driven, struggling with his own demons, as he set down in his work an experience that was genuinely open to the world and to the love of all things rather than to mere rote learning and repetition; or to a mythology praised to reality; or to an over-weaned, gentle-megalomaniac Christian small form of self. For Rev. Thomas as creative poet saw beyond the routines, rigours and blind-affirmations of his revealed religion to its beating heart; he saw through the altar piece and the walls of his chapel on Anglesey to God as nature. It was a shift in attitude with which Thomas could step onto a moorland in Wales and proclaim that it:

> "... was like a church to me.
> I entered it on soft foot,
> Breath held like a cap in the hand."
> *From "The Moor" by R.S. Thomas (in Morgan 1966).*

Religion, any religion, became acceptable to the older boy, not for its prescribed knowledge of the world and mankind, but only for its measure of honesty. There are uncertainties in the world, things that we do not know, and this can entail fear. Closed religious-minds block out the unknown with spurious knowledge, faith and affirmation and may thus be abused and diminished by those who understand and manipulate this point. With meditations such as these, the older boy came to understand that it was the small form of self that introduced *evil* to religion; that a person in conformity with only his or her society's opportunities for satisfying the immediate demands of physical and psychological need was the embodiment of the evils of the small self.

Goodness, for the older boy, became equivalent to experience of a greater, an expanded, self that possessed a presence beyond that of doctrine, rite, ritual, and dogma. William Blake (1757–1827) starts his poem *Auguries of Innocence* with an experience of the greater self:

"To see a world in a grain of sand,
And a heaven in a wild flower,
Hold infinity in the palm of your hand,
And eternity in an hour."

But he ends his masterpiece with a warning. Blake counterpoises his experiences of "sweet delight" those of the smaller self, the night dwellers:

"Some are born to sweet delight,
Some are born to endless night.

We are led to believe a lie
When we see not thro' the eye,
Which was born in a night to perish in a night,
When the soul slept in beams of light.

God appears, and God is light,
To those poor souls who dwell in night;
But does a human form display
To those who dwell in realms of day."

Auguries of Innocence, William Blake (1863).

After Thoughts

One fine blindingly-sunny but exceedingly cold and frosty early-spring day in the Derbyshire Peak District, when snowdrops were displaying their pure-white flowers in sheltered corners, the older boy was walking and thinking of the ancient Goths in their equally cold, northern, pagan world. He considered that those people would have found nature very alive because it had been replete with their diverse gods and spirits in all their forests, lakes, rivers, seasons, and seas and in the sun. He went home and phoned Grey Beard in Gothenburg.

Grey Beard was in his office in the Handelshögskolan. He was far more mindful of accounting, business case studies and social science theory than natural deities. He had had only four days in which to prepare an application for research funding to be submitted to a Swedish pension fund. Grey Beard listened quietly to the older boy for a few moments and then said: "Politicians and business leaders perform a double act of trickery. They set the agenda and define what is available and then pretend to ask people what they want. They are just like my wife. I have total freedom of choice providing that I decide for something that she also wants."

The older boy tried to interject but Grey Beard was far too pre-occupied with his work-in-hand to reflect in that moment. Grey Beard cut in and apologised for lacking the time for talk; he then hung up.

The older boy searched the World Wide Web for help. He did not know for sure what kind of help he needed other than something to do with mysticism and reality and openness to a nature that is very much alive. Within ten minutes he was reading and considering Weber's words: "The fate of our times is characterized by rationalization and intellectualization and, above all, by the 'disenchantment of the world'." (Max Weber in *Science as a Vocation*, 1918–1919). The older boy did not feel disenchanted, but he wondered who did.

He searched wider using the terms "nature", "enchantment", "order" and, since he was thinking of ringing QC in Being, "Way" and "Dao". Lao Tzu's *Tao Te Ching* appeared on his screen, and he read:

> "The way that can be spoken of
> Is not the constant way;
> The name that can be named
> Is not the constant name.
> The nameless was the beginning of heaven and earth;
> The named was the mother of the myriad creatures."

Here, he was thinking, an unexplained mystery was made known, institutionalised and held in the form of knowing something but of not knowing what. A mystery circumnavigated, mapped out, planned, caught, tamed and laid out for centuries at the feet — or above the heads — of one of the world's oldest civilisations. A lynch-pin for that distant and strange other-world Chinese civilisation, where it had been held fully known, but only by its edges; with generations of Chinese people teetering on the brink, open to the darkest secrets but never once crossing that edge, never being unable to slide down into its dark, impenetrable recesses. They had been forever agape, in awe, a whole civilisation built on the uncertainties of wonder; a society of lived enchantment at the bare, throbbing, threatening, embarrassing mysterious edge of its own unknown being; an ancient pragmatic, knowledgeable and able society kept alive, uncertain, sensitive to the inexplicable gap, that all-healing, un-healing wound in reason and knowledge which was consequently, very much and unavoidable so, open.

He thought it would be useful to ask QC for her opinion. Impatiently he typed the numerous digits into his phone to get a call to China at the cheapest rate. He began his conversation with QC with tentative caution, restraining himself from releasing his enthusiastic flood of ideas with which QC would be overcome. QC cut him short. She was driving, or rather sitting, on Beijing's fourth ring road in a long traffic jam. QC was prepared to listen, but the older boy did not talk to drivers at the wheel. He apologised for interrupting. He hung up.

Day-to-day living appeared unassailable, self-justifying, urgent and irrepressible. Universal, eternal mysteries of life and death mean little when faced with the necessities and immediacies of getting from A to B and getting on. QC might, might not, respond warmly to his ideas; that was another mystery but one he might solve eventually. And it was by means of this idea of "mysteries that we can solve", first used in relation to QC, that the older boy came to perceive the primal role of knowledge within society. After some thought, he formulated and justified to himself the following definition: "The prime purpose of civilisation is to solve mysteries".

Solving Mysteries

In a matter of hours after calling Beijing, the older boy's civilisations-solving-mysteries project was taking shape. This project would be a rational interrogation, not of mystery, but of mysteries solved. It was not an abandonment of any of his other thoughts or distractions; it would be fully inclusive of the Potteries small boy by the canal; of

Josiah Wedgewood; of that African shoreline with two trendy young people, the particle exchange universe, the !Kung Bushmen and the VIGAs; of the Goths, the Göta Älv and its cold wind, the Feskekörka, Swedish accountants, Grey Beard and sustainable business models; of the Baroque; of China ancient and modern; of the Han and QC; of Descartes, western rationality; and, he had to admit to himself but almost as an afterthought, of Foucault and epistemes.

His analytical test for civilisations-solving-mysteries quickly became equivalent to a test for what is taken as reality. It seemed to be a sensible way to proceed, but unlike Descartes' similar line of enquiry, the older boy sought an answer, not from within reason but from all quarters including science and opinion. Of all the people that could be on the telephone line into my study, of all their words in books and papers and on the World Wide Web, he was asking of himself, are some more in touch with reality than others? Is Wall Street, Madison Avenue, Fleet Street, Downing Street, the White House, or Mao's Mausoleum in Tiananmen a better place to get to know reality than in a cold wind in Sweden, along a dry riverbed during a drought in Africa, besides an ocean's shore or sitting alone in a tiny room in a cold cottage in northern England?

He gave his project academic credentials with a literature review of "scientific realism". Within the Philosophy of Science community, questions of reality were far from settled. It was a subject of current debate (Leplin, 1997; Kukla, 1998; Cartwright, 1999; Giere, 1998; and Niiniluoto, 2002). In the year 2011, after so many centuries of knowledge accumulation, reasoning and many lifetimes of thought in the Western world, the older boy found it reassuring, even pleasing, that philosophers still do not know for certain what can be taken as real.

The older boy learned that realism in science gravitates around two ideas:

(i) science gives us knowledge of independent phenomena; and
(ii) it is possible to have real scientific knowledge even in cases when the phenomena are not observable but are conjectured from hypotheses and theories.

Chapter 6 — Modern Knowledge   **137**

Both of these arguments want to say that if you obtain knowledge and understanding derived from evidence that has been studied, filtered and approved by people skilled in looking at things and events as objectively as possible then you have good reason to believe that the knowledge does indeed represent reality; or that those who claim to know reality have provided reliable evidence that atoms, molecules, compounds, electricity, stars, galaxies, climates, flora, fauna, ecosystems, people and the rest of the universe are as they say.

If you disagree with what scientists say, then you might (i) be on the verge of a scientific breakthrough provided you can support your claim with reliable new evidence or a reworking of old evidence, or (ii) be a crank of one kind or another who is wanting to select, amend or ignore reliable evidence to support whatever fantasies guide your mind.

Most of the scientific knowledge and understanding based on reliable evidence is not disputed. The scientific accounts of the realities of temperature, electricity and gravity are well known and respected; holding a burning branch by the hot end, standing on top of an exposed hill during a lightning storm or falling off a cliff will reinforce these realities for anyone who cares to try these experiments.

Other phenomena may be just as apparent but occurring on non-human time or spatial scales so that only trained and knowledgeable eyes can see and appreciate the effects. You do not for example see many people "surfing" continents as they glide over the surface of the earth by centimetres a year on a current of magma, nor do people hide away because somewhere in our galaxy a star has gone supernova and has emitted more energy in a few weeks than our sun could emit in its entire lifetime.

But science postulates other phenomena that are so strange that they require us to cross from that with which we are familiar to totally alien, barely believable worlds. We may see the sun in the sky and we do not expect to find it at the bottom of a swimming pool; but at the level of the smallest parts of the universe, the quantum worlds, physical location is not definite. Those who study the quantum world deal with probabilistic knowledge not certainties. In the quantum world, the sun being in the sky and at the bottom of the swimming pool at the same time, or a cat being simultaneously alive and dead, are acceptable and real probabilities.

Those who observe and explain phenomena in the quantum particle world deal with mystery as daily currency. Their mysteries are as great, as far beyond normal experience and as significant as any imagined by the world's great religions. What we commonly know of time and space is challenged when two particles interact spontaneously over a distance as wide as our galaxy, the Milky Way, 9×10^{17} kilometres across. Indeed, the basic idea of objectivity, of studying things as they are in themselves, disappears in the quantum world, because the very act of observing, just looking, changes what there is to see.

For those who study the world at the edges of our knowledge, there must be awe, wonder and enchantment. One mysterious edge of Modern civilisation lies in the quantum world. It follows that scientific knowledge of the quantum world may in some respects assume the same kind of power normally attributed to religion. But the older boy could not, at that point in his enquiries, see how this knowledge could affect other lives. Visions of awe and wonder no doubt help people acquire something grand and enduring and in this way, for this reason alone, such experiences can lift people out of the meanness and isolation of the small self and thereby help solve one fundamental problem of sight. Experiences of awe and wonder derived from observing and thinking about nature must surely mean that nature, for at least a few people, is not dead. Conversely, the death of nature must correspond to something in the death of man.

Mystery Solving in Europe

The older boy took time off research to be pleased with himself. For a few weeks he contented himself with teaching and administration at the university. It gave time for his ideas to settle.

At length, after the first orchids had bloomed in sunnier dales and swallows were nesting beneath eaves, he too felt the need to create. He returned to his previous anchorage, the sheltered thought-space that he had created for himself with that working paper with the title

Passive Nature in European Thought. It was after all still unfinished. He developed notes with the intention of eventually writing another working paper, a kind of sequel to the first. Some of these notes are reproduced below.

Notes on Scientific Realism in European Thought & Civilisation

In 1543, Copernicus published "On the Revolutions of the Celestial Spheres" to explain how the earth and other planets revolve around the sun and this achieved two things:

1. It showed that scientific versions of reality may go against common-sense for people accepted the evidence of their own eyes insomuch as the sun crossed the sky as it revolved around the earth; and
2. It established that science is in the business of revealing reality.

By 1610, when Galileo published "The Starry Messenger" and supported Copernicus' theory with telescopic observations, the intensity of the reaction from established society shows the strength of the opposition to realism or, conversely, the persistence of what people believe they see with their own eyes. Even "scientists" opposed Galileo because they did not trust telescopes but did trust their own eyes; they thought that telescopes deceived their eyes.

Newton's mathematics and his theory of gravity illustrated that simple laws could govern the motion of the moon and planets. This was a powerful validation of both mechanism, the belief that the universe was like a machine, and scientific realism, the belief that science revealed physical realities.

In the Enlightenment, mechanism was the dominant scientific view of the universe and, just as with a machine, it was believed that nature could be broken down into parts with each new piece of knowledge adding to the last. This was the foundation for the notion of progress that still dominates the Modern age.

As far as technology, expertise and reality allowed, Modern science came to be rooted in empirical evidence. This was in marked contrast to Mediaeval science which relied on strict logical procedures to get to know the world. Logical methods also came to support empirical evidence in "logical empiricism" put forward

140   *Intrinsic Sustainable Development*

by Hempel (1905–1997); an understanding that required the use of logic to derive the theoretical entities that are necessary for understanding nature, but which cannot in themselves be proved by evidence. Logical empiricists are scientific realists who extend empirical evidence with logic to develop theories which, like the factual evidence they explain, they argue really do exist. Just as the "mechanistic" exploration of nature was progressive, so too was logical empiricism for each successive theory was held to be closer to reality than the theory before.

Kuhn (1922–1996) challenged the logical empiricist's view of scientific progress. Kuhn proposed that scientific change occurring with revolutions in the thoughts of the scientific community. He introduced the idea of a "paradigm", a word that means pattern or template in ancient Greek such as those used to help stonemasons cut consistently shaped marble columns. By giving the scientific community a role in accepting or rejecting scientific theories, Kuhn broke the direct link between scientific progress and reality.

Feyerabend (1924–1994) further weakened the logical empiricist's claims by pointing out that universal theories from Aristotle to Newton and to Einstein have been overturned during the "progress" of science and that such major upheavals reveal that we have no right to believe that any of them correspond to reality. He argued that the triumph of one scientific paradigm superseding another is comparable to one myth replacing another and that science is a cultural manifestation which cannot provide an objective view of reality.

Latour (1947–) argued that the objects of scientific study are socially constructed within a laboratory. This means that they cannot be attributed with any wider reality. This means that science exists only in the instruments of science and in the minds of scientists, but only as a form of culture. Latour does not deny scientific realism, but he extends its definition. He argues that we should pay close attention to the various, contradictory institutions and ideas that bring people together and inspire them to act; this, for Latour, is empirical science. Thereby he has redefined what is real to include anything that a person claims as a source of motivation for action.

The older boy reviewed his notes on scientific realism. His notion of the progress that science is making in revealing reality had been "socialised" by Kuhn, Feyerabend and Latour, but not destroyed.

After all, one paradigm being replaced by another is merely say-ing that there are cadres and vested interests within the scientific communities; such groups may persist for a long time, but even-tually reality will out. A new generation of scientists will form their own cadres, develop their own vested interests with PhDs, careers and articles within the new paradigm and set themselves up to propound their understanding both against older, and also against newer ones. Paradigms bring a human social dimension to the methodology of science, but they do nothing to refute underlying realism.

"Feyerabend and Latour may be correct," he mused, "but so what?" Science necessarily exists as culture and as myth; this is merely a recognition of the way science permeates, influences and is interpreted by society. It is the human face of science. Among sci-entists there is a culture, a high-minded culture with a larger than life purpose and this can for some rise above the meanness of the small self. Furthermore, hypotheses are the myths of science; they are the mysterious creation of fabulous explanations which can exist without a realistic foundation especially in the early stages of some empiri-cal sciences or forever in some very theoretical sciences. Scientific hypotheses may come and go; they are manifestations of a healthy scientific imagination.

"But whether or not science says something about reality," he asked himself, "who knows for sure? If we knew for sure, then that would be the end of scientific enquiry." Science is necessarily open-minded in marked contrast to a religion. A scientific claim stands for ever - but only as a claim; resilient, persistent and close to reality it may be, but it is nonetheless just a claim and it may be mistaken. The possibility of mistaken claims brings beauty and life to scientific enquiry; any scientific claim may be revised at any time. That is why mistakes are healthy and open-minded.

"What we can assume regarding science and reality," he even-tually concluded, "is that there is likely to be a very close match, since so much of our scientific knowledge *works*. It intervenes in the world and gives the results we expect or which can be even-tually explained with more science. This is of course not true for all scientific knowledge which means that science itself will always be a living, active and liberating pursuit. Indeed, science is the mark of open minds, the *sine qua non* of an open society in contrast to revealed religion that stands for closed minds in a closed society."

It became obvious to the older boy at this point that any understanding of the life or death of nature is likely to have been settled in some other, less-scientific arena of contestation. What science had to say about mechanism in nature or otherwise was only part of the story. A more complete account needs to say something about how science interacts with society; or rather what society makes of the reality that science reveals.

In this regard, Feyerabend, Latour and their supporters were unhelpful. By attempting to extract the pursuit and revelation of reality from science, they put science on a level with religion and hence introduced the societal closures that that implied. If "Civilisations are mysteries solved" is indeed true, then the open-ended pursuit of reality by scientists was far preferable to the closures of dogmatic assertions and unfounded claims by clerics. "People need reality." He was thinking, "No sensible person claims to be unreal and if that reality does not come from scientific enquiry, it will come from religious dogma."

So the older boy turned his attention to those who had accepted scientific realism and considered its social integration. Karl Marx was the first to receive attention, for he more than anyone had taken a form of scientific realism and applied it to society with the grandest and most influential of effects. The scientific understanding of real nature as a deterministic machine that could be analysed into parts, manipulated and redirected to serve man's progressive purposes may have come directly from mechanism, but it was applied with equal directness by Marx and used to "deify" class conflict.

The older boy found out that Marxism has been considerably modified since Marx's death and that it still instructs various strands of Critical Theory. Far from denying scientific realism, Critical Theory assumes that there are realities underpinning social phenomena and hence it is essential to undertake social critiques so that these underlying realities may be revealed.

Chapter 6 — Modern Knowledge   **143**

Critical theorists argue that their criticisms and revelations of underlying social realities will make the world a better place. The Frankfurt School for example wanted "to liberate human beings from the circumstances that enslave them" (Horkheimer, 1982, p. 244). The older boy also discovered with some pleasure, that the Frankfurt School did possess a measure of unity with nature; at least insofar as other creatures were argued to suffer alongside mankind in the hands of a calculative, instrumental form of reason (Adorno and Horkheimer, 1979).

But for the older boy there was a deep dilemma to do with taking an objective scientific approach to studies of society. Societies were after all the product of human will, maybe strongly collective or maybe strongly individualistic, but nonetheless a very human will. The older boy's dilemma had to do with intentional subjective reality. This had also been a problem for the Frankfurt School and critical theorists in general. If social reality is the product of man-made, subjective intentions, then self-interest cannot be excluded and the question of nature's real state and influence on society becomes once more just a matter of opinion.

Jürgen Habermas (1929–) had recognized this problem. Indeed he dedicated his life to finding a solution to this very problem. He looked for an alternative conception of rationality that does not let objective reason slip into forms of subjective self-interest. He found it in a "communication free from domination" which enabled a "rational consensus" and an "ideal speech situation" which could, under certain conditions, be justified to all those who would be affected by a decision (Habermas, 1979). However, the older boy could find little in Habermas that went beyond forms of social consensus; Habermas replaced individual self-interest with social self-interest. He took no step towards the science of any greater world.

Remaining within the Critical Theory tradition, the older boy then read Giddens. In Giddens, social "reality" is determined for and by a reflexive combination of the structures that are the result of societal and human intervention. This was Gidden's Structuration Theory. It lies somewhere between Marx's strong mechanistic structuralism and the Frankfurt School's human agency. For Giddens: "The social systems, in which structure is recursively implicated, on the contrary, comprise the situated activities of human agents, reproduced across time and space." (Giddens, 1984, p. 25).

There was a nod in Giddens to the relationship between society and scientific studies of the wider world: "In a complicated inter-weaving of reflexivity, widespread reflexive awareness of the reflex-ive nature of systems currently transforming ecological patterns is both necessary and likely to emerge" (Giddens, 1991, p. 222). But such examples of the <u>content</u> of societal change as opposed to the <u>processes</u> of societal change are not that frequent in Giddens, so the older boy concluded that without any clear transformative content Giddens' Structuration Theory would tend to support the status quo and would in that way be insensitive to any understanding of the state of nature, either alive or dead.

After so much work and so many disappointments, it was with an increasingly heavy heart that the older boy approached his last and most recent social science, realist author, Roy Bhaskar. These are the older boy's notes on Bhaskar.

Roy Bhaskar, British Philosopher Born 1944

Bhaskar (1978; 1979 and 1986) has been successful in recent years in developing a form of realism for the social sciences. Bhaskar includes the reasons and accounts that people accept and make use of in their lives among the category of things that we can regard as real; i.e. he asserts that our reasons and accounts have an existence just as real as the solid objects of scientific enquiry.

For Bhaskar, acquiring knowledge of social reality is an activity that starts with the interpretation of people's reasons. Accounts for these are the best guide to understanding the structures and pro-cesses that shape our lives. This approach echoes Durkheim's (1966 [1894], p. 103) observation: "Society is not a mere sum of individuals. Rather, the system formed by the association represents a specific reality which has its own characteristics". For Durkheim, there are social facts that are real insofar as they were external to an indi-vidual. But Bhaskar goes beyond Durkheim. He proposes that the existence of such social facts "depends upon the intentional activ-ity of human beings" (Bhaskar 1989, p. 81) and it is this inten-tional activity that creates the social reality in which we spend our lives.

True to his words, Bhaskar uses his own intentionality to structure his work. In his book "Dialectic: The Pulse of Freedom", Bhaskar (1993) explains how his idea of social reality serves human emancipation in two steps:

i. use people's own words and intentions to define the reality of social structures and processes; and then
ii. employ this knowledge of "reality" to create new social structures and processes that emancipate people.

Bhaskar then argues that there is "social realism" but that it is subjective and the best we can hope for is to replace restricting social structures and processes with emancipatory ones. This is an unsatisfactory observation, since it defines social realism as self-referential; it has nothing to say that will open minds and societies to all that we know and, more importantly, to all that we do not know, to all those mysteries and enchantments of which we are constituted.

Furthermore, there is a fundamental problem with Bhaskar's approach that has been previously identified by Hegel. In his critique of Natural Rights theories, Hegel noted that such theories attempt to provide universally-justified normative visions of human behaviour with methods that start by simply assuming the importance of the normative visions in question. Hegel argued that in those kinds of cases "...the guiding principle for the *a priori* is the *a posteriori*." (Benhabib, 1986, p. 24). Bhaskar makes the same mistake of putting the *a posteriori* cart before the *a priori* horse. This slight of hand which proceeds by converting what may be just local, specific and contextual into something universally applicable does not make for good science as Kemp (2005, p. 185) observes: "In neither the natural or the social scientific case do the philosophical arguments of critical realism take the lead, in the sense of convincingly establishing claims about some domain prior to research in that domain".

After all these efforts, the older boy began to appreciate that realism may not provide anything close to the simple solution he sought. Realism was a highly contested word open to a variety of interpretations in the social sciences; it ranged in meaning from what is hidden and in need of the revelations of critique to any thought or impulse that mankind has ever acted on. This caused the older boy to falter in his purpose and to doubt himself. Without a clear and simple understanding of what is real, the older boy felt unable to navigate through even his own thoughts and they began to turn around upon themselves as if in a whirlpool. However, in the heady, sea-sickness of swirling chaotic thoughts, the older boy found unity.

His melee of distractions was energised, made even more turbulent, and in their moment of greatest abandonment, of lost direction, of confusion, of anxiety and despair, they formed a single, unifying structure. The older boy's many and various dissociated distractions, his business entrepreneurs, the particle exchange universe, the accounting representations, !Kung Bushmen, the counter-revolutionary Baroque, passive nature, Descartes' rationality and the pressing need for sustainability, were united in the ordered turmoil to be found around his purposeful, deep, unfathomed but structured whirlpool.

As if by divine intervention, the older boy suddenly realised and understood the significance of an episteme. He thumbed one of the many academic papers that were lying on the desk in his study. He found the words he wanted, and he read: "My contention is that the coherence of Foucault's project lies in the singularity of its aim: to unearth the stratum of experience that governs the thought and practice of the historical epochs that have shaped the present age. Foucault's work was an examination of the conditions in and through which we have come to be what we are; it thus continually poses, for us, but one central question: what is our present?" (Thompson, 2008, p.1).

He read Thompson's paper thoroughly. He found: "It [Foucault's research] seeks to isolate the strictures that govern knowledge and practice, the work of critique, so that we can clearly see where and how we might begin to constitute ourselves otherwise, the task of enlightenment." (*ibid.*, p.18). The older boy was now thinking that nobody would choose willingly to live in a whirlpool, but it has come to represent the totality of my knowledge of my world: it has become my world. He was thinking that this situation was unstable; whirlpools can come and go leaving no trace. He began to ask himself "Is this also Foucault? Did he too think in this way? Did Foucault find a way to live with the whirlpool? Can Foucault help me understand what is going on?" He could not answer himself and so he returned to his copy of "The Order of Things" (Foucault, 1970) and read.

A few weeks later, the older boy had acquired the following understanding of the Modern view and of the world in which most of us live our lives.

The Modern Episteme

The older boy now believed in Foucault's illustration of the Classical episteme as a Rational Table bordered by a philosophy strong in metaphysics and an epistemology based on mathesis and taxinomia; he illustrated this with Figure 1. He also accepted that the Modern episteme required more than the two dimensions of that Classical Table. Kant's questioning of the origins of representations resulted in a third dimension for knowledge which the older boy illustrated with Figure 2. Within Figure 2 there are the three dimensions that now form an epistemological space open for analysis in the three directions of:

(i) Philosophical reflection,
(ii) Formal thought and mathematisation,
(iii) Empirical origins.

He now believed in Foucault's representations, because he had recourse to no other such archaeology of the ordering of knowledge and because his readings did indicate that different orderings of knowledge had existed in the past. Besides, it was becoming of secondary importance to the older boy whether or not Foucault was sufficiently accurate, thorough and painstaking to have accumulated enough evidence to support his particular explanations, since he now intended to use Foucault's work to identify a new ordering; an ordering of knowledge that the older boy realised retrospectively had been his principal preoccupation for some time.

To this end, he represented in a third illustration, Figure 3, the principal working elements of the Modern episteme. "From this foundation," he argued to himself, "I will be able to perceive the impact of changes brought about by a wholly new episteme."

Intrinsic Sustainable Development

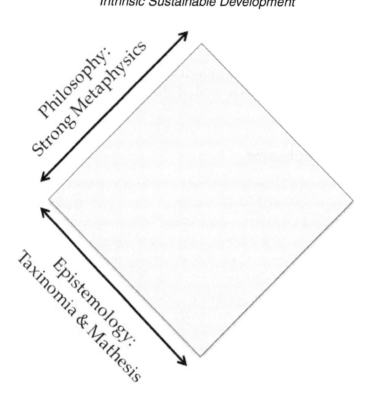

Fig. 1.   The Classical Episteme.

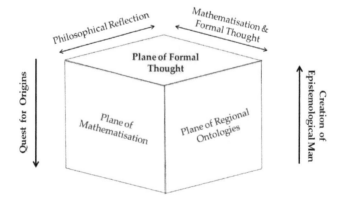

Fig. 2.   The Modern Episteme.

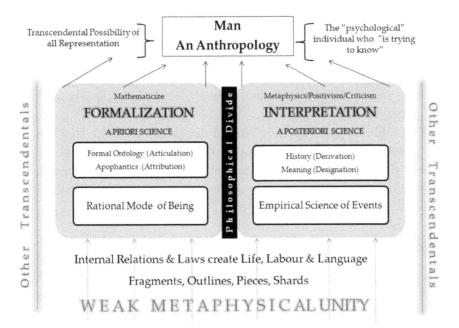

Fig. 3.   Details of the Modern Episteme.

His Figure 3 provided a cross section of that third dimension introduced by the Modern episteme. It was as if the uncertainty introduced by Kant's question had initiated a drilling-down into the table, or an opening of deep holes within the table in the search for origins. This was represented by the older boy both as both the downward-pointed arrow for "Empirical Origins" in Figure 2 and as a cross-section through one of these Modern holes as per Figure 3.

The older boy made notes to help him understand and remember the key elements of Foucault's explanation of the creation of the Modern episteme. Some of his notes are provided below.

Point One: Epistemic Change from Classical to Modern

The Classical episteme has a foundation based on the face-value acceptance of things more or less as they appeared in a systematic, rational ordering. However towards the end of the eighteenth century, epistemological questioning and new forms of knowledge went beyond the Classical episteme's limits of representation. When the German philosopher Immanuel Kant asked "What makes representation possible?", he effectively challenged the foundation and the Classical ordering of knowledge which thereafter was destined to appear naïve and dogmatic.

This added a third epistemological dimension to break free from the Classical Table. The older boy thought of this breaking-free as a form of drilling down into the Modern episteme's three-dimensional space and he represented a cross section of one of these drill-holes in Figure 3.

Point Two: Modern Origins

Kant's question resolved itself into a search for origins within the Modern episteme. But these origins are inaccessible, beyond our gaze. Only in the heart of things does cohesion still hold sovereign and secret sway over each and every part of visible beings.

Starting at the bottom of Figure 3, the older boy illustrated a foundation for knowledge which reflects the unity at the origin of things. In this region, things begin their differentiation into visibility; they are present here as fragments, outlines, pieces, and shards and they then offer themselves, though very partially, to our representation (Foucault, 1970, p. 239). In short, in the Modern episteme the foundation unity is based on weak metaphysics and it may be found only in fragments.

Point Three: New Forms of Knowledge

For Foucault, Kant's question "What makes representation possible?" represents the start of the Modern episteme which remains dominant to this day. By means of this questioning, the great empirical regions of the Classical Age, general grammar, natural history and exchange, becoming transformed into their Modern equivalents of philology, biology and political economy.

Furthermore in Classical thought time, as a sequence of chronologies, merely scanned the prior and more fundamental space of the table because this table contained representations of all that is known. Time past and present, finite and infinite were once unified in the Classical Table, as with everything else, no matter whether fact or fantasy, for it had a strong metaphysical foundation in God's created world.

The Modern episteme is very different from the Classical, for it now has successions, sequences of events in time that determine what we know; time has become historical. It is historical time that bestows order on the fragments, outlines, pieces and shards that the Modern episteme discovers as it tries to approach the origins of knowledge. The older boy placed the emergence of the new Modern forms of knowledge together with its analysis by shards and succession towards the bottom of the cross-section of the hole in Figure 3. For Foucault, the empirical regions of philology, biology and political economy emerge as discontinuous, organic structures arising from the never-to-be-fully-attained origins and consist of internal relations and laws between their elements. The internal relations and laws are organized according to analogy and succession (*ibid.*, p. 218). "This", the older boy had noted in the margin, "is Foucault's equivalent to order forming in my own conceptual whirlpool."

In this way, the transformation from Classical to Modern is clearly not a simple replacement in which new forms of knowledge slipped into the space occupied by the old; instead it necessitated the creation of a new epistemological space for knowledge "... in an area where those [Classical] forms of knowledge did not exist, in the space they left blank, in the deep gaps that were filled with the murmur of their ontological continuum" (*ibid.*, p. 207). In this way, the new great empirical regions escaped from the Classical Order as Modern forms of philology, biology and political economy were created around *Language, Living Beings* and *Need*. In Figure 3, the older boy followed Foucault and represented and substantiated these three great empirical areas of the Modern episteme as the "identification of internal relations and laws".

Point Four: A Philosophical Consequence of the Modern Episteme

The Modern Episteme possesses an almost infinite series of consequences notably including the emergence of discrete empirical fields and a transcendental theme.

The transcendental theme is the direct descendent of Kant's question. It is concerned with representations from the point of view of what in general makes them possible (*ibid.*, pp. 243–244) and hence constitutes a philosophical enquiry. The older boy had this theme starting with the expression "Rational Mode of Being" in Figure 3. As the figure shows, this area supports an *a priori* science, a pure formal deductive science based on logic and mathematics.

Figure 3 also has a column for *a posteriori* sciences, those empirical sciences which employ deductive forms only in fragments and in strictly localised fields. These are represented in Figure 3 with the expression "Empirical Science of Events". They also include interpretation and Foucault's metaphysics/positivism/criticism triangle of the object (*ibid.*, p. 246).

These empirical fields question the conditions of a relation between representations from the point of view of the being itself that is represented; those realities that are removed from reality to the degree to which they are the foundation of what is given to us and reaches us and are the force of labour , the energy of life and the power of speech (*ibid.*, p. 244). In this way labour, life, and language appear in the Modern episteme as so many "transcendentals" which make possible objective knowledge. Labour, life and language correspond to Kant's general transcendental field, but they differ from it in two important ways:

1. They are situated with the object and, in a way, beyond it to totalise phenomena and express the *a priori* coherence of empirical multiplicities as a foundation in the form of a being whose enigmatic reality constitutes, prior to all knowledge, the order and connection of what it has to know (*ibid.*, p. 244);

2. They concern the domain of *a posteriori* truths and the principles of their synthesis and not Kant's *a priori* synthesis of all possible experience (*ibid.*, p. 244).

The first difference, the transcendental located in objects, explains those metaphysical doctrines that develop on the basis of transcendental objectives, such as the Word of God, Will, Life (*ibid.*, pp. 244–245).

The second difference, the transcendentals concerned with *a posteriori* synthesis, explains the appearance of "positivism", a whole layer of phenomena given to experience whose rationality and interconnection rest on an objective foundation which it is not possible to bring to light (*ibid.*, p. 245).

The older boy was particularly concerned to understand the links between the Modern episteme and the Classical. This was because he wanted to identify a new episteme to replace the Modern and he needed to better understand the processes of such a transformation. To help clarify the links between Classical and Modern epistemes, the older boy included terms from Foucault's description of the Classical episteme in Figure 3 as "Formal Ontology (Articulation)", "Apophantics (Attribution)", "History (Derivation), and "Meaning (Designation)". For those who appreciate such distinctions (although it is not really necessary for the development of the older boy's arguments), the older boy illustrated his thinking behind the inclusion of these terms with Figure 4. This last figure takes the four corners of the Classical Table (Attribution, Articulation, Designation and Derivation), splits them according to their referential powers to either "Things" or "Words", and tracks them (by means of Apophantics, Formal Ontology, Meaning and History) to either the "Formalisation" or the "Interpretation" of knowledge.

The older boy interpreted Foucault as meaning that the "Other" and the "Transcendental" are active in making Modern knowledge not only at the level of foundational cohesion and the origin, but all the way through the Modern thought processes, at all stages. This is why the older boy surrounded his columnar representation of

Intrinsic Sustainable Development

Modern thought processes in Figure 3 with the "Other" as well as the "Transcendental".

Point Five: No Strong Metaphysical Continuum in the Modern Episteme

The older boy followed Foucault and did not take presence of the "Other" and the "Transcendental" to mean that there was a strong metaphysical continuum in the Modern episteme as there had been in the Classical: there is then no strong metaphysical continuum in the Modern episteme. It follows that the possibility of a universal synthesis can now not be considered within the Modern episteme. "No wonder," the older boy had written in the margin beside this point, "we make such a hash of sustainable development."

This lack of universal synthesis creates an epistemological vacuum which in the Modern episteme is occupied by the unifying forces of formalization or mathematicization. But this occupation is more functionally implicit than realised, which explains why all hasty mathematicization or naïve formularization of the empirical seems like "pre-critical" dogmatism and a return to the platitudes of Ideology (*ibid*, p. 246).

Point Six: The Modern Episteme's Two Schools of Philosophy

Since from Kant's question onwards, knowledge can no longer be deployed against the background of a unified and unifying mathesis working within an accepted metaphysical continuum, two problems of relations arose between on the one hand the formal field and the transcendental and, on the other hand, the domain of empiricity and the transcendental foundation of knowledge (*ibid.*, p. 247). In both these cases the philosophical thought concerned with universality is on a different level from that of the field of real knowledge. It is constituted as:

> either a pure reflection capable of providing a foundation such as Fichte's undertaking to deduce genetically the totality of the transcendental domain from the pure, universal, empty laws of

Chapter 6 — Modern Knowledge   **155**

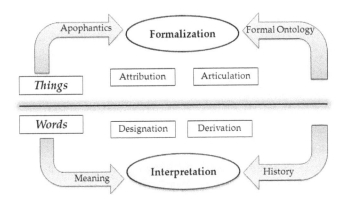

Fig. 4.   Derivation of the Two Philosophical Fields of the Modern Episteme.

thought (*ibid.*, p. 248; and Martin, 1997), which is now typified by so-called Analytical philosophy (Critchley, 2001) and the quest for a truth based in things (the above-the-line Formalization process of "Things" in Figure 4);

or a resumption capable of revealing in such as Hegel's phenomenology when the totality of the empirical domain was taken back into the interior of a consciousness revealing itself to itself as spirit (Foucault, 1970, p. 248), and hence leading to the so-called Continental School of Philosophy (Critchley, 2001) and the quest for a truth based in statements (the below-the-line Interpretation process of "Words" in Figure 4).

Point Seven: Epistemological Man

Foucault was heavily influenced by Nietzsche. They both ascribe a pivotal role to a new form of Man. The lack of a strong metaphysical continuum gives rise to the inability of the Modern episteme to reach the origins of things. Such origins are always to be approached, but never to be attained. This creates an epistemological need to explain from whence Modern knowledge arises. Foucault argues that this need is met in the Modern episteme by the creation of Man in a unique epistemological role, an epistemological man. The older boy illustrated this role of Epistemological Man by sitting him at the top of the cross-section through the hole in Figure 3, as well as by having him follow an upward pointing arrow alongside the three dimensional epistemological space of the Modern episteme in Figure 2.

So the Modern episteme's never-to-be-attained approach to origins is compensated for by an Epistemological Man who both defines and is defined by the self-same Modern knowledge which he thereby creates in an endlessly repetitive, reflexive doublet. Hence at the summit of Modern knowledge of the human sciences, sits the "psychological" individual who from the depth of his own history, or on the basis of the tradition handed to him "is trying to know" (Foucault, 1970, pp. 239–240). It can thus be argued that Modern knowledge in the human sciences is a form of anthropology.

In the Modern episteme, Epistemological Man is the source of the same positive forms of knowledge that define him. The human sciences are not then based on analyses of what man is by nature but rather on analyses that extend from what man is in his positivity as a living, speaking, labouring being (*ibid.*, pp. 352–353). Hence western culture has constituted, under the name of man, a being who, by one and the same interplay of reasons, must be a positive domain of knowledge and cannot be an object of science (*ibid.*, pp. 366–367).

Point Eight: History

As discussed above, from the 19th century onwards, temporal series and the analogies that connect distinct organic structures to one another were the source of the ordering of knowledge in the Modern episteme. This creates a new role for history. History was now to deploy, in a temporal series, the analogies that connect distinct organic structures to one another. History now gives place to analogical organic structures just as Order had opened the way to successive identities and differences in the Classical episteme; from the 19th century onwards, History defines the birthplace of the empirical (*ibid.*, p. 219).

Things in the Modern episteme received a historicity proper to them which freed them from the continuous space that had imposed the same chronology on them as on men in the Classical episteme.

The result was that nature no longer speaks to man of the creation or end of the world; or of his dependency or of his approaching judgement. Nature no longer speaks to man of anything but natural time (*ibid.*, p. 368).

Point Nine: Finitude

Within a natural time that starts and finishes, the great empirical regions of life, labour, and language become the forms of finitude that characterize man's mode of being (*ibid.*, p. 362).

Man's reflexive doublet imposes itself on all forms of Modern positive knowledge with the consequence that finitude, with its own truth, is posited in time; it is the time of epistemological man, and from then on time is therefore finite. Consequently the great dream of an end to history becomes the utopia of Modern systems of thought (*ibid.*, p. 263).

At the end of the 19th century, Nietzsche took the end of time and transformed it into the death of God as the springboard for the great leap of the superman. He once again took up the great continuous chain of History in order to bend it around into the infinity of the eternal return. Nietzsche burned the intermingling promises of the dialectic and anthropology (*ibid.*, p. 263).

Perhaps all we have here, in the concrete forms of the unconscious and History, is the two faces of that finitude, which, by discovering that it was its own foundation, caused the figure of man to appear in the 19th century. A finitude without infinity is no doubt a finitude that has never finished, that is always on recession with relation to itself, that always has something still to think at the very moment when it thinks, that always has time to think again what it has thought (*ibid.*, p. 372).

In modern thought, historicism and the analytic of finitude confront one another. Historicism is a means of validating, for itself, the perpetual critical relation at play between History and the human sciences. But it established itself at the level of the positivities: the positive knowledge of man is limited by the historical positivity of the knowing subject, so the moment of finitude is dissolved in the play of a relativity from which it cannot escape and which itself has value as an absolute (*ibid.*, p. 372).

Point Ten: Anthropologization

If in Figure 2 each of the three dimensions of knowledge remains in its own dimension, there is no danger of overlap. However, Foucault argues that each of these dimensions is linked by intermediary planes that are difficult to define with the consequence that the slightest movement along one of these planes sends thought tumbling over into the whole space, the complete domain occupied by the human sciences. The older boy imagined that this phenomena may also be illustrated by considering a knowledgeable person deep within the particular hole of their own empirical region; it is natural, perhaps inevitable, that such a person would know and understand the rest of the space of the Modern Episteme, the other holes, by means of the knowledge acquired primarily in his own hole. This, according to Foucault, is the greatest threat to knowledge in Modern times; i.e., the danger of one human science spilling over, falling outside its rightful domain, (occupying other holes as the older boy saw it) and reducing, consuming, reforming other dimensions of knowledge in its own image, in a "psychologism", a "sociologism" and an "anthropologism" (*ibid.*, p. 348).

"And," thought the older boy, "'an economism', a 'socialism', a 'pseudo-scientism', a 'human-biologism', a 'professionalism', a 'managerialism', an 'accountingism', a 'consumerism', 'a hedonism', and an '-ism' for any damn hole you happen to occupy in the human sciences. The relativists and subjectivists are indeed correct to argue that there is no space for objectivity in the modern world."

Specialisation has its roots in the formative epistemological processes of the Modern Episteme; it is a primary, not a secondary, phenomena. "Presumably," the older boy had noted with emphasis in the margin alongside this point, "this embedded form of specialisation means that the Modern episteme can never become sustainable."

The Process of Freedom

With these thoughts and illustrations, the older boy felt able to bury Foucault, to add him and his work to the selfsame archaeological strata from which they had arisen. The older boy was now able to move on from the Modern episteme; to see it for what it was looking as it were from the outside and that — that very act of objective observation — was itself the herald of new times, of a new episteme.

It was time for the older boy to make his own discoveries in the uppermost layers of the archaeology of knowledge; in those layers so fresh that they had been in the processes of sedimentation during Foucault's life; existing only as unsettled, partly formed ideas in air and only lightly resting on the surface of the grounding of knowledge. But now, the older boy felt, these new ideas had gained some weight; they were piling up around mankind, gaining density and becoming themselves buried for future archaeologists.

He found clues in the work of Foucault to help him. There was of course the question of language. For Foucault had raised the question "if language is emerging with greater and greater insistence in a unity that we ought to think but cannot as yet do so, is this not a sign that the whole of this configuration is now about to topple; that man is in the process of perishing as the being of language continues to shine ever brighter upon our horizon? Ought we not to admit that, since language is here once more, man will return to that serene non-existence?" (*ibid.*, p. 386). But it seemed of no use to the older boy at that stage in his understanding; he felt very much as if he was venturing out into unknown territory very much on his own.

As he turned over the sediments, as he dusted down intellectual artefacts and reassembled fractured and damaged sets of ideas, the older boy did begin to create something new and in that process he sensed freedom, a profound, soaring freedom; a freedom from the embrace of received ideas.

Intrinsic Sustainable Development

"Art requires neither complaisance nor politeness; nothing but faith — faith and freedom."

> — *From a letter from Gustave Flaubert (1821–1880) to Léon Laurent-Pichat on October 2, 1856 (Flaubert, 1953).*

CHAPTER 7 — SQUARE-PEG BUSINESS

An Everyday Enormity

An understanding of episteme change begs a question. To answer that question became a part of the older boy's everyday experience. It introduced a profound and world-shaking critique to all his encounters. It distanced him from the world and embedded him thoroughly, thoughtfully and sensitively within it. It led him to rail against the oppressive enormity of the everyday.

This question became central for the older boy. It rose above, enveloped, permeated, overcame, departed, renewed, discredited and elevated his several distractions. The question was "Do we have a new episteme?"

With time, the older boy could answer "yes". But, before he could provide support for his affirmation by describing a new episteme, he sought supporting evidence for the recognition of epistemic change in historic consequences. Furthermore, since his interest in epistemic change was nothing if not practical, he sought this evidence in changing attitudes to business.

The Religious Business

Seeking evidence for epistemic change made its own place within the older boy's daily routine. When for example QC rang from Beijing with a research idea, the older boy's questioning was not displaced, it continued in the background.

QC's idea was to conduct a capability audit within Yorkshire to find suitable environmental skills, knowledge and products for exporting to China. Her logic was that the UK's old industrial cities

161

had once been as dirty and polluted as parts of China but they had now cleaned up their act. Maybe they could help China do the same, and make money as they did so.

To assess the viability of such an audit and to gather ideas and partners to support his bid for funding, he made a series of visits. One of the first was to a civil engineer who was working on a building powered by fuel-cells. This expert was employed by a large engineering consultancy with an office in a refurbished church near Sheffield city centre. She was appreciative of his efforts, but felt that her work on fuel-cells was not yet ready for export. Nonetheless the older boy did gain from the meeting.

The inner space of the refurbished church had been partitioned to provide modern cellular office space for around two dozen employees. The walls and exterior of the church were Gothic, or rather a Victorian vision of the Gothic, and hence in this way they represented a yearning for past certainties as did Gothenburg's Feskekörka.

During this meeting, it had occurred to the older boy that we, just as much as the Victorians, could not build a true Gothic church again. We could copy in detail what the original Gothic architects and builders had done and reproduce a fair imitation but it would no more be a Gothic church than a computer simulation reproduces the flight of a bird.

Such copies are not real. They lack the full impetus of the life that first created them. For the bird, it is evolution, the aeons of minute action and revision that exploited the boundaries of feather, atmosphere and gravity that gives it something that computers can only imitate. For the church, it is attitude, understanding, a way of ordering knowledge of the world, that engendered a specific kind of answer, something which, with all our other knowledge, we can now only observe from the outside.

The older boy began looking for the kind of business that would have been part of the world of a true Gothic church. The mediaeval world had been god-given. His handwork was to be found, read and interpreted in every facet, every phenomenon, small or large, of the lived environment. Mediaeval scholars made no distinction between reading the bible and reading God's other creations in the world at large. The church would have dominated business; it could not have been otherwise given their episteme.

Mediaeval religious institutions were necessarily powerful and wealthy. Monasteries were essentially mediaeval production centres, "factories", where people were organised to create wealth — pious wealth.

Back at home, the older boy searched the bible to find out more about the relations between mediaeval business and their religious episteme. He found out that the Old Testament prohibits charging for money-lending in some twenty two individual passages for example: Exodus 22: 24–25 proclaims that "If you lend money to one of your poor neighbours among my people, you shall not act like an extortioner toward him by demanding interest from him"; whilst Deuteronomy, 15: 1–11, demands that at the end of every seventh year all outstanding debts are to be cancelled.

But even if some mediaeval entrepreneur could have pulled together the finance to fund a new venture, the older boy considered that he or she would have quickly found out that their society provided neither the goals, nor the incentives nor the legitimacy by means of which they might have prospered:

- "Next a word to you who are rich. Weep and wail over the miserable fate overtaking you: your riches...will be evidence against you and consume your flesh like fire." James 5: 1;
- "If you wish to be perfect, go, sell what you have and give to the poor...Again I say to you, it is easier for a camel to pass through the eye of a needle than for one who is rich to enter the kingdom of heaven." Jesus in Matthew 19: 21–24;
- "All possessions are by nature unrighteous", Saint Clement of Alexandria (Titus Flavius Clemens, c. 150–c. 215 AD), a Christian theologian;
- "That bread which you keep belongs to the hungry." Saint Basil the Great (330–379 AD), Bishop of Caesarea Mazaca;
- "A man who is a merchant can seldom if ever please God." Saint Jerome (c. 347–420 AD) who translated the Bible into Latin;

Intrinsic Sustainable Development

- "How did you become rich?. . . The root and origin of it must have been injustice." Saint John Chrysostom (c. 347–407 AD), Archbishop of Constantinople; and
- "Business is in itself an evil." Saint Augustine of Hippo (354–430 AD), one of the important figures in the development of Western Christianity.

In just one morning's study, it became clear to the older boy that we cannot enter and appreciate a world that thinks in ways so alien to our own without great difficulty and with the ever-present risk that we would lose our identity. Episteme change is a very personal affair. He continued his study.

Thomas Aquinas (1225–1274) wrote about the mediaeval "economy". Aquinas was a Dominican monk, an Italian philosopher and one of the most influential thinkers of the Middle Ages. He combined the ideas of Aristotle with Christian laws. Like Aristotle, he touched on a wide range of subjects, but Aquinas' purpose was to develop a system of thought that combined the worldly and the divine with seamless unity. Within this system, Aquinas attempted to define "fairness" in monetary transactions and trade.

Aquinas disagreed with Aristotle who had argued that tradesmen break rules of justice whenever they sell items at prices higher than their purchase price, i.e., whenever they make a profit. Aquinas realised that tradesmen deserved returns that covered not only their out-of-pocket expenses but also included a payment for their own labour and risk-taking. Aquinas therefore suggested that society should be prepared to tolerate the activity of traders as long as their gains from trade were moderate and their wealth was used for the benefit of the entire community. Hence the "economic policy" proposed by Aquinas was based on intervention and regulation in order to achieve equity and fairness in society.

Aquinas developed the concept of a "Just Price" that was to be determined by market place activity moderated by informed and compassionate judgement. The market price of food for example would have been reduced if the customer was starving. Aquinas had argued that there was no guarantee that the just price could be

Chapter 7 — Square-Peg Business   **165**

reached automatically by the operations of the market. He had no faith in the ability of markets to tend towards supply and demand equilibriums with fair and balanced exchanges. In his view, price controls and other forms of market regulation were essential to curb the selfish excesses that would otherwise dominate trade.

For later mediaeval writers, who built on Aquinas' economic ideas, the Just Price came to be seen as the value of an item that allowed producers to maintain their financial status in society and not to exceed it. The Just Price was thereby linked to long term costs which included an allowance for a reasonable profit.

From the 13th century on, craftsmen and traders began to group themselves by streets to attract customers and to keep an eye on the competition. These loose groups eventually became guilds whose role was to look after the craftsmen and traders. But customers did not trust them. Customers had little information and idea about the nature and cost of their purchases; the skills and arts of apothecaries were for example mysterious to lay people. Consequently, the market control and validation that the Just Price provided was both required and necessary — it endured.

From around 1150 to 1300, the population of Europe increased from about 50 to 70 million people. By 1400 that population was back to around 45 million, or about the same as it had been over two hundred years earlier. Influenza, smallpox, war and the Black Death killed Europeans in large numbers and emerging markets had added to this considerable death toll. Changes in demand for food had encouraged landowners and peasants alike to prefer stockbreeding, market gardening and cash crops to the growing of grain. Cash received for these other produce meant that grain could be purchased from large-scale, more efficient producers, in good times. Grain production fell continually during the 14th century as production was switched to more lucrative agricultural produce with the result that when famine came it devastated the poor who did not have the cash for trade.

Whole villages were wiped out and the survivors must have been traumatised. The sheer scale of their problems, together with the rise of markets and a powerful class of merchants meant that the authority of the church was weakened. Increased trade across

Europe resulted in a sophisticated banking system being developed and interest-based lending became far too important to be further restrained by the Church. The potential profits for money-lenders were far too high to be ignored.

Religious constraints on business activity lingered, but ways were found to avoid them. In England during the 15th century, the annual return expected by "sleeping partners", a polite term for money-lenders, was in excess of 10%. The Church still disapproved of such large gains; so interest payments were concealed in legal technicalities such as by combining a loan with an exchange of funds from one country's currency to another's and interest payments then being disguised as commission on foreign exchange transactions. This was for the older boy a clear example of the interrelations between a change in episteme and practical action; the one reinforcing and being reinforced by the other.

So there was no great revolution that brought the mediaeval episteme to a close; just a whittling away, a series of small victories. New and old epistemes existed side by side, balancing and opposing each other in the judgement of the people. Very slowly one side gained weight and the other side lost weight as compromises blurred distinctions, constraints were circumvented, and arguments began to group minds around other ways of ordering knowledge. The clarity, simplicity, unity and purpose of lives lived in the constant presence of God's hidden meanings and truths in mediaeval Europe was removed, possibly forever, by man reinventing and elevating himself and his institutions in the Renaissance.

"More than anything," the older boy wondered as he rounded off his morning's study by walking alongside the river, "how has the integrity, the wholeness, the complete life view of the mediaeval episteme been lost? The needs of sustainable development had brought holism, systems, life-cycles, the totalities of environmental and social impacts and accounting and series of other techniques to the fore of innovation as we try to recover something of the mediaeval episteme. McLuhan's global village is approaching reality with the World Wide Web and daily news reports from across the whole planet."

"Perhaps," he asked himself, "unsustainable development is a necessary consequence of the loss of unity in the ordering of our knowledge."

Banker Business

On the Thursday of the following week, the older boy had the opportunity to attended a meeting of a local green business club to promote the environmental capability audit. The meeting was held in the commercial centre of Sheffield. The meeting went well.

Afterwards the older boy walked through the city centre to his university office. His thoughts were with the audit, with the technologies, innovations, skills, values, ideas, motivations and perspectives that had created the environmental turn-around in the region. The fragmentation of knowledge in the modern episteme could not have done this. There was some kind of new awareness, a new synthesis that, for empirical reasons, had to be put in place.

The mediaeval religious controls on business were long gone, vestigial and easy to dismiss. But what had replaced them? He thought that technological change was a relevant factor. The refinement and expansion of the human capacity to innovate and adapt seemed ineluctable. He remembered that even way back in mediaeval Europe, technological innovations could be revolutionary. Long distance transportation had once been undertaken by four-wheeled ox-wagons with an escort of guards making perilous journeys along muddy roads; this was slow, expensive and dangerous. The development of the fast three-masted Carrack changed this situation; it probably had a bigger impact on trade in the Europe of the day than containerisation was to have centuries later. Once a two tonnes consignment of goods travelling by road for the 720 kilometres between Lübeck and Danzig (now Gdask) on the Baltic coast would have taken about 14 days to complete. A fast Carrack cutting through the relatively far-safer sea crossed between the two ports in just 4 days without an escort and with a massive 120 tonnes payload. Fortunes were to be made from cost reductions on this scale: 72% less time taken and a 6000% increase in carrying capacity.

But it was to be institutional innovation that had brought about far greater change in Europe. Payment for business transactions made across Europe had once been made with money. Such money was in unrestricted circulation. It came in many varieties of silver and gold, from different mints of varying repute; the professional expertise of the moneychanger had been an important, essential and stabilising control. Such moneychangers acted as fledgling bankers for they would also hold safe the monetary deposits and securities of merchants who had to travel in dangerous surroundings. Moneychangers could also provide travelling merchants with evidence of their monetary deposits for those business transactions made far away from home; this evidence took the form of a letter stating the amount of money held in deposit and it performed the function of a modern banker's cheque.

During the 14th century, the moneychanger's letter of deposit was transformed into a bill of exchange. For such bills to work, overseas offices had to be established in main centres of trade. Money would be paid to the local office of a foreign vendor and a bill of exchange issued; that bill travelled with the merchant to be handed over in payment. In this way, goods could be ordered, received and paid for between London and Florence without any movement of hard currency. Bills of exchange provided a valuable service and that, of course, was not free. A new revenue stream was thus created and taken by bankers and since it could be earned with relatively little use of time and resources; it was easily replicated and applied to all long distance trade transactions. Bankers became wealthy and powerful.

By these means, Bologna, Bruges, Florence, Milan, Rome and Venice flourished as banking centres. Many other cities were soon to follow. Great banker families include many famous names such as the Italian Medici and Strozzi families as well as the German Fuggers and Welsers of Augsburg who were destined in the fullness of time to acquire not only many Italian bankers' assets, but also much of their power and influence. The economic power of rich banking families came with significant political influence in their own cities and in royal and papal courts.

Trade and banking was so successful that it came to rival the wealth and influence of the royal courts. Whilst the interests of the church may have been weakened by the rise of commerce and its new attitudes and values, the court remained strong.

A French trader Jacques Cœur (1395–1456) became very successful by founding a lucrative trade between France and the Levant. He was so successful that he came to the King's attention and Charles VII of France made him master of the royal mint. Jacques' ships eventually came to ply all known trade routes; he employed 300 managers in offices across France; he established colleges in Paris; and he provided funds for the king's military ambitions.

Eventually, Jacque became too powerful. He was dealing in everything from money and arms, furs and jewels, brocades and wool, to brokerage, banking and farming. His commercial empire controlled virtually all trade in France. Other merchants could not make enough profits to sustain their basic activities and they became debtors to Cœur; so did significant numbers of courtiers, many members of the French royal family and even the King of France himself.

The world of commerce had challenged that of clerics and was winning; now it was challenging that of royalty. Royalty however was forged in battlefields and for Charles VII, truth was merely another weapon.

When the king's mistress died in 1450, a rumour was spread that she had been poisoned. Those courtiers in debt to Cœur grasped the opportunity; they accused Jacques Cœur of the murder though no evidence was produced. Charles acted quickly. On the 31st July 1451, Jacque Cœur was arrested and his property seized by the King who urgently needed more money to conduct war in Aquitaine.

Jacque and his empire had perished before other, more supportive attitudes had been widely established. But the institutions of trade and banking now had an entry into Europe and for centuries they were to support the power of kings — before overthrowing it.

The date of the end of the European Middle Ages is often taken as 1453, when the Turks took Constantinople. A new age is said to have dawned. Aquinas's religious arguments against usury became distant history. By the 1500's, regulations against usury had been weakened across Europe. Even Church members accepted interest-based lending as part of everyday life. In the 16th century, Domingo de Soto, a religious Spaniard, argued that receiving interest from a banker was a good thing, for not only did Domingo get richer but the banker used the money to make more profits. But even then, Domingo felt it necessary to make the point that banking practices were not inherently evil.

The transition from *evil* money lenders to the *good* of banking was an essential part of the arrival of the new age in Europe — the Renaissance. God had not departed from Europe, but European man was now forging a more secular side to his own identity in which banking was prominent. The Renaissance was an age marked by new ideas, mixed with those from the distant, Classical past as man searched for a new identity, a "Humanism" by means of which European man climbed out of the cradle of God and stood on his own feet — or rather on his own *banker's* feet, for that is how he now supported himself.

During most of the 15th century, the circulation of wealth had been limited to rich merchants and the owners of silver mines in central Europe. But in 1492 Christopher Columbus discovered America. Subsequent Portuguese and Spanish explorers wasted no time in exploiting the New World's vast silver and gold resources. From 1530 onwards, shiploads of silver and gold arrived regularly in Europe; this input of wealth caused unprecedented price rises. To manage this new wealth, trading associations had to extend their banking systems, credit houses developed ever more sophisticated techniques, uses of bills of exchange multiplied and letters of credit were introduced.

Precious metals now formed the foundation of Renaissance trade. For Renaissance thinkers, the ability of money to serve both as a measure and a representation of all exchange commodities rested on its intrinsic value. For this reason, fine metals were in themselves marks of wealth: "Its buried brightness was sufficient indication that it was at the same time a hidden presence and a visible signature of all the wealth of the world." (Foucault, 1970, p. 174).

Such fine metals were treated no differently than any other thing in the Renaissance ordering of knowledge. European man may be forging an identity other than that prescribed by the Bible, but the whole world, from fireside to mountain top, was still God's world. It was still as if presented in a book waiting to be read, interpreted and revealed. The mediaeval legacy of omnipotent divinity had not disappeared in the Renaissance world; it had simply been modified. The signs that were to be read equally in great books and in the world, and the resemblances to be drawn, still existed in the foundations of their knowledge which remained necessarily full and complete within their Great Chain of Being.

New attitudes, values and institutions sat alongside the old. Fine and precious metals might shine like stars and represent all the wealth and meaning of the world — but from now on bankers would have their cut.

The Rationalising Business

A month later, in Paris after attending a seminar on EU funding opportunities, the older boy took two days off. On the first day of his holiday, he visited the Louvre with a colleague from Siena. During the morning of the second day, he escorted her on a tour of the Eiffel tower. The queue to ascend the tower had been so long that the older boy became tired by the crowds of tourists in spite of his charming companion. She departed mid-afternoon by train for her home in Italy. For the rest of the afternoon the older boy began strolling as a kind of backdoor, away-from-crowds tourism to get to know Paris the better along her back streets. He made several stops at pavement cafes usually for coffee but around five o'clock he experimented with a Ricard and a carafe of water.

In the welcome sunshine of a quiet Parisian suburb, the older boy could reflect. The EU did have a funding scheme suitable for his environmental capabilities audit but he would have to involve other researchers and other regions across Europe to obtain it. But that was not what he reflected on that afternoon.

In Paris, he returned to Foucault. He wanted to develop his knowledge and understanding of business and epistemes. More specifically, he wanted to take his understanding into the age that Foucault had called Classical; the age that had been marked by Descartes, the French philosopher. It was in the Classical age that nature's passivity had seemed sealed by the success of Descartes' mechanism philosophy. Nature could indeed have been laid at the feet of traders and bankers ready to serve any purpose, for a profit. But how had Europe actually coped with the turn of events of a new episteme; with the new opportunities that technological change and sources of vast wealth had brought; and with the passing of the Renaissance episteme, that vast and deeply embedded ordering of knowledge and source of values, meanings and rights? How did these changes affect business: then and now?

Reflection at that level is fine for Parisian street cafes on sunny afternoon but it was not until six weeks had passed back home that he felt he was making real progress with this particular study. It was in the 17th century that money in itself, not precious metals, was to become foundational for trade; an important link was thereby lost with the Renaissance episteme for money was man-made and hence it lacked anything of God's hidden meaning and truth.

The establishment of colonies had meant that home nations did not depend wholly on other nations for the acquisition of wealth by exchange. The great volume of bullion arriving from colonies became the basis of wealth. Nations sought to maintain this wealth through positive balances of trade. In this way, it was the exchange properties of money itself that came to dominate in place of its intrinsic representational value and its immediate exchange relation to goods.

The mediaeval and Renaissance circle of "preciousness", of gold and silver's concealed meaning and resemblance, had been broken — from now on money was money. There could no longer be the possibility of a "Just Price"; nothing in any given commodity indicates, by any intrinsic character, the quantity of money that should be paid for it. Trade was now just a matter of exchanges, of markets and of circulations of money and goods (Foucault, 1970, p. 184).

Hence to be worth something within the Classical episteme was first of all to be capable of substitution within the processes of exchange as either the value created in the act of exchange or as value found in things themselves anterior to the exchange (*ibid.*, p. 190).

The anchoring of wealth in signs, representations and the Great Chain of Being had passed; making sense of the Classical episteme's new ideas and values, rationalising them, would take time and effort. Many minds would be applied to this task.

Thomas Hobbes

In England, Thomas Hobbes (1588–1679) was born the second son of a wayward English vicar. Like Descartes and Newton, Hobbes experienced an intellectual awakening, but for Hobbes this revelation was catalysed specifically by the geometry of Pythagoras. Hobbes was described by his friend John Aubrey in the book *Brief Lives* as falling in love with geometry and being swept away by its "irresistible deductive power and compulsive certainty".

Hobbes was also impressed by his friends Galileo Galilei and William Harvey, the English physician. In his book *De Cive*, Concerning the Citizen, Hobbes claims to have established a "civil philosophy" that was to be the political equivalent of natural philosophy, or what we now call physics. This was to be a new science of the state and it was to be mechanistic. In the introduction to the book, Hobbes wrote: ". . . everything is best understood by its constitutive causes. For as in a watch . . . the matter, figure and motion of the wheels cannot be well known, except it be taken insunder and viewed in parts; to make a more curious search into the rights of states and duties of subjects, it is necessary (I say, not to take them insunder, but yet that) they be so considered as if they were dissolved."

His method of analysing the behaviour of men was indeed to take society apart or, more specifically, to imaginatively remove the laws and practices that enable men to live together and to then consider what remains. What remains is, for Hobbes, a vision of a state of nature. In his masterpiece *Leviathan* (1651), Hobbes put forward his political arguments and many other ideas including this famous description of natural man that entails ". . . a war of every man, against every man. . . And the life of man, solitary, poor, nasty, brutish and short" (in *Leviathan* Chapter 13). If we are not careful, Hobbes argued, then we will slip back to this unpleasant condition and our only security is to concentrate all the powers of a state into the hands of one man or an assembly of men.

Hobbes had no experience of natural society, whatever that may be. His view of society was based on what he found mainly in England at the time; an England coming to grips with many new ideas and opportunities, and not least among these was the market economy. Pepper (1996, p. 148) observes with regard to Hobbes' Leviathan: "This painted a dismal picture of human nature; one which reflected the market economy that was then beginning to develop."

For Hobbes' life in a state of nature was a condition to be avoided, but this did not mean that the laws of nature could be suppressed or ignored. Hobbes had a clear understanding of a law of nature as "a precept or general rule, found out by reason, by which a man is forbidden to do that which is destructive to his life or taketh away the means of preserving the same" (in *Leviathan*, chapter 14). For Hobbes, inescapable laws explain why a rational man who understands the true, unpleasant state of nature will readily submit to political power, any political power for his own sense of self-preservation and will "naturally" avoid any threat of a return to a state of nature. Hence, Hobbes' understanding of liberty involves being obedient to man-made laws, principally laws of state.

It appeared to the older boy that in God's absence, Hobbes wanted man to impose his own ineluctable laws. There was no recourse here to any knowledge of nature, either active or passive; nature was more or less irrelevant.

John Locke

John Locke (1632–1704) adopted Hobbes' broad analysis of human nature and accepted that there were laws of nature governing human society just as they governed the physical universe. Locke had been borne into the minor gentry of Somerset in England. He went to Oxford in 1652, where he became acquainted with Robert Boyle, the leading English scientist of his day. Boyle was then the spokesperson for the corpuscular philosophy that had developed from Descartes' description of mechanistic "corpuscles". In later life, Locke would count Isaac Newton among his friends.

In his *Essay Concerning Human Understanding* (1691), Locke applied a corpuscular understanding to the origin of ideas. He classified ideas into simple and complex ones, where simple ideas included such as "cold", "red" and "bitter" and they were simple because no other ideas were contained within them; they could neither be created nor destroyed, just like atoms. Also like atoms, simple ideas were the building blocks of more complex ideas, ones that could be created and destroyed. For example, the simple idea of "horse" may be built in different combinations of complex ideas according to how a person relates to a horse and to the idea of horse; a once horse lover may change their mind and come to hate the beasts and so create and destroy several sets of complex ideas.

Just as Locke's friend and mentor Robert Boyle had explained, the behaviour of gases in terms of particles in motion obediently conforming to a law of nature,[1] Locke argued that people were similarly in motion in society and obedient to societal laws. Locke was a devout protestant and for him these societal laws came from God. The laws from God, according to Locke, grant each man natural rights such as a right to life, to liberty (providing our actions do not infringe the rights of others), to property in our own bodies, and to the products of our own labour. These arguments were put forward in his *Essay* and that book was a huge success. It remained the single most influential book in European philosophy for at least two hundred years; and it underpins many rights to this day.

In the second of his *Two Treatise of Government* (1690), Locke argued that before civil society existed and man was living in a state of nature, his rights to property were limited to that which he himself could use; for example, he had rights to the amount of grain that he and his family could eat. In these "natural" circumstances a man had no rights to a surplus since that surplus would spoil and hence be denied to others.

---

[1]Boyle's Law states that $PV = \text{constant}$ where P is the pressure on a gas and V is the volume of that gas.

As societies developed, Locke argued that state-of-nature societies would become unstable since men would frequently and necessarily restrict the rights of others as they lived in close proximity. For this reason, Locke argued that men must join together by means of a social contract. In a society so formed, the king or ruling body of men has the primary function of enforcing the God-given laws that protect God-given rights to property.

For a society bound by such a contract, Locke then wanted to prove that a person would gain other rights; rights that would extend to having possessions in excess of immediate personal needs. Such a justification was necessary for Locke for he, like his scientific friends, was an empiricist; the fact was that some people in Locke's society did already own more than their personal needs and this required an explanation. According to his own arguments, property ownership was not a right if that property was going to spoil; Locke got around this by identifying a kind of wealth that was not subject to decay. Locke proclaimed that *money* does not decay and hence there is no argument for limiting a person's right to the amount of money owned.

Having excesses of money then becomes a God-given right according to Locke. This right applies, no matter how poor and desperate a neighbour may be. Locke's arguments for God-given rights are still used to support excesses of wealth in our own societies, but Locke did set one proviso that is now often forgotten. A person may have an excess of monetary wealth, according to Locke, but only if that excess is used to convert more of Earth's resources for the eventual benefit of all mankind; a person had no right to excesses of wealth that perish from uselessness.

"Locke wrote and ordered his knowledge within the Classical episteme," concluded the older boy, "but his arguments apply today. Capitalism needed John Locke."

David Hume

Hume (1711–1776) had a gift for friendship and was an exceptionally good-natured and attractive man. Modern biographers of Hume cannot find evidence of him being responsible for any mean or malicious act. Hume was born in Edinburgh as the second son of a minor laird seven years after the death of John Locke. Hume too enjoyed an intellectual revelation that was to set the course of his life; an experience that came to Hume when he was eighteen years of age and it prompted him to write *A Treatise of Human Nature*. This book took eight years to finish. It is large and revolutionary but it sold very few copies; as Hume himself famously remarked, "It fell dead-born from the press".

His *Treatise* has the subtitle: *Being an attempt to introduce the experimental method of reasoning into moral subjects*. In Hume's day, 'moral subjects' was a phrase understood very widely to include not only moral philosophy but also a broad selection of what we now call the social sciences, such as politics and economics. It was an attempt to discover what our understandings could deal with. In this way it was a successor to Locke's *Essay*; but Hume introduced other dimensions to his arguments, those of human nature, of psychology, and of the logical limits to knowledge. For Hume, everything that we know depends on the constitution of the "knowing agent", i.e., on man. Hence, following Hume, all knowledge is dependent on human nature. These were radical ideas indeed.

Hume sought to answer a riddle concerning man's nature. He wanted simple solutions obtained by simple means. He achieved all of this and furthermore he explained his ideas with clarity and elegance; nonetheless, his solutions were often at odds with popular opinion.

For example, Hume regarded religious beliefs as distortions of fundamentally sound principles of human nature. So it was a human nature free of divine intervention, influence and rights that Hume wanted to observe and to know.

But Hume was his own enemy. He posed a question that was to remove forever the possibility of uncomplicated and direct learning from observations of nature. He asked what basis do we have for drawing universal conclusions from repeated observations of the same event? So even though our experience may teach us that a rubber ball will bounce back when thrown at a hard floor, there was, for Hume, no valid revelation in this experiment other than the blunt, *unconnected* fact of a ball bouncing.

178   *Intrinsic Sustainable Development*

Hume argued that the deduction of a cause and a set of *necessarily* connected events for a bouncing ball is merely a "perception of the mind", just a thought without any correspondence in reality. A ball may bounce 1,000 times and we may deduce a theory of the elasticity of rubber to explain why the ball bounces, but this does not mean that on the 1001st try, the ball will bounce as before. Hume claimed that what is happening is that our experience has generated within us a habit of "expecting" and it is this habit that our consciousness transforms into the idea of a *necessary* causal connection. Hence the fact that we expect the sun to rise each morning has to do with our mental constructions, perceptions in our minds, and not with a logically verifiable property of the world external to ourselves. With similar ideas, Hume also argued that virtue, vice, beauty and ugliness do not exist outside our minds.

Such a profound denial of the possibility of knowledge of causality was to liberate no less a person than Albert Einstein. This greatest of all scientists once remarked that he would never have dared to overthrow Newton's well established view of the universe if he had not read Hume.

Such a profound denial of the possibility of knowledge of causality is also entirely appropriate for the Classical episteme. For a detached observer looking over the two-dimensional table of all possible knowledge, there exists no logical connection with that table. Furthermore the order of knowledge imposed on things on the Classical table was entirely man-made. The imposition of identities and differences was a product of rational minds.

But Hume worked at the edge of the Classical episteme. He anticipated its final demise with the emphasis he placed on the "psychologisation" of knowledge. It is not too surprising, therefore, that Kant's response to Hume overthrew the Classical episteme.

When in 1776 the Americans made their Declaration of Independence, Hume was dying with a protracted bowel disorder. James Boswell, Hume's biographer, visited Hume in those last days and expected to find a terrified atheist confronted by the appalling finality of an irreligious life. It greatly disturbed Boswell to find Hume to be his cheerful and pleasant self.

"Perhaps," considered the older boy, "Hume had found other intimations of immortality in his life dedicated to original, creative thought."

The Liberty Business

Two months later, in New York attending a conference to present a paper on sustainable business models, the older boy was greatly enjoying his hotel in Washington Square. The food, jazz and echoes of Bob Dylan all added to his enjoyment. He took a boat trip around the Statue of Liberty and ate in Times Square as he watched electronic billboards mixing the serious business of making money with fashion and films in various forms of "finacialtainment". It was hard to see the antiquity in these presentations, but the older boy knew it was there.

The latter decades of the eighteenth century are known as the Enlightenment. They were inspired by powerful beliefs in the abilities of reason and science to improve the lot of mankind. The *Encyclopédie* was published in France between 1751 and 1772 as a systematic dictionary of the sciences, arts, and crafts and was intended to change the way that people think. It was a culmination and proclamation of the Classical episteme's achievements in ordering and revealing knowledge. Enlightenment ideas were to prove profoundly revolutionary in practice as in theory; they gave justification and purpose to the French Revolution and, via writers such as Montesquieu and Thomas Jefferson, to the American Declaration of Independence and to the Constitution of the United States of America. The Classical episteme came of age.

Jean-Jacques Rousseau (1712–1788) published *Du Contrat Social* in his fiftieth year. He argues that the general will, not a social contract, should rule society. In chapter one of his book, Rousseau observed that "L'homme est né libre, et partout il est dans les fers" (Man was born free, and everywhere he is in chains). These are the most famous political words ever written.

Echoing Hobbes, Rousseau also observed in *Du Contrat Social* that if we all were coerced to follow the general will, then we would be "forced to be free". This attitude, of course, proved very useful for the French, and other, revolutionary assemblies.

It would be difficult to overestimate the influence that Enlightenment thinkers have had on our own times. Thomas Paine (1737–1809) for example wrote *Common Sense* (1776), an appeal for American independence, and he also published *The Rights of Man* (in two parts, 1791 and 1792) which justifies the French revolution and gives praise to both the new French Republic and the American constitution. In response to *The Rights of Man*, one of the first British feminists, Mary Godwin (1759–1809), produced a *Vindication of the Rights of Women* (1792), a courageous attack on the conventions of the day and on the dominance of men.

The Founding Fathers of the United States of America made use of Enlightenment ideals to write constitutional principles for their new country. Some of these principles were taken to be universal; they were to apply to all people of all nations and cultures. In the USA, these principles helped to create a society in which Capitalism was to flourish.

"Liberty, when it begins to take root, is a plant of rapid growth."
> George Washington (1732–1799), first president of the United States of America from 1789 to1797.

"Property is surely a right of mankind as real as liberty."
> John Adams (1735–1826), leading champion of American Independence, and second President of the United States of America from 1797 to 1801.

"The exercise of a free trade with all parts of the world [is] possessed by [a people] as of natural right."
> Thomas Jefferson (1743–1826), principal author of the American Declaration of Independence (1776), and third President of the United States of America from 1801 to 1809.

The Independent Organic Business

Over the rest of the summer recess, the older boy left his episteme project well alone. During fine sunny and warm days when his garden was replete with flowers and butterflies and a pair of buzzards was soaring and calling high above, he pressed on with his environmental capabilities audit.

It was only when leaves were golden that a sense of greater, ineluctable change came back to the older boy. A change of season is dramatic and pronounced in the Peak District. The open skies, flowers and diverse and delicate plant life, swallows, rooks, warm air temperatures and light clothing of summer quickly give way to warm clothing, open wood-fires, weak sunlight, ice, snow, strong winds and deep depressions. But it was the epistemological and consequential cultural changes that took place during the decades around 1800 that interested the older boy most during that particular autumn.

He started with an observation: "The French and American revolutions were not caused by epistemic change, which has no power to do anything. Epistemes are the world, not the cause of any particular event or thing within it."

As the 18th century closed and the 19th opened in Europe, epistemes changed from Classical to Modern according to Foucault's archaeological narrative. The cause of change was not simply Kant's questioning of the origin of representations which marks a noteworthy position, a milestone, in the process of changing episteme. The causes of change, the causes of new attitudes to the world, European culture, social institutions as well as the causes of the French and American revolutions were many and various, detailed and sweeping at all levels of understanding and analysis. They were of both structural and contingent kinds.

"The struggle that mankind undertakes to be able to make its own decisions and to take some control of its destiny may well be," thought the older boy, "a structural property of change, but the discovery of America had been pure contingent fact. Mankind may struggle everywhere and forever to be free of Rousseau's chains, but the American War of Independence would not have happened if the American continent did not exist or had not been discovered."

Kant's questioning of the origin of representations was itself a major event, but it was only part of a process of greater change, the long transition from a Classical to a Modern episteme, which is even now incomplete. Whilst Kant's questioning may mark a clear epistemological separation between the two epistemes, memories, values and attitudes do not separate so readily.

The distancing of mankind from nature had not been present in the Renaissance episteme, according to Foucault. Nature, man and sacred texts were then all parts of God's creation within the Great Chain of Being. It was within the Classical episteme that Descartes caused the clear separation of man's thinking mind from both nature and from his own body. The philosophy of Mechanism, its many practical applications and its outstanding scientific successes, deepened this divide.

For Aristotle, nature had been alive and active. It was the ground out of which the human world had grown. For the Christians, at war with pagans in ancient Rome, a prominent, formative role for nature was not at all appropriate for their message that to die painfully for their one and only God was the ultimate source of meaning for humanity. In the Middle Ages a reworking of the Master, of Aristotle, had been both necessary and thorough; it was necessary so that Christianity could gain profound and ancient philosophical roots. It was thorough, for God's agency had to displace nature in each and every quarter. Nature became the passive medium within which God's will could be revealed to be at work. Without this deep-grained Christian attitude that regarded nature as passive, Descartes' dualism and his philosophy of Mechanism would have been inconceivable.

But just as the Classical episteme was reaching its giddy, "liberating" heights, the Physiocrats were already starting to formulate an ordering of knowledge that lay well beyond that two-dimensional table. In the middle of the 18th century, the Physiocrats were developing the first theories of economics. They argued that the wealth of nations was derived solely from land development and that productive agricultural labour was the origin of national wealth. Their economic arguments that labour was the *origin* of wealth lay outside the understanding that wealth was a given, just an item to be found on the table, to be simply taken and used as in mercantilism. Physiocrats such as Anne-Robert-Jacques Turgot (1727–1781) and François Quesnay (1694–1774) defined an *origin* for wealth and by doing so they were heralds of a new age, one that did not take the origins of knowledge as a given.

The Physiocrats raised a question about origins in economics; but a similar epistemological question was to be asked. It was Kant who had questioned *origin* within a philosophical understanding.

The new order of knowledge and its new attitudes were to have the usual, world-changing consequences. This is the start of our own episteme, the Modern; the order of knowledge with which we grew. One prominent Physiocrat, Pierre Samuel du Pont de Nemours, emigrated to America. His son was to found a company called "E.I. du Pont de Nemours et Compagnie" and that company, DuPont, is now the world's second largest chemicals company.

Adam Smith

As David Hume lay on his death bed, he read a newly published book by Adam Smith, an *Inquiry into the Nature and Causes of the Wealth of Nations*. Hume declared this book a masterpiece.

Adam Smith's masterpiece was published in 1776, at a time when the Classical episteme was reaching its culmination and harbingers of a change in episteme were emerging. So just as for the economics of the Physiocrats, Smith's book was written within a dominating passive nature attitude and mechanistic understanding of society, but it was about something very different.

Smith (1723–1790) established a comprehensive analysis of the economic origins of wealth that was revolutionary, circumspect and appealing. So persuasive were his arguments that they not only provided the world with a new understanding of the wealth-creating process, they laid the intellectual foundation for economic expansion. D. R. Butler of the Adam Smith Institute argues: "The Wealth of Nations changed our understanding of the economic world just as Newton's Principia changed our understanding of the physical world." (ASI, 2010).

Smith identified the functions by means of which economic entities could grow: "In North America... fifty or sixty pounds is often found a sufficient stock to begin a plantation with. The purchase and improvement of uncultivated land, is there the most profitable employment of the smallest as well as of the greatest capitals, and the most direct road to all the fortune and illustration which can be acquired in that country. Such land, indeed, is in North America to be had almost for nothing, or at a price much below the price of the natural produce; a thing impossible in Europe, or, indeed, in any country where all lands have long been private property.'' (Smith, 2007, pp. 505–506).

For Foucault, Adam Smith had formulated a principle of order that was irreducible to the analysis of representation in the Classical episteme. He had unearthed labour, the toil and time, the working-day, that gives pattern to and uses up a man's life. With Adam Smith, knowledge of wealth begins to overflow the space assigned on that table of the Classical Age, where it had been lodged within ''ideology'', inside the analysis of representation. After Smith, wealth has two domains with dimensions that lie well outside the table: (i) the anthropology that questions man in his essence, in his finitude, in his relation with time, and in the imminence of his death; and (ii) the objects of his needs in which he invests his time (Foucault, 1970, p. 225).

After Smith, the relative values of things are not created by other objects or other needs in the continuous circulation of the markets; it is the *origin* of things, the activity that has produced them, the days and hours required for their manufacture, extraction, or transportation that now constitutes their real price. It is on the basis of this essential nucleus, this *origin*, that exchanges can be accomplished and that market processes can find their point of rest (*ibid.*, p. 238). The time of economics was now to be the interior time of an organic structure which grows in accordance with its own necessity and develops in accordance with autochthonous laws; it is now the time of capital and production (*ibid.*, p. 226).

With more precision, Adam Smith did privilege labour, but he also introduced a confusion that arose because of the dominance of representations of exchange in the Classical episteme. For Smith, all merchandise represented a certain labour and all labour could represent a certain quantity of merchandise. It was Ricardo who destroyed the unity of that notion. Ricardo argued that it is the worker's energy, toil, and time that are bought and sold, and it is thus the activity itself that is at the origin of the value of things and not their exchange value (*ibid.*, p. 253). For Ricardo labour is the producing activity and the source of all value (*ibid.*, p. 254).

This replacement of exchange by activities as the source of value gives rise to a series, since economic activities take place one after the other; a great linear, homogenous series, of production arises and this in turn introduces, by its very existence, the possibility of a continuous historical time (*ibid.*, p. 255). Hence Ricardo made possible the articulation of economics on history; "Wealth" is now organized and accumulated in a temporal sequence and the mode of being of economics is now linked to the time of successive productions (*ibid.*, p. 255–6).

However, men die and so the human economy is henceforth labouring under the threat of death. Also a population needs new resources or is doomed to extinction. Finite human time and the need to find new resources means that economics exists in a perpetual and fundamental situation of scarcity within a nature that is seen to be passive and mostly scarce. Man risks his life for increasingly harder to win resources (*ibid.*, p. 256–7). So it is no longer within the interplay of representation that economics exists, but near that perilous region where life is confronted with death and therefore economics has to be referred to an anthropology, to the biological properties of the human species. Foucault concludes that the positivity of economics is situated in an *anthropological hollow* where Homo oeconomicus wears out, wastes his life in evading the imminence of death (*ibid.*, p. 257).

Man is a finite being and Kant's questioning of origins made the question of finitude more fundamental than the analysis of representations. After Ricardo, economics became an anthropology that attempts to assign concrete forms to finitude. In Classical thought, the economy possessed an ever-open, ever-changing future within the two-dimensional space of the table of all knowledge and all of time. In Modern thought, economic history exists only in so far as man is a finite being (*ibid.*, p. 257). The more man makes himself at home in the world, the further he advances his possession of nature and the more strongly he feels the pressure of his own finitude, the closer he comes to his own death (*ibid.*, p. 259). Modern economics is thus inextricably entwined with the Modern episteme, its anthropology, psychology and man's finitude.

Smith and Ricardo gave economics a form of autonomy; economics became an entity with its own rights and inner functions that, if properly understood and nurtured, could grow and provide wealth for the world — at least for those who own capital. Smith also provided the understanding required for the creation of the independent organic business; a form of business with its own life that grows by means of its own inner functions, just as other forms of natural life (but one which had been created by man to serve man). The rigid mechanistic understanding of the Classical episteme had been surpassed with knowledge of an economics that reproduced and grew according to its own intrinsic and creative functions. In this way, independent organic structures that are the mark of the Modern episteme would come to replace the rigid mechanisms, identities and differences of the Classical episteme. But the organic structures created by the Modern episteme were created by man for man. Nature remained passive, immaterial, and irrelevant except as a provider of resources for these independent, living-business institutions.

Today, the Adam Smith Institute promotes *The Wealth of Nations* for the great book that it is and its protagonists explain: "Adam Smith railed against this restrictive, regulated, 'mercantilist' system, and showed convincingly how the principles of free trade, competition, and choice would spur economic development, reduce poverty, and precipitate the social and moral improvement of humankind. To illustrate his concepts, he scoured the world for examples that remain just as vivid today: from the diamond mines of Golconda to the price of Chinese silver in Peru; from the fisheries of Holland to the plight of Irish prostitutes in London. And so persuasive were his arguments that they not only provided the world with a new understanding of the wealth-creating process; they laid the intellectual foundation for the great era of free trade and economic expansion that dominated the Nineteenth Century." (ASI, 2010).

The American economist Milton Friedman (1912–2006) is one of the best known advocates of Smith's work. Friedman was a Nobel Laureate and he was described by *The Economist* as "the most influential economist of the second half of the 20th century... possibly of all of it". By means of Friedman's book *Capitalism and Freedom* (1962), the independent organic structures that are capitalist businesses were able to outgrow the societies in which they had been created and nurtured. In that book, Friedman argued for further reductions in state power in favour of free markets as a means of creating political and social freedom as well as a means of solving a range of social and political problems. Friedman's influential ideas were put into practice by governments around the world in the 1980's including those of Ronald Reagan in the U.S.A. and Margaret Thatcher in the UK.

In chapter eight of *Capitalism and Freedom*, Friedman makes use of Adam Smith's "invisible-hand" in an attempt to reconcile social responsibility and the independent, organic economic entities. Friedman argued that the "correct" understanding of a free economy allowed for one and only one social responsibility for business, that of gaining more money and increasing profits. After all, Friedman continued, how can private individuals decide on just what "social interest" really is and similarly how can "businessmen" [sic] know what "social responsibility" is? But this lack of knowledge does not matter for Friedman since it is the workings of an "invisible hand" that will distribute wealth more widely in society. So by unleashing the independent organic economic structures, a few people, those with the capital, might *en route* become rich but all of mankind would ultimately benefit as "invisible hands" did their work.

The older boy could now recognise the evolution of Capitalism's immense power. As he looked back over the intellectual history of Europe and America, Capitalism had had a long period of gestation. "It is," thought the older boy, "a very easy mistake to regard this history of events as a progressive form of evolution. It is easy to link historical facts and to make a story that brings us unavoidable to the present day without considering that those facts and events could have been very different. Others could have made up very different

188   *Intrinsic Sustainable Development*

stories and believed, uncompromisingly, in their own different, but unique and purposeful, destinies.''

Square-Peg Business

The older boy was stumped. His knew that his work had reached a turning point. He now wanted to follow a new road, to find new stories, perhaps even a new episteme, but he was motionless — or rather not moving either forwards or backwards — but spinning, twisting, contorting himself mentally on the same spot. At that point in his understanding where the Modern episteme and its institutions were clearly failing, he could not see another way forward and his energy internalised itself: rooting out and modifying old ways; tweaking concepts and modifying theories; generating new control and regulatory devices to try and compress his problematic ideas into something manageable; and finding comfort with the many others who were doing the same.

In an attempt to free himself of Foucault's reading of the Modern episteme, the older boy returned to the ten points he had identified as key features of the Modern episteme. He related these points to Modern business and its institutions and put them in a Word document which he then printed so that he might persistently review them, perhaps tentatively turn them into a new way forward and, hence eventually, let them lead him to new ways of thinking.

For a Phoenix Rising from the Ashes of the Modern

  i. **The change from Classical to Modern**
     A shift from *wealth* as a given to an *economics* with origins and production functions.
 ii. **Modern origins**
     The foundations of Modern economics and accounting are constantly sought, but never to be attained.
iii. **New forms of knowledge**
     Modern economics and accounting formed as independent entities with their own internal relations and laws.

iv. **Philosophical consequences of the Modern episteme**
   Economic theory uses a belief in its own *a priori* coherence to select *a posteriori* truths.

v. **No metaphysical continuum in the Modern episteme**
   The lack of a strong metaphysical continuum in the Modern episteme is compensated by the strong mathematical formularization of both economics and accounting.

vi. **The Modern episteme's two schools of philosophy**
   Capitalism and Communism are interdependent.

vii. **Epistemological man**
   Modern economics and accounting is conceived by man for man.

viii. **History**
   Economics regards itself as the culmination of history.

ix. **Finitude**
   Time is money.

x. **Anthropologization**
   Economism is pervasive.

The older boy folded his "phoenix" page and carried it everywhere for several weeks. He had hoped that all his *distractions* would work on these clearly enumerated thoughts and produce something new. But they did not. He wrote so many notes on the "phoenix" that he had to reprint the page over ten times. In time he came to judge the page as clever, insightful and perhaps accurate here and there, but as no way forward; it was part of the turning, the vigorous spinning, the agitated contortions on the spot that he was performing at that ought-to-be, junction of ways: "Me and the rest of the world," he thought to himself.

He then looked for inspiration in the works of others. When some fact or statement or story impressed itself on him, he made a note and hoped that somehow a conceptual crystallization would take place. His new notes were to be a melting pot of hot, fluid ideas which just might reform, grow with structure and purpose — just as a crystal grows — if the right focal point or particular idea could be found. A sample of his notes is reproduced below.

Consequences of Square-Peg Business

Critiques of the Ordering of Knowledge in the Modern Episteme

- Point six of the Draft Declaration on the Human Environment prepared in 1972 at the UN Conference on the Human Environment held in Stockholm said: "A point has been reached in history when we must shape our actions throughout the world with a more prudent care for their environmental consequences. Through ignorance or indifference we can do massive and irreversible harm to the earthly environment on which our life and well being depend." The conference authors also claim that: "... through fuller knowledge and wiser action, we can achieve for ourselves and our posteriorty a better life in an environment more in keeping with human needs and hopes." (UN, 1972).

- Foundational radical thoughts from Rachel Carson's *Silent Spring* (1962), Garret Hardin's *Tragedy of the Commons* (1968), *Blueprint for Survival* in a 1972 issue of the Ecologist magazine, and the Club of Rome's *Limits to Growth* report (Meadows *et al.*, 1972).

- "In the conventional economic view, corporations are simply neutral providers of the goods and services that people want. They exist to serve society's needs (and make a profit in the process). This view dismisses corporate crimes as mere accidents, at worst errors of judgement, which will ultimately be corrected, since market forces have everyone's best interests at heart. Don't they?" (Corporate Watch, 2010).

- John Dewey (1859–1952), the influential American pragmatist philosopher, argued that: "As long as politics is the shadow cast on society by big business, the attenuation of the shadow will not change the substance" (Westbrook, 1991, p. 440).

- Speth (1942–) writes: "John Maynard Keynes, writing eighty years ago, looked forward to the day when the 'economic problem' would be a thing of the past"; and "This means that the economic problem is not — if we look into the future — the permanent problem of the human race" (Speth, 2008, p. 107).

Extinctions as Evidence of Square-Peg Business Damage

- In 1497 the Venetian explorer John Cabot set sail from Bristol to the New Found Land, to America. En route he came across abundant fish and his crew reported that all they had to do was lower a basket in the sea and it would come up full of cod. After WWII, hundreds of factory trawlers, mainly from Eastern Europe, arrived on the Grand Banks of the North Atlantic and it was reported that all you could see at night were dragger lights as far as the eye could see, just like a city in the sea.

  In 1977 the Canadian government imposed an exclusive 200-mile zone around its coast to protect fish stocks but the attitude of the Canadians had been that if other countries could make so much money from the fish so would they. Fishing the Grand Banks with advanced technology continued until the 1980's when cod populations in the area collapsed to bring an end to nearly 500-years of human exploitation of cod. When the cod population crashed, so did the Canadian society that depended on cod fishing: 40,000 Canadians lost their jobs.

- Life on Earth has suffered at least five major extinctions in the past, but today the "'sixth extinction'... is being caused not by meteors or other environmental changes, but by ourselves, our species Homo sapiens." (Eldredge 1998, p. IX).

Break-out Institutions

- Business and Human Rights Resource Centre (2010) wants to:
  - Encourage companies to respect human rights, avoid harm to people, and maximise their positive contribution,
  - Provide easy, one-stop access to information for companies, non-governmental organizations (NGOs) and others, both practitioners and those new to the subject, and
  - To facilitate constructive, informed decision-making and public discussion.
- Andrew Simms, Director of the New Economics Foundation (NEF, 2010), says "Debt-fuelled over-consumption not only brought the financial system to the edge of collapse. It is pushing many of our natural life support systems toward a precipice. Politicians tell

192   *Intrinsic Sustainable Development*

us to get back to business as usual, but if we bankrupt critical ecosystems, no amount of government spending will bring them back."

- UNEP's Global Outlook 2000 blamed societal attitudes: "... a wasteful and invasive consumer society, coupled with continued population growth, is threatening to destroy the resources on which human life is based" (UNEP, 1999, p. 362).

- The "Vision 2050 Report" from the World Business Council for Sustainable Development reports that: "We have what is needed to live well, within the limits of the planet: the scientific knowledge, proven and emerging technologies, financial assets and instant communications. Nevertheless, today our societies are on a dangerously unsustainable track. The story is one of growth in populations and consumption (in most countries) compounded by inertia stemming from inadequate governance and policy responses necessary to manage this growth. The result is degradation of the environment and societies." (WBCSD, 2010, p. 2).

Sustainable Corporations?

- Many indices purport to assess the sustainability of corporations: CRO's best 100 Corporate Citizens, Oekom Corporate Ratings, Bloomberg Sustainability Reporting Initiative, FTS4Good Index Series, GoodGuide, Newsweek's Green Rankings, Vigeo Ratings, Dow Jones Sustainability Index, Covalence Ethical Quote Rankings, the Global 100 Most Sustainable Corporations in the World (Corporate Knights), KLD 400 Social Index, Asset4 ESG Ratings, Wal-Mart Sustainability Index, Fortune's Most Admired Companies and Hang Seng.

But these indices provide *relative* measures between corporations: they may all be unsustainable with a different ordering of knowledge. Such corporations often work with Elkington's "Triple Bottom Line" (1997). This concept provides a measure of business performance based on social, environmental and economic bottom-lines. The TBL effectively casts the environment and society as additional costs which have to be managed and reduced or eliminated; for it has only one top line, economic performance. A "Triple Top Line" is urgently needed!

The CSR Dilemma

- Corporate Social Responsibility (CSR) has been proposed as a way to bridge the gap between business and societal objectives and action. But CSR is a vague concept; it encompasses a broad range of activities previously known as corporate philanthropy, corporate community involvement, ethics, sustainability, legitimation and stakeholder dialogue. In short, CSR is a collection of many management and business ideas that adds nothing new (Van Oosterhout and Heugens 2006).
- CSR is a reworking of the Modern episteme's inevitable conflict between business and society, Capitalism and Marxism: "Since companies cannot act in any wider interest than the interest of their shareholders to make profit, CSR is of limited use in creating social change. Since CSR is also a vehicle for companies to thwart attempts to control corporate power and to gain access to markets, CSR is a problem not a solution." (Corporate Watch, 2006, p. 26).

One wet day in Sheffield when rain fell so hard that it bounced from the pavement outside the coffee bar, that conceptual crystallisation process, the focal point around which a whole new arrangement of thought would occur, still eluded the older boy. Then it occurred to him that he might have been looking in the wrong places. He had been looking into business, economics and social theories and practices for inspiration: but what if these compartments of knowledge were in themselves products of the Modern episteme's ordering of knowledge in the human sciences? What if these sophisticated and extensive bodies of knowledge were parts of the problem and not the solution? What if the simple solution he sought for sustainability was to be found elsewhere in knowledge? After all, both the Renaissance and the Classical epistemes had had strong metaphysical foundations, their knowledge had been fully synthesised, holistic and complete; albeit by God.

Since the older boy would have to validate any ideas he might eventually generate, he could not in the first instance consider belief-based systems of thought. So the began to explore the understandings, scientific knowledge and evidence that we now have of the natural world.

> "But the age of chivalry is gone. That of sophisters, economists, and calculators, has succeeded; and the glory of Europe is extinguished forever."
>
> – *Edmund Burke in Reflections on the Revolution in France (1790).*

PART III

PRIMAL KNOWLEDGE

CHAPTER 8 — BREAKING FREE

Chongming Island

Warm mist enveloped Wusong Port on the Shanghai waterfront and totally concealed the dockland railway, barriers, warehouses and walkways. Crowds slipped into invisibility in the murky distance. But Queen's Chinglish knew where she was going. She strode out briskly and talked on her mobile phone with her "link" in the government department of Chongming Island. She arranged access to the private salon for herself and the older boy on the ferry across the mouth of the Yangtze River.

The ferry was full. On the deck, QC squeezed between families of Chinese people and stepped over bags to lead the way to the salon. Three people were already sitting there and QC greeted them in Chinese, and discovered their business. A flask of warm water stood on the table; the older boy poured some into a plastic beaker and sipped his drink. When the engine started, talk was difficult, so the five people sat silently for the journey and closed their eyes. The older boy fell asleep.

QC and the older boy had visited the Shanghai exposition the previous day. They were now going to speak with the government officials who administered Chongming Island regarding the transfer from Europe of environmental management expertise and services. The older boy and QC had created the China Europe Responsible Trade (CERT) network to promote both the commercial and academic aspects of their work.

Chongming Island lies in the mouth of the Yangtze River. Contentiously QC's "link" in Beijing had called the island "China's third largest" after Hainan and *Taiwan*. Chongming is an alluvial island growing by centimetres a year as the Yangtze deposits silt on her sea-ward side to extend the bird sanctuary.

QC thought that Chongming Island would offer many opportunities for their CERT network. The island was only some 25 kilometres from Shanghai but still retained considerable green space. Until 2009 the ferry had been the only way to get to Chongming Island and that fact had protected it; now with the opening of the Shanghai Yangtze-River Tunnel and Bridge for the Shanghai Exposition, development of the island would be rapid. QC had suggested that they took the ferry out to the island and return by the tunnel and bridge to better appreciate the implications of that construction for the island.

They arrived to a clear sky and a modern ferry terminal. Government officials met them and wasted no time in starting their day of meetings and visits. QC and the older boy returned to their hotel rooms late in the afternoon to rest. Before the evening meal, they took a walk and entered a tea-house to talk. The tea-house was dark and they sat in hanging wicker basket-seats. The waitress wore a green silk ch'i-p'ao with a small curling leaf motif woven with a royal blue thread.

"It was an interesting day," said the older boy. "I am sure something will come of it." QC agreed. "But we must make progress with your PhD. We do not have much time. I leave tomorrow."

The tea came. It was Oolong tea and they watched the leaves uncurl and grow within the glass tea pot. "I hope this tea is good for thinking," the older boy said.

"Of course! It is *green* tea with many health benefits."

"Do you remember," the older boy began, "I once mentioned I was working on Foucault?"

"No."

"It was in passing. I said little at the time because I then judged his work not appropriate and too marginal for you."

"So what has changed?"

"A couple of things. I now think Foucault's work on epistemes is too important to ignore. The opportunity is too great to miss, both for CERT business and your PhD. CERT and your PhD are ostensibly about changing business practice but what they both come down to is changing attitudes. Change attitudes and new ways of doing things in practice will follow."

"I think that's more easy to say than do."

"So are many things. But I think we should try. After all, you don't need to tackle Foucault head on. We need to know only the principles he used and how he applied them. The greater part of his work, his descriptions of previous epistemes, I have already summarised."

"Okay," she said with a shrug of her shoulders. It was hard for her as Chinese to go against her teacher.

The older boy then explained that an episteme was a way of ordering knowledge and that different cultures and ages had different epistemes. "In Mediaeval Europe," he said, "the world was understood to be God-given. Knowledge of that world was to be gained by unearthing *His* hidden meanings, either in books or the world at large. In those days, gaining knowledge from the world was the same as interpreting a book to find its hidden meaning. Knowledge was then *unearthed* and built up by identifying resemblances among the revealed meanings. It was all underpinned or kept together because Mediaeval Europeans accepted an undivided, God-given world."

QC had many questions, most of which the older boy answered directly. But QC however was astute; she quickly sought relevance to the present day. "But few think like that now," she said. "We have books for communication that is all. Earth is Earth with its own way. Why this Mediaeval episteme of interest to business now? We do not need Mediaeval confusion."

"We do not," the older boy answered. "You are very quick to see ancient flaws, but can you do the same for your own times?"

QC did not answer. She felt that she should answer and, consequently, she felt a loss of face.

"That's not fair of me," he consoled her. "Few can do that in the way I mean."

"Then why you ask me for the not possible? That helps little."

"I want to raise the possibility of you leaving your own episteme. I want you to start thinking that such a thing may be possible."

QC immediately asked "But where shall I go?" That question was left hanging in the air.

The older boy proceeded to tell her about the Classical episteme, about Descartes, the famous doubt and the birth of rationalism and mechanism. He continued: "Classical man sat looking over a two-dimensional table that contained all knowledge from fact to fable, from past to future, from earth to heaven. Nothing was left out. This was still a God-given world but now man discerned a role for himself applying rational order, identifying identities and differences, constructing an ordered totality of all things known. Past and future, finite and infinite, fact and fantasy were all treated the same. Man began to stand alone as he got to know God's rational mind."

"This changed the world?" she asked incredulously, for it was too philosophical for her pragmatic inclination.

"It changed man's *attitude* to the world. The knowledge of Mediaeval and Renaissance men would have looked naïve and childish in comparison to the emerging great Classical rational ordering."

"I find it hard to believe," said QC. "They were still Europeans. We Chinese have had many emperors and revolutions, but we still Chinese."

At that point in time, the older boy did not have enough knowledge of either ancient Chinese thinking or the emerging episteme to appreciate the significance of her words. If he had been able to make the connection, he could have proceeded much more quickly. As it was, he stayed with his local thought: "They were still Europeans. But in effect, their new way of ordering knowledge created a revolutionary new Europe."

"You are revolutionary?" she asked with caution, for this she certainly did not want to bring to her home country.

"No," he answered almost as a laugh. "I'm no revolutionary as you mean. Nor were the men of the Classical age. We are dealing with scholarly revelations, not bloody revolutions. They are unavoidable and impartial but admittedly they bring change."

These points assembling quickly one after another were too much even for QC's nimble mind. She sipped her tea. She asked the waitress for more hot water for topping up the tea pot.

"But my thesis has plenty already," she gently argued. "Do I really need more complications of past ages and scholarly revelations?"

"I want your work to be relevant. If you change the ordering of knowledge, you change knowledge itself and hence our basic attitudes to ourselves and the world in which we live. We would have different aspirations and different ways of reaching for them. Different values, cultures, life trajectories."

They sipped tea. QC looked down at her cup.

The older boy persisted. He proceeded to explain about Kant's questioning of representations and how this marked another turning point in the developing European episteme. It heralded the Modern age into which they had both been born. The older boy explained that he thought it very significant that the Modern episteme sought the origins of things but never found them. "Instead," he continued, "Modern minds found man alone, all alone, defining *his* world by himself for himself, without God."

QC had listened attentively as the older boy introduced the Modern episteme. He used diagrams to illustrate his talk.

"I do not like these ideas," she said. "You think Foucault has dictated what we think and say."

"Your reaction is not uncommon," the older boy sympathised. "Many people don't like the idea that their knowledge is somehow determined by structures beyond their control. They do not like the idea that they are forced to think in a particular way, a way imposed by some French would-be philosopher. But Foucault is only the messenger. He neither created nor imposed any episteme: thought does that to itself."

"That's small compensation," she replied distractedly.

"You mean small *consolation*."

"Yes thank you, I do. But it still does not seem very *pleasant*. It seems confining."

"It may be confining for some, but for those pursuing the ideas of a new episteme it is liberating to cast off the old ways. Foucault stands for freedom. The freedom to be tomorrow what you are not today."

"I'm not sure I like that either. I am me and I'd like to be me tomorrow."

"But why should your notion of 'me' not change?" he asked. "Everything else changes. Please keep an open mind."

"But this Modern episteme is so complicated," she replied. "These diagrams mean so little to me. How can they change my mind? Where would I go?"

"You would *go* into a new episteme," he replied. "In a new episteme, you would be different. You would have no choice."

Their arguments were becoming circular; she did not want that. "You have a new episteme?" she asked to break free.

"I think so. It is really beginning to look that way. I can now clearly see the inadequacies of the Modern episteme. How its thoughts are trapped within its own reflexive logic, in its own quest for origins finding only epistemological man. Even those who purport to break-out, the critiques of the Modern, they remain trapped within this whirlpool of human self-reflecting knowledge. They are able to define themselves only in Modern episteme terms as *post-modernists*. But my work is not just negative. I can see somewhere else to go."

"Where is it that you go?" she asked.

"Into natural science," he answered. "I spent too long within the Modern episteme looking for a way out, too long within the human sciences alone. It was my mistake, but it is perhaps pardonable. After all, the Classical and the Modern epistemes originated within thought reflecting on thought itself."

QC looked at her watch. She would like to leave him now. Step away from his bombardment of ideas.

"I have something simple for you, but we must now look at the scientific evidence," he said ignoring her body language. "We must persist. Trust me a little longer."

The Chinese character for teacher, 老师 (lǎo shī), conveys many things including old people, a venerable person, experienced or of long standing and the order of birth of the children in a family which in turn indicates affection or familiarity. All of these meanings formed part of QC's relationship with the older boy. It was in her nature to trust a teacher.

Evidence for a New Episteme

Following his trip to Chongming Island, the older boy maintained an almost daily communication with QC as he built up a case for a new episteme. He started with the scientific evidence. This evidence had not been available at the start of the Modern episteme.

He advised QC over the phone: "Let's follow the scientists and reveal the implications of what they say." Over the next few weeks, he sent QC several files by email and explained them during conversations over Skype.

First File: Biological Evolution

The theory of evolution was once controversial in scientific circles, but this is no longer the case. The functioning of DNA has provided the mechanism for evolution that Darwin had lacked. Evolution by common descent whereby a group of organisms share a common ancestor is now established.

Darwin's idea was that the *natural selection* of new variants happens continually within populations. A small percentage of these variants cause their bearers to produce more offspring than others. These variants thrive and supplant their less productive competitors so that many repetitions of selection led to a species being modified over time.

Prior to Darwin, Lamarck (1744–1829) had published a theory of evolution in 1809. Lamarck argued that species came continually from non-living sources and that whilst they were initially very primitive they would increase in complexity over time. He also argued that organisms could adjust to their environments and that such adjustments could be passed on to offsprings. Lamarck also believed species never went extinct, but they would change into newer forms. Lamarck's ideas belong to the Classical episteme in which all things and all of time were already present in their totality in the world and change happened *to* things as they moved across that great table as part of the predestined cosmic processes set in place by God.

Charles Darwin published his "On the Origin of Species" in 1859. He thought within the Modern episteme. He transformed the predestined *natural history* of the Classical episteme into a *biology* with intrinsic origins. Darwin made nature intrinsically active; after Darwin, nature was seen to perform the miracles of evolution on her own.

Interdependence not independence

Life evolved on Earth over a period of about 3.55 billion years. During this time evolution created many new species, 99% of which perished. Nonetheless for all this time, there were interactive and interdependent relationships between species and the physical environment: evolving species changed their physical environment and a changing physical environment changed species.

Admittedly, this was not always a mutually beneficial situation, since some changes could prove disastrous. For 90% of geological time the Earth's atmosphere had contained little oxygen but evolving forms of bacteria that used the anoxic atmosphere produced oxygen as waste. These bacteria were so successful that they effectively "poisoned" themselves; their oxygen waste product was to build up and cause their own mass extinctions. Some oxygen-poisoning survivors, the anaerobic bacteria, had to hide from the newly oxygen-rich atmosphere in places such as offshore, deep-sea muds and our intestines, where they still survive to this day.

We now recognise that different forms of life are necessarily dependent on other forms of life and on the environment. Knowledge of these relationships indicates a form of knowledge other than that of the Modern episteme which had created discrete, *in*dependent entities. As Foucault noted, in the Modern episteme from Cuvier onwards, biology became regional and autonomous with the consequence that the living being wrapped itself in its own existence (Foucault 1970, p. 273). In the emerging episteme, life is known to be highly *inter*dependent.

Cooperation not Competition

This is admittedly just an aspect of the previous change from independence to interdependence. It is worth emphasising for its implications for the small self and Modern economic theory. Spencer's false reading of Darwin's theory that "survival of the fittest" gave eminence to competition in natural selection, has been challenged by diverse people from poets to hard-minded scientists, all of whom regard *cooperation* and not *competition* as the dominant behavioural trait in life. Eugene Odum (1913–2002), the great American ecologist, wrote: "Cooperation for mutual benefit, a survival strategy very common in natural systems, is one that humanity needs to emulate" (Goldsmith 1992, pp. 210–215).

Adaption not Progress

Darwin's evolutionary theory has been, perhaps inextricably, linked to the modern concept of progress. I don't want to labour this point, but it was inevitable that this happened because of the Modern's episteme use of "History". It was only in the Modern episteme that progress became a movement in time as "History" gave place to the analogical organic structures of knowledge just as Order had once opened the way to successive identities and differences in the Classical episteme (Foucault 1970, p. 219).

But this notion of progress in evolution is not supported by evidence. The evolution of life is frequently represented by a tree diagram which has mankind standing on its top above all other forms of life at some pinnacle of evolution — how self-centred! This is simply not true. All species descended from common ancestors and as time passed, different lineages of organisms were modified as they adapted to differing environments, but no living organisms today are our ancestors: every extant living species is as fully "progressed" as we are. Many species are evidently much "progressed" than our own because they have endured so very much longer and they have not destroyed their environments.

Complex urban societies are not more evolved than those of food foragers. They are *both* highly evolved, but in different ways. All evolved human societies must have the ability to fit into their ecosystem by either adjusting or participating. But sometimes humankind makes the wrong decision. We seem to be able to hold on to other ideas that encourage us to think ourselves above the need for such adjusting or participating. Progress is one such idea: "We must avoid falling into the ethnocentric trap of equating change with progress..." (Haviland *et al.*, 2008; p. 155).

Over Skype a day after he had emailed the first file to QC, the older boy asked of her: "Do you begin to appreciate how new knowledge of life challenges the foundation of the Modern episteme and its institutions?" QC said that she did not. "Biological evolution seems to have little to do with Kant's question or Modern economics or business practice." The older boy sent a second file.

Second File: Ecology

You might wonder why I have a file on ecology. After all it seems to add little to the properties of living things mentioned in the first file such as co-operation, competition, and interdependence. But ecology does make further powerful conceptual contributions.

Remember how Linnaeus had a holistic attitude in which nature, God, the material, the social and the spiritual were intertwined in an "economy of nature" which had ancient roots in 'physicotheology'? Well, Ernst Haeckel, the German biologist (1834–1919), introduced the term "ecology" to expand the "economy of nature" concept and include more specific terms such as geographic distribution, cycle of nature, balance, biogeochemical cycle, nutrition chains, and niches.

Haeckel defined ecology as an inclusive concept embracing other ideas such as the inorganic and organic conditions, friendly and hostile relations between animals and plants and, in short, the great complexity of relations that makes life what it is. In this way Haeckel's life, though lived within the Modern episteme, had a vision that went far beyond it. The Modern episteme sought the discrete origins of things within themselves but Haeckel found holistic origins in ecology.

Lynn White makes this distinction clear in the following quotation: "Whereas the laboratory method's power lies precisely in its isolation of the phenomenon to be studied, ecological science is, on principle, anti-isolationist. It is the science of totalities. As such it is antiscientific, as science at present is usually conceived and practised." (Goldsmith 1992, p. 11).

Indeed, much has been written to change this Modern attitude and to see ourselves with ecological eyes. For example: "Ecology, community and lifestyle", a philosophical view of active nature in deep ecology (Naess 1990); "Dwellers in the Land: the bioregional vision", draws out a vision of development focused on ecological and cultural diversity (Sale 1985); "Mutual Aid: a factor of evolution", a classic argument stressing the importance of cooperation in nonhuman and human animals that illustrates active nature interdependence and interaction (Kropotkin [1920] 1987); "Ecological Communication", an extension of the concept of "ecology" to include connections between social systems and the surrounding environment as well as a review of the development of the notion of "environment" from the mediaeval to the modern definition which separates social systems from the external environment (Luhmann 1989); "The Ecology of Freedom", the foundations of an "ecological society" (Bookchin 1982); and a "A Sand County Almanac" which contains Leopold's famous Land Ethic which changes the role of mankind from conqueror of the land-community to plain member and citizen who respects his fellow-members and the community." (Leopold [1948] 1989).

The Geological Society of London is aiding this transition. They have proposed a new geological epoch, The Anthropocene, the Age of Man: "It is this vision of how things change that grounds our 'economic ethics for the Anthropocene'. What we can see all around us, if we put on the 3-D glasses provided here, are ethical practices of economy that involve the being-in-common of humans and the more-than-human world. Each of these practices is involved in building a community economy, in which sustenance and interdependence are key values and ethical negotiations center on the interrelated issues of necessity, surplus, consumption and commons." (Gibson-Graham and Roelvink, 2009, p. 343).

In his next conversation with QC, the older boy made much of the need to disabuse the Modern episteme's of its embedded separation from nature. He pressed the point home with examples. "Excuse me," QC interrupted with annoyance, "Chinese know about links with nature. We have ancient *Dao*."

Third File: Diversity

You probably know that diversity plays important roles in ecology, referring to both the different genes, species and ecosystems as well as being a defining property of a mature ecosystem. I doubt if I would have mentioned it in a separate file had I not come across a wonderful conference paper by the Italian geographer Adalberto Vallega (1934–2006). He presented at the International Workshop on Cultures and Civilisations for Human Development in Rome, 2005. The title of his presentation was "Diversity: A Multi-faceted Concept".

Vallega argued that international policies have evolved in recent decades because of an intense interaction between science and policy. He cites the Convention on Climatic Change and the Convention on Biological Diversity as examples of a deep change in which life sciences took the lead. During the 1990s, Vallega said that the concept of diversity acquired a political role in two ways:

i. As a 'sense of diversity' which was concerned with the protection of individual ecosystems, endangered and threatened fauna and flora as well as the preservation of small human communities; and
ii. With regard to the 'topical extent of diversity' which lead to a discussion about scale and the meaning and significance of local, regional and global ecosystems.

For Vallega these changes were not just changes in focus, of using the same knowledge but applying it in a different context. For him these changes happened because of an epistemological change from what he identified as "Positivist and structuralist approaches" to "Constructivism, complexity-based approaches". We'll deal in detail with this change later, but for now just remember that Vallega presented evidence for an "epistemological divorce" in science with physical and chemical sciences being led by positivist approaches and analytical methods and biological and ecological sciences moving towards complexity-based approaches and axiomatic methods. His "epistemological divorce" (Vallega 2005) is evidence of an episteme emerging.

Chapter 8 — Breaking Free   **209**

QC and the older boy did not speak after the third file. She had sent him an email asking if he knew the ancient Chinese concept of "all under heaven"; ". . . seems a bit like diversity" she had written.

Fourth File: Entropy

We cannot prepare our own epistemological arguments just yet, since we need some more new knowledge from science. In this file we shall consider "entropy", the thermodynamic measure of *dis*order, or of work available in a system. It seems to be a fundamental property that drives the universe.

Entropy has taken some of the work-load off God by providing an explanation of the energy available to change things. It is a measure of the potential of energy to flow and bring change just as much as water on a mountain "wants" to flow to the sea. Entropy measures this kind of potential, the innate potential for energy to flow and bring about change.

It is a scientific idea that was not available at the start of the Modern episteme. Admittedly it had many Modern contributors to its development such as Lazare Carnot (1753–1823) and his son Sadi (1796–1832). Rudolf Clausius (1822–1888), one of the founders of thermodynamics, is often attributed with the discovery of entropy, together with James Clerk Maxwell (1831–1879), Josiah Gibbs (1839–1903) and Ludwig Boltzmann (1844–1906).

Entropy is a fundamental concept and it applies to natural and human activities. Think of entropy as a measure of disorder such that higher entropy means higher levels of *dis*order. The energy in our universe wants to flow from low entropy states, high states of order, to lower entropy states, high states of disorder. Our universe works by increasing disorder.

An explosion is an example of extreme entropy: order becomes disorder in milliseconds. More slowly an ice cube melts because of entropy: the cube receives energy from the surrounding air because the molecules in frozen water are more ordered than those in liquid water. When you pour milk into a cup of coffee the two liquids will mix because the entropy of separate coffee and milk is lower than that for mixed milk and coffee.

Intrinsic Sustainable Development

Entropy is not purely for physical phenomena. It can be applied to many things. Because higher order implies greater instability: lower entropy states have a higher potential for change. This can be applied equally effectively to molecules in motion and peoples in societies. A highly ordered restricted society is a low entropy condition with a high potential for change and this society needs to draw in energy from outside itself to stop this change happening. Much policing and legislating is required to maintain this society in a low entropy, highly ordered state.

On a technical point, the entropy of a closed system always increases. A closed system is isolated so that no matter or energy can enter or leave. This is the Second Law of Thermodynamics.

The universe is a closed system and hence its entropy always increases. But within the universe there are many subsystems that are open, that do have matter and energy exchanges with an exterior environment. Within an open system, entropy can decrease as well as increase since energy and matter is exchanged with its environment so that in effect total entropy (of system and its exterior environment) still increases.

Biological systems are open systems. They locally decrease entropy — increase order — to make living things. They can do this because of sunlight; sunlight comes from outside the open biological systems and allows them to decrease their own entropy (meanwhile, the total net entropy of the solar system increases to compensate).

It follows that if we want to keep the increase of entropy of a local system to a low value, we must make the system as open as possible. The separate entities of Modern episteme want to have a highly ordered system that serves only human needs; i.e., we try and design and operate a closed system. This makes human systems low in entropy (highly ordered) and hence unstable which is why we are experiencing unsustainable development.

Our present human system is too closed and simplistic; it does not interact enough with other systems and strive for openness. We need more complex open systemic relations to become more stable and more sustainable;

Chapter 8 — Breaking Free   **211**

we need to design systems that provide benefits for non-human as well as human forms of life. I think we are intuitively aware of this fact.

During their subsequent Skype conversation, QC had expressed a great interest in entropy in societies but confessed that she needed to better understand the concept. "Just remember," the older boy advised, "how much energy is needed by the Chinese authorities to maintain order in your closed society." Without hesitating QC added "... or by America in a closed Capitalist economic system."

Fifth File: Chaos Theory

It is not just lucky that we find a solution to our problems at the very moment that a solution is required. Chaos theory came as we entered a whole new world of understanding. But we did not create Chaos Theory: "Chaos is found everywhere in nature, sometimes even in the beating of a human heart." (Percival 1992, p.11).

Descartes' graphical representations of algebraic equations and the differential calculus developed by Newton and Leibnitz are outstanding inventions. Their astonishing success permitted many natural relationships to be both explained and predicted. But in spite of their elegant simplicity and enormous explanatory power, these linear mathematical representations or linear equations remain significantly incomplete.

These mathematical representations are called "linear equations" because they can be represented by a straight line on a graph. They provide predictable results. When you know the speed of an aeroplane and the duration of the flight, you can set up a simple linear equation to calculate the distance travelled. The laws of the mechanical world that Descartes and Galileo had discovered could be expressed in simple algebraic equations or graphically using Cartesian coordinates. But even for Descartes, Galileo and their contemporaries there remained an insolvable problem.

Their simple linear equations were fine for representing the flight of a plane (or, for the sake of historic accuracy, a horse) if the speed was constant. As soon as the plane

212   *Intrinsic Sustainable Development*

accelerates or decelerates, straight-line graphical relationship and their equations do not apply; if you plot the
speed of an accelerating or decelerating body you will get
a curve, not a straight line. When moving bodies accel-
erate or decelerate, their speed changes in an instant and
this could not be expressed mathematically — that is,
before the genius of Isaac Newton.

Newton's differential calculus solved this problem by
approximating each part of the accelerating and decelerating curve with a triangle. He effectively selected two points
on the curve, drew a straight line between these two points
and treated that line as the hypotenuse of a right angle
triangle; and given the values of two sides in a right angle
triangle finding the value of the third side is elementary.
So given the time and distance taken in travelling between
two points on the accelerating or decelerating curve, Newton could find an approximate value for speed. But if the
triangle calculation is repeated infinitely for smaller and
smaller distances along the curve, then at some point the
approximated value for speed becomes *the* value for speed
for all intents and purposes. This is the basis for Newton's
equations of motion which were non-linear but nonetheless determinative and wholly appropriate for a describing
a mechanistic universe.

In the early days, Newton's equations were brilliantly
applied to many phenomena, including tidal flows, vibrat-
ing strings and elastic bodies down to the smallest detail.
It was impressive evidence for the causal and deterministic Mechanistic philosophy. Many different applications
of Mechanistic mathematics were used to model nature.
But finding solutions for these models eluded scientist and
engineers: ". . . to *set up* the equations is one thing, to
solve them quite another." (Stewart 1989, p. 38).

The core problem was taking the mathematical descriptions from applications of the simple to the complex; from
the behaviour of one or two entities considered in isolation to their behaviour with three or four others, or a
dozen others, or an infinity of others. For example dealing
with the relative motion of one or two bodies in motion or
one or two planets pulling each other with gravity could
be handled with existing mathematics but the relative

motions of many bodies, or many planets, pulling each other in different directions could not.

James Clerk Maxwell (1831–1879), the Scottish physicist and mathematician, came up with one kind of solution. He considered Boyle's law that accurately described the relation between temperature, volume and the pressure of a gas. If two of these values were known, the third could be calculated using the gas law. This law presented a paradox: how could a simple and accurate linear equation represent the motion of a very large, potentially infinite, number of gas particles in motion, pulling each other in many different directions?

Maxwell's answer was that it was the *average behaviour* of the particles that gave rise to the observed regularity. With this insight, physicists quickly explained the properties of a gas in terms of the motion of many gas molecules: ". . . the pressure of a gas is the force caused by the molecules' average push, while the temperature turned out to be proportional to their average energy of motion." (Capra 1997, p. 121).

This averaging of behaviour was well described by the branch of mathematics known as statistics which had been developing since the seventeenth century. Hence, no matter how complex and unpredictable the behaviour of the individual components of a phenomenon might be, the averaging of their behaviour gave precise, deterministic and predictable results. It was a form of statistical mechanics and this came to underpin the new science of thermodynamics and its representations of entropy.

Even complex phenomena could now be described by the mathematics of linear equations, or approximations to linear equations. The attitude of scientists that enabled them to look at the uncertainties and complications of natural and man-made phenomena and see an underlying predictable simplicity was the foundation for what is known as "Classical Science". Mathematical representations supported Classical Science in many incredibly accurate and wide-ranging applications throughout the first half of the twentieth century. But in the 1970's, scientists began to perceive another kind of order and that was *chaotic*; it was not predicable or deterministic but was nonetheless well ordered. This identified a need for Chaos Theory for as Gleick observes: "Where chaos begins, classical science ends." (Gleick 1987, p. 3).

The ancient Greek meaning of the word *khaos* is "vast chasm or void". This is precisely where scientists stood with the coming of Chaos Theory, at the edge of a great chaotic chasm or void within which classical science knowledge and attitudes did not work. Even now Chaos Theory lacks an agreed scientific definition, partly because it has applications that range from the quantum world, to life, to the behaviours of humans and their institutions and to cosmology. In fact, just about everything displays chaotic behaviour. Roderick Jensen of Yale University offered a definition of Chaos Theory: "The irregular, unpredictable behaviour of deterministic, nonlinear dynamical systems." (Gleick 1987, p. 306).

In short, Chaos Theory describes the behaviour of dynamic systems that are in themselves deterministic, but which are rendered *unpredictable* by their initial random conditions. So once set up, the outcomes of these dynamical systems may be predicted, but even very small differences in their initial conditions can create very divergent outcomes; so that longer-term predictions are generally not possible. This is well known as the "Butterfly Effect" whereby the flapping of a butterfly's wing in an Amazon forest is said to have the potential to alter a developing global weather system and change its trajectory.

Patterns in chaotic systems have been identified using topological approaches which would not have been possible without modern computers. In the mathematics of dynamical chaotic systems, "attractors" are objects, or sets, towards which the system evolves. You can see this in action by rolling a marble around the inside of a bowl; it will revolve and come to rest at the centre. In this case, the attractor is a point. Attractors can also be curves, like the orbits of planets. But in chaotic dynamical systems, the attractors are usually fractals, or in other words, geometric shapes that can be split into parts, each of which is an approximate reduced-size copy of the whole.

You must have seen the many beautiful fractals that were produced on computers some years ago; the

Mandelbrot set was a very famous example. Fractals are common in nature: many plants, crystals, clouds, mountains, and rivers display fractal properties. Indeed the Mandelbrot set was found to be so common in the creation of natural features that it has been called the "Thumbprint of God" (Mandelbrot 1982).

Chaotic systems typically do not evolve to a point or to curves: they evolve to fractal forms which possess great detail, complexity and beauty. These fractal forms are known as "strange attractors". They are the source of the many patterns found in nature.

In summary, chaos is a new mathematical representation of the world: it was not available to the thinkers who established the Modern episteme and its institutions. It marks a significant point of change in our approach to knowledge. "Traditionally, scientists have looked for the simplest view of the world around us. Now, mathematics and computer power have produced a theory that helps researchers to understand the complexities of nature. The theory of chaos touches all disciplines." (Percival 1992, p. 11).

Unfortunately, our existing social institutions are pre-chaotic. They were established when linear equations ruled — or promised to rule, if we had enough computing power and social obedience. They retain many attitudes and practices typified by linear equations.

"I guess you may not like the idea of increasing Chaos," the older boy said to QC. "My life is already chaotic," she replied.

Sixth File: Dissipative Systems

Now, this file is really going somewhere QC, trust me. Please ask yourself what is the link between a chaotic, dynamic system evolving towards a fractal strange attractor and life? I do not expect an answer.

Ilya Prigogine (1917–2003) was a Russian-born Belgian physicist, who provided an answer to that question. He won a Nobel Prize in 1977 for doing so. He had realised that life, and many other dynamical systems, do not reach an equilibrium. Once set up, such systems constantly evolve; there is no rest to be had at any time from any such equilibrium — just as in life. You constantly have to move forward, change and adapt like in those moments when you trip and fall forwards and then you have to run fast to stop yourself toppling over and hitting the ground. Sometimes you can stop yourself falling, but imagine that you once do not manage to do so; then take the ground away; then you are caught burning much energy in a constant, never-ending fall. That is what Prigogine (1985) had in mind for his "far-from-equilibrium" dynamical systems — they fit life well I think.

"Far-from-equilibrium" dynamical systems require a constant exchange of energy and entropy with their environment. They are necessarily open systems. If you are going to run fast, forever, you too would consume much food, water and air.

Because much energy passes through these systems, Prigogine called them *dissipative* structures. They are a way of dispersing energy and hence of following that cosmic requirement of increasing entropy (or disorder) whilst creating a dynamic, local increase in order. Nature and ourselves are united in this respect; we are restless and constantly dissipating energy and evolving towards some fractal "strange attractor" in a "far-from-equilibrium", never-to-rest system.

After discussing dissipative structures and their significance for over one hour, QC complained that she would not sleep now with this thought of endless falling. It was after eleven in the evening in Beijing for the older boy had not called until mid afternoon. Nonetheless she said goodnight. The older boy carried on working and prepared and sent the seventh file before the end of the day.

Seventh File: Bifurcation and Autopoiesis

Good day, I hope you have slept well in spite of all the restless turbulence! We now need to consider how things are created. I think this file is best appreciated from an undifferentiated, uniform perspective, from that of isotropy. Isotropy means uniformity in all directions of space and time.

Chapter 8 — Breaking Free   **217**

What Prigogine realised is that his "far-from-equilibrium" systems start with some seemingly unimportant, but unpredictable, event, as in chaos theory. It is that same flapping of a butterfly's wing that determines the course of global phenomena, like weather patterns. We have no way of knowing when or how that butterfly will flap its wings or which butterfly, among the millions, will be the one to affect the start of the next system. Similarly whilst the "far-from-equilibrium", dissipative, thermodynamic system has a deterministic structure, its origin is unpredictable. And this, according to Prigogine, breaks *isotropy*, "space ceases to be isotropic" (Prigogine and Stengers 1985, p. 171).

Imagine that things are stable and isotropic for some time, so that there is continuity and stability. We could then have a good idea of how the future will turn out because of what we know of the past. But now imagine other times without stable and isotopic conditions so that our past experiences no longer point to a way forward. Just like me. When I am in the London I know, I am happy to find my way around, but in Beijing, I am lost. I then need your knowledge of those very different Chinese streets.

That point of change, going from London to Beijing, the butterfly flapping its wing and starting a whole new weather system, the egg falling to the floor and breaking, mark points in time when old systems, old given conditions, no longer apply. This is the point at which new systems, new "far-from-equilibrium", dissipative, thermodynamic systems, begin. It is a point when the old stable, more or less predictable trajectories change their direction. These changes in trajectory are called "bifurcation" points; it is at these points that systems "choose" between one or more possible futures. The results of bifurcation points are unpredictable; as Prigogine puts it "This mixture of necessity and chance constitutes the history of the system" (*ibid.*, p. 170). At bifurcation points, nature creates its own, indeterminate, anisotropic futures; this is the end of certainty (Prigogine 1997).

Nature is thus a mixture of steady, predictable order within the structures that the stable thermodynamic systems create, and unpredictable indeterminacy at bifurcation points. Intrinsic properties of the world "choose" the future insofar as it originates within existing systems, but this does not imply any form of intention; the future is just a mixture of chance and historical context: what exists at that moment, and the new, unpredictable, dissipative, thermodynamic systems.

There are many ways in which nature "chooses" or "selects". Many different kinds of forces in quantum and cosmic worlds "select" relationships to create new things and new worlds. But life selects in its own unique way; a way that ultimately implies at least a modicum of consciousness.

Living cells exist alongside other cells within their environments in complex, dissipative, thermodynamic systems. We know that life creates new life and that sometimes new forms of new life emerge, having encountered and having been redirected along a new trajectory at a bifurcation point. Indeed the morphological complexity of forms of life can now be defined not only in terms of the numbers of different kinds of cells in an organism, but by the history of its development trajectories: the number of bifurcation points crossed during its development.

Famously, the Chileans Humberto Maturana (1928-) and his pupil Francisco Javier Varela García (1946–2001) argued that *consciousness* exerts its influence on bifurcation points in all living organisms. Their unique combined knowledge of biology, philosophy and neuroscience gave them integrative vision of life reconstituting and creatively exceeding its old self with a kind of self-poetry, an "autopoiesis".

Maturana had been working hard to achieve a simple change of attitude; he struggled to regard mind and consciousness as a process and not a state or condition. This may not seem very much to you now, but it was revolutionary in its day. It placed the processes of knowing, cognition, at the fore of centre stage in the theatre of life.

With Varela's knowledge of neuroscience, the pair worked closely together to develop and proclaim the "Santiago Theory of Cognition" which claims:

> "Living systems are cognitive systems, and living as a process is a process of cognition. This statement is valid for all organisms, with or without a nervous system." (Maturana and Varela 1980, p. 13).

This means that Maturana and Varela believe that you cannot separate life and cognition; they are one and the same (Maturana and Varela 1987). According to the Santiago Theory, every living organism renews itself, maintains its overall identity amidst cyclic ongoing energy and material exchanges with its environment. But in addition to self-renewal, every living organism also develops itself, creates something new in its organisation out of the selfsame ongoing interactions with the environment and its own intrinsic dynamics. For this reason, living systems are said to respond *autonomously* to changes in their environment.

Sometimes a living system responds to a particular interaction with its environment; sometimes it does not respond. And this is the significance of the Santiago Theory:

> "... the living system not only specifies its structural changes; it also specifies which disturbances from the environment trigger them." (Capra 2003, p. 32).

Living systems choose for themselves if they will react or not. They determine if they will create a bifurcation point or not.

A living organism "creates" the reality of the world in which it lives. I may enter a room with my dog, but he experiences the realities of a world that is radically different from my own. His sense of smell, his personal priorities and prior experiences, his life needs and their means of satisfaction, and his point of view mean that our two worlds may overlap, but they are not at all the same.

With time, the living organism's selected interactions with its environment alter its future behaviour. It learns from past experience with the consequence that life's structures are always a record of prior development.

Intrinsic Sustainable Development

Autopoiesis has many applications. Niklas Luhmann made extensive use of autopoiesis to better understand and analyse society (Luhmann 1986 & 1995). Stuart Kauffman, the American theoretical biologist and complex systems researcher, has greatly developed the concept of self-organisation. He argues contentiously that biological systems and organisms might rely as much upon self-organization and far-from-equilibrium dynamics as upon Darwinian natural selection. He also applies principles of self-organization to social and economic systems (Kauffman 1995). Bitbol and Luisi (2004) argue for the importance of autopoiesis for "defining life at the edge" which they see as a necessary, but not sufficient, condition for life.

In "Sync: the emerging science of spontaneous order", Steven Strogatz draws the following conclusion for the mathematical theories of self-organisation: "For reasons I wish I understood, the spectacle of sync strikes a chord in us, somewhere deep in our soul. It's a wonderful and terrifying thing. Unlike many other phenomena, the witnessing of it touches people at a primal level. Maybe we instinctively realize that if we ever find the source of spontaneous order, we will have discovered the secret of the universe." (Strogatz 2004, p. 289).

It was evident during their Skype conversation that QC had not slept well. She was nonplussed with more theory. The older boy tested her interest with practical issues by asking how could a business person make decisions within all this complexity, uncertainty and varied autopoietic realities. She said that "she didn't have a clue" and their chat ended. The older boy waited a week before dispatching his eight file.

Eight File: Complexity

It must be hard for you to believe that this is a way to break free — my files have become so intellectual, so complex! However there is something simple and real to be found within all of this but I doubt if you would believe me without all this other evidence and argument.

Chapter 8 — Breaking Free   **221**

But I need not apologise for these difficulties. They are not of my making, or of Foucault's. They are more or less consequences of the Modern episteme. We will soon be able to recognise a new episteme. The trouble is that we will tend to look at it from the grand expanses of the old one.

Take the science of complexity for example. It is what we must consider next, for it has roots in all seven preceding files: it is their culmination, their inevitable consequence, as well as their detailed, formal enactment or application.

Furthermore, complexity will give the world back to humanity. Sir Roger Penrose, Emeritus Rouse Ball Professor of Mathematics at Oxford University, seems to believe something similar. He considers that "... sciences seems to have driven us to accept that we are merely small parts of a world governed in full detail (even if perhaps ultimately just probabilistically) by very precise mathematical laws" and he concludes: "Yet it is hard to avoid an uncomfortable feeling that there must always be something missing from this picture" (Penrose, 1989, p. 579). Your freedom lies precisely in what is missing from the Modern episteme.

But first we have to answer the question "What is the science of complexity?" For many scientists working in the area of complexity, there is no answer or, rather, no agreed single answer. It is too complex! So we have to sneak up on an answer or we will not even get close to it.

Complexity is a systems science. It studies the intricate relationships between parts in systems and is necessarily a computer-based science for it would not be possible to perform the many necessary calculations without the aid of computers. But fear not, it is not just another wishful human science trying to fit the world into a few abstract formulations. For me, the science of complexity studies *joined-up reality*. It is human reality struggling to be more real.

Complexity science is a representation of complex behaviours, especially when they emerge and create something new. It studies self-organization, adaptation and long-term evolution in complex natural and man-made systems where elements join capabilities to become something greater than the sum of their individual capabilities. As I said, they encompass all our files. They are usually dynamical and

222   *Intrinsic Sustainable Development*

non-linear. The complex systems have a composition, structure, internal interrelationships that evolve in response to their environments. They modify themselves in a non-linear manner.

The complex systems may form out of chaos, but they can show enduring high levels of stability and coordination despite environmental disruptions and this applies to both natural and even those man-made systems which lack any central operational planning and control. But do not think that complex-systems scientists are easily discovering and directing many examples of entropy-driven, far-from-equilibrium thermodynamics situations. For one thing, these scientists cannot find a foundation for their work.

Physics lacks a unified theory and cannot help. Complex systems themselves exhibit emergent properties, so why should the emergent formulations of a complex systems scientist be any different? Once they pin down an idea, they have essentially created something new, a new emergent property, at least in language. Should that new entity not defy old definitions? As Mitchell concludes her review of complexity science: "This is the nature of science — an endless cycle of proud proposing and disdainful doubting" (Mitchell, 2009, p. 295). I think that she is on the right track. She ends her book with the observation that for the future of the science of complexity: "What's needed is the ability to see their deep relationships and how they fit into a coherent whole — what might be referred to as 'the simplicity on the other side of complexity'" (*ibid.*, p. 303).

But such simplicity is, for many, unreachable at the moment. Perhaps simplicity will always elude us, for, as Prigogine records: "The irreducible plurality of perspectives on the same reality expresses the impossibility of a divine point of view from which the whole of reality is visible" (Prigogine and Stengers, 1985, p. 225).

Indeed complexity science is in its infancy and we, humankind, are still overawed by its many implications. Johnson's book "Simply Complexity: A Clear Guide to Complexity Theory" provides examples of complexity theory applications in financial markets, traffic and transport, career path development, marriage, war, terrorism, spread of diseases, the quantum world and infinity and beyond (Johnson, 2007).

Chapter 8 — Breaking Free   **223**

The times really are a-changing. In 1998, Byrne was able to provide an introduction to complexity theory and its applications in the social sciences. In 2003, Berkes *et al.* edited a book that challenges established views about the role of equilibriums in ecology and the management of social systems, arguing that they do not fit with observations of instability and reorganization. In 2008, Ramalingam and Jones provided a working paper with the title "Exploring the Science of Complexity: Ideas and implications for development and humanitarian efforts" for the ODI. The ODI, Overseas Development Institute, is the UK's think tank on international development and humanitarian issues. The ODI's mission is to inspire and inform policy and practice which lead to the reduction of poverty, the alleviation of suffering and the achievement of sustainable livelihoods in developing countries.

In their 2004 book, Jørgensen and Svirezhev examine the foundations of a Thermodynamic Theory for ecological systems. In 2008, Norberg and Cumming, systems ecologists, published a book with the title "Complexity Theory for a Sustainable Future" that crosses from ecology to sociology by using community-based, conservation studies of the management of complex adaptive systems.

Right now, Complexity Theory has much promise, but perhaps the age-old desire for completeness in knowledge will remain elusive. Barrow, the astronomer, recognises a practical limit to our knowledge: "There remain intractable problems that require so much computational time to solve that they are for all practical purposes insoluble" (Barrow, 1999, p. 117). He also identifies a theoretical limit to knowledge: "A new type of impossibility has emerged..., one that can be proved to exist, one that limits our most vigorous systems of reasoning, and one that threatens consequences for all our applications of reasoning to understand the Universe around us." (*ibid.*, p. 217). Nonetheless, complexity theory applied to things that we do know about is likely to be an invaluable aid in finding our way to happy and prosperous futures — if we learn how to use it appropriately.

In 2006, Burdyuzha of the Russian Academy of Sciences, Moscow, was editor of a book with the title "The Future of Life and the Future of our Civilization". This book is dedicated to the memory of Carl Sagan, the American astronomer.

Within that book, Kirilyuk argues that sustainability will be achieved only by a transition to another level of civilization since our current one has reached the end of its established system of *complexity*. Such a transition, Kirilyuk notes, will be achievable only by changes *in all aspects of life* (Kirilyuk 2006).

But what if our next level of civilization was actually an old one? What if we need to reach back into a prior order of knowledge, ancient ways of regarding our selves and the world about? We would still have to change and it would be future directed, but we would nonetheless be learning from the past, or rather melding ancient wisdom with present knowledge. Does this make you feel more or less comfortable? One thing is certain, because of complexity, any new civilisation will emphasize how we must all work together: "Finally, complex systems research has emphasised above all interdisciplinary collaboration, which is seen as essential for progress on the most important scientific problems of our day." (Mitchell, 2009, p. 300).

Whether we make something entirely new and independent or synthesize past, present and future is a question that will have to wait for an answer. I am afraid that we have not quite finished our present series of files. After the revolutions realised and promised by Complexity Theory you might feel justified in wanting no more ideas and that the time has come to make our own contribution by identifying a new episteme. Well you are right! But there is one simple, very human matter, an attitude that we must bring to the fore of our minds. I'll deal with that in the next and last file.

The ninth file took the older boy two weeks to prepare. After listening to Bob Dylan's "The Times they are a changin'", QC developed a taste for the singer. She sang with gusto over Skype:

> "Come writers and critics,
> Who prophesize with your pen
> And keep your eyes wide
> The chance won't come again
> And don't speak too soon
> For the wheel's still in spin".

She told the older boy that it was meant for him.

Ninth File: Active Nature

QC as a graduate chemist you should appreciate that nature is intrinsically active. The elements, molecules and compounds have their own intrinsic properties that cause them to behave as they do. The theories that chemistry uses are reliable; they are precise, infallible and generic enough in theory and practice to confirm the *existence* of nature's own causal powers. Chemists, I am sure, believe that nature is active. So do biologists, geologists, botanists and physicists; they all work with the conviction that nature is active. Any other conviction is redundant, unnecessary, confusing and misguided.

Ellis argues: "... the idea that things are intrinsically disposed to behave as they do is already widely accepted in fields such as physics and chemistry" (Ellis, 2002, p. 145). Chalmers says something similar: "Things happen in the world of their own accord, and they happen because entities in the world possess the capacity or power or disposition or tendency to act or behave in the way that they do... Once we admit such things as dispositions, tendencies, powers and capacities into our characterisation of material systems, then laws can be taken as characterising those dispositions, tendencies, powers or capacities." (Chalmers, 1999, p. 218).

Children regard the natural world as active; as being composed of entities that have their own characteristics (Gelman, 2003). As adults we are immersed in an active world. With a moment's reflection, it can hardly be otherwise. The cause and effect relationships that constitute ourselves and our lives are obvious and inescapable: kicking a ball and the ball soaring through the air, scoring a goal or breaking a window; jumping into water, causing a splash and waves; typing at a keyboard and sending innumerable electronic pulses through the machine before me to make letters, words, sentences and meaning appear on a screen; or just holding someone's hand. We are indeed concatenations of cause and effects; of events causing, following, influencing, determining, creating, modifying and ordering other events. As Ellis expresses it: "We are in the world, and manifestly interacting with it. So the origin of our concept of cause is not really a mystery. It can seem mysterious only if one starts out with a Humean conception of reality, and conceives oneself to be a detached and passive observer of it." (Ellis, 2002, p. 105). Our actions, our unconscious and possibly even conscious selves, intervene in these event chains. They cause their own fractures, eruptions and harmonies. At some level of understanding, humankind has always known this.

Pagans located their gods in nature. The Presocratic, Essentialist philosophers of ancient Greek knew nature was active. Aristotle, the Philosopher, was a biologist, perhaps the world's greatest; he too knew that nature was very much alive and that all the institutions, meaning and purpose we seem to own are actually derivatives of natural attributes.

Sometime in our past, somewhere in the clouds at the top of mountains and volcanoes, in the depths of chasms, caves and deep underground rivers, in lightening, storms, unending oceans and the limitless heavens, another kind of world was imagined. It was often an abstract, untouchable, invisible world of ultimate powers and origins that was to be accessed only by a select few who would use it to provide explanations for all kinds of things. This other world was used to underpin order in societies; it also underpinned the *power* that imposed the order.

Order is indeed the story that I am now writing. It is about how we explain things and bring order to our knowledge. Plato relied on a perfect other, totally-abstract world for the teleology of all things on Earth. Because he had a vision of a perfect world, Nature for Plato became decrepit, an incompletely formed world of imperfection and decay. Jews, Christians and Muslims effectively allocated the perfections of a perfect but imaginary heaven to their one God and relied on Him to provide order and meaning for their secular worlds. Nature was transformed by these monotheists into (i) pagan enemy, and then (ii) into His work, His ordering, His meaning, His purpose, and His revelation.

By denuding nature of her own causal powers, the monotheists prepared for the Europe of Descartes and his Philosophy of Mechanism. In a world conceived as a machine, the power of rationalism to explore, interpret and define is impregnable. So the Classical Episteme's attempt at the impossible, a totality of knowledge based on the sole representations of man's rational order, is a reasonable enterprise. This is especially true if you bear in mind that their knowledge was protected, dehumanised, made possible, governed, directed, eternalised, imbued with meaning and truth, by the benevolence of the rational mind of their omnipotent Christian God. Nature in consequence was totally denatured.

But it was from the very centre of the Classical that David Hume had brought that episteme down. It was Hume who had shown that the detached, patiently and delicately observing and ordering rational mind was without foundation; without any connection between the careful order it brought to the world and existence itself; that there was no logical or empirical connection between observation and the observed concatenations of cause and effect. In this way the last vestiges of knowledge of nature-in-herself or of a God-given natural world was rooted out by Hume. All that was left after Hume was the knowing observer himself; i.e. man and his psychologies.

Given this scenario at the end of the Classical episteme, Kant's question, the Modern episteme and, eventually, unsustainable development were inevitable. That bottomless pit; the falling; the accelerating motion; the élan; the artificial progress, purpose, direction and meaning; the stranger's isolated, unconnected small self; the loneliness; the widespread sickness; and terrible wars; all became, possible, necessary, consequential upon adoption of the Modern episteme.

Nature and God had breathed life. The Modern episteme forgot how to breathe.

For in the Modern episteme, the world is truly of mankind's making, an unconscious autopoietic product. Man is now the measure of all things. Hence the necessary presence of extrinsic, life-giving forces such as electricity, élan vital, spirit, aliens, celebrity, competition, markets and neo-classical economics amongst our many secular theologies; the essential harbingers of those external forces so necessary to compensate for the death of nature.

Man could no longer see the world around him without seeing himself. In philosophical terms, Kant had identified two categories of knowledge which are:

i. *a posteriori* knowledge as being derived from experience either directly by observation or indirectly by inference and ultimately from something that is known in a particular way; and

ii. *a priori* knowledge that is knowledge that we have independently of experience.

A priori knowledge was for Kant always true. It was a form of truth that was necessary, yesterday, today and tomorrow and it will be true universally, wherever we go.

The *a posteriori* knowledge was for Kant always subject to change; it was a contingent form of truth. Following Hume, Kant argued that we can never be sure that what we *observe* in the world today will be true for tomorrow.

Kant also distinguished "analytical judgements" as those which were true in the meanings of their words; and "synthetic judgements" whose truth depends on some real connection external to the judgment itself.

Kant maintained that synthetic *a priori* judgments provide the basis for significant portions of human knowledge since arithmetic and geometry are made of such judgments and in turn natural science depends on these for its power to explain and predict. On the other hand, *a posteriori* knowledge, knowledge dependent on observation, was contingent and hence was an unreliable foundation for Kantian knowledge.

Reliable knowledge was now the sole property of the mind of man insofar as it was mind and only mind that could discern universal *a priori* truths. Observations of existence, of nature were contingent and unreliable. Nature was thus *necessarily* passive in the making of the Modern episteme.

To base knowledge on observations of nature, we have to have a category of knowledge that is *a posteriori* (i.e., based on observations) and *necessary* (i.e., not contingent). Knowledge of water is, for example, not something that can be known *a priori*, it has to be observed. But, and here's the rub, it is also *necessary* not contingent. If "water" did not behave as water in all places at all times then, quite simply, we are not dealing with water; we are dealing with something other. Our knowledge of water is *necessary* and *a posteriori*. Water is in itself water; it has its own properties, propensities and causal powers. If we let water have its own properties and causal powers, then we must allow nature to have the same; hence nature is intrinsically active and its laws are *necessary* and *a posteriori*. This might not seem much of a claim to a chemist, QC, but believe me, it is a very radical proposition that "... flies in the face of both the Anglo-American and German traditions of metaphysics" (Ellis, 2002, p. 109).

It is a fact that *Passive* nature thinking remains hugely influential in the world today: "The view that things in nature are essentially passive, and obedient to nature's laws, was widely shared by philosophers of all persuasions in the eighteenth century, as indeed it has been ever since. It was accepted, not only by Descartes, Newton and Hume, but also by Locke and Kant, and therefore by the founding fathers of all the major philosophical traditions of western Europe." (Ellis 2002, p. 2). But this is no mere philosophical issue; many institutions that inform and guide our societies, the economics, laws, corporations, and the political systems as well as the innumerable attitudes, assumptions, practices, meanings, aspirations and values that shape day-to-day life also have their roots in passive nature thinking. We are crippled QC, weighed-down, held-back, stunted, diminished by our intellectual inheritance. We need to set ourselves free from these encumbrances. We need to move on from the confines of the Modern episteme.

QC listened patiently while the older boy talked more about the religious and philosophical foundations for Passive nature thinking. Then she told him with pride: "We keep **Ch'i** in China. It means 'air' or 'breath' and a living force in all nature things. We keep our own health by balancing Ch'i in Chinese medicine."

CHAPTER 9 — THE PRIMAL EPISTEME

Aristotle's Spring

Within the fragile warmth of an early spring day, the older boy took a walk. He became hot in the sun as he climbed, but was chilled when the sun slipped behind clouds as he walked the paths that followed contours of the dale.

In the rough limestone grasslands, there was a rich diversity of plant life. He recognised the early purple orchids, cowslips, campion, saxifrage, leadwort but there was a exuberant abundance and variation in the low-level foliage that clung to every undulation in the ground and about which he knew very little. This rich, exotic diversity contrasted strongly with the stark empty winter and was, in the older boy's appreciation, flamboyant.

In his rucksack, in addition to water, coffee, a sandwich and a biscuit, the older boy carried a notebook, a pencil with sharpener, and a few academic papers either complete or as selected individual pages downloaded from the web. He carried with him information about Aristotle. He did so because the old Master was emerging as someone important in his studies.

The older boy had read about a TV documentary in the making that would visit the Greek island of Lesvos, where Aristotle had arrived after the death of Plato. It was there, beside a lagoon rich with the diversity of life, that Aristotle would study forms of life so efficiently that posterity would grant him the nickname the "father of biology".

Aristotle's name kept on cropping up in many places. For example, the older boy read Capra's book "The Hidden Connections". Capra's arguments were for a new synthesis of life, drawing on self-generating networks, patterns of organisation, dissipative structures and processes of cognition derived from autopoiesis. To appreciate the workings of a living cell, Capra had used the three perspectives of process, form and matter which he had linked together by placing them at each corner of an equilateral triangle. As Capra explained for the metabolism of a cell: "It consists of a network (*form*) of chemical reactions (*process*), which involve the production of the cell's components (*matter*), and which respond cognitively, i.e. through self-directed structural changes (*process*), to disturbances from the environment." (Capra, 2003, p. 62).

The key points of Capra's arguments are that:

(i) the distinction between living and dead matter is a specific network pattern of relationships which in themselves are non-material; and

(ii) structural changes in such network patterns of relationships are *cognitive* processes which are nonetheless embedded in the body itself, i.e. the non-material cognitive processes involving complexity and self-creating organisation are immaterial, but they do not exist apart from matter.

To apply this cognitive process to the study of social reality, Capra introduced a fourth dimension to the triangle of three perspectives of form, process and matter. He added the perspective *meaning* to accommodate the workings of human reflective consciousness. Capra then had a pyramid to extend the three dimensions of his earlier triangle.

It is at this point in Capra's argument that Aristotle (384–322 BC) makes a contribution. Aristotle explained the origins of things by means of four causes:

- A **Material Cause** which answers the question "From what is a thing made?" This could be wood, flesh, water, or bronze etc.
- A **Formal Cause** which deals with the arrangement or pattern that the thing creates for itself such as the proportion of the length of two strings in a lyre as the formal cause of one note being an

octave from another. This was how Aristotle himself explained a formal cause.

- An **Efficient Cause** which refers to the way in which the thing was brought about and is thought of as the primary principle of change or stability. This could be the act of chiselling a marble statue, the giving of advice or some inception for a person.
- A **Final Cause** which refers to the question "Why?" which for man could be to live within reason. For walking it could be health or for a seed it could be the final plant and it is hence the ultimate purpose, end, aim, or goal.

Capra argues that Aristotle's four causes are similar to, but not the same as, his own pyramid of matter, form, process and meaning (Capra, 2003, p. 65). The principal point of differentiation being the assertion of the scientific world that Aristotle's Final Cause, equivalent to Capra's "meaning", plays no role whatsoever in the non-material world: the material world is, for science, without meaning.

However, the older boy found meaning in the diversity of the life he was encountering that morning, within the fecund Derbyshire Dales. It was a meaning that had to do with autopoiesis and the self-organisation of far-from-equilibrium thermodynamic processes, the transcendence capabilities of minds, and being a part of nature. He sat down on a convenient bench, drank coffee and ate his biscuit.

As he relaxed, he thumbed a paper from the 2003 Annual Conference of the International Society for the System Sciences which coincidently had taken place in Greece. It was about complexity, ecosystems and Aristotle. In this paper was a speculative argument that a more complete account of life required all four of Aristotle's causes; that modern science's focus on only Aristotle's material and efficient causes was misleading. It was no longer adequate to simply relegate Aristotle's formal and final causes to the realm of Platonic idealism or computational simplicity. Computations, the paper argued, are now too complex to allow that to happen: "Life, psychological choice, quantum phenomena, and the origin of the universe each raises questions of causal origins, which cannot logically be addressed from the mechanistic viewpoint. An understanding of

234   *Intrinsic Sustainable Development*

formal and final cause is therefore needed to understand what is life and living." (Kineman 2003, abstract).

The older boy reread Kineman's conclusions several times: "This is, in fact, the assumption of ecological economics --- that natural ecosystems can be managed in terms of ecological goods and services to mankind. This assumption is valid only if it is possible for human values, through intuition and empathy, to reflect ecosystemic ones that are shared by other organisms. Once again, we rely on the commonalities of living systems, and the belief that the human organism is in some way more inclusive than most others --- but these are grand assumptions. There is no test that can determine if such intuitions are correct, or to ensure that human values reflect natural ones, except by practicing them and experiencing the result. Nevertheless, the existence of natural functions in a causal relationship should not be doubted merely because they cannot be directly observed. They are implicit realities, based on observation of nonclassical system behaviors that are consistent with a relational model of structure and function that appears to be fundamental to living systems in general. The question is whether we have got them right, not whether or not they exist. Hence the ultimate success of goods and services assessment lies in the likelihood that by including a wide enough range of human values and intuitions, the natural set will have been approximated. It thus becomes very important, both scientifically and socially, in ecosystem management to incorporate the greatest diversity of interested parties --- the stakeholders --- in the design of management plans." (Kineman 2003, conclusion).

The older boy then read several pages about "being and becoming" from "Heidegger and Aristotle: the two-foldness of Being" (Burgen, 2005). He began wondering again just how science, complexity, philosophy, business and accounting might be connected. He had long ago realised that reality itself is joined up. He struggled to put an author's name to a quotation that came now to his mind's eye, "Look deep into nature, and you will understand everything better". Just as he remembered the name *Albert Einstein*, ease overcame him and he fell asleep sitting upright on the bench.

In such a position, he was permitted only a momentary sleep. He shortly rose, packed his rucksack and carried on exploring the many small flowers in a brilliant, and sudden, warm flood of sunlight.

All Under Heaven

His next stop, ninety minutes later, was on the exposed edge of a craggy limestone outcrop. He sat a little back from the edge in a cranny that supported his back, allowed his legs to dangle over the edge, and provide magnificent views over the River Wye. He sipped his water. He re-read the attachment to an email that he had received two days previously and had printed in his home office; it was from QC in Beijing. Her attachment was an eight-page essay in which she summarized the work of the contemporary Chinese philosopher Zhao Tingyang whom she had seen on TV. QC introduced her essay by describing it as "extra bricks for bridge builders".

QC argued that even foundational social theorists in the West such as Habermas were prevented from fully realising the integration they sought. For example Habermas described a "communicative rationality" as a foundation for social theory and epistemology, but it was still based on "inter-subjectivity". This, she argued, is to be expected, since Western thinking is caught in, at the best, an "*inter-ness*" between subjects or nation-states, and not a "transcendence" over these subjects. This is the point, she wrote, that Zhao makes in his book "All-under-heaven 'Tian Xia' System" (Zhao, 2005). The alternative to discrete subjects or nation-states proposed by Zhao, QC explained, is what the ancient Chinese imagined as Tian Xia (天 下) or "All under Heaven".

For Zhao, Tian Xia has three levels of meaning. The first one is geographical. This refers to the "di" (earth) in the traditional Chinese triad of earth, heaven and people. The Second is psychological and refers to the mentalities of all peoples on earth. Tian Xia in this sense includes all the people on earth and under heaven. The third meaning is an ethical-political mix with ideals of Utopia where everybody under heaven treats everybody else like members of a single family.

Tian Xia, she concluded, captures all the meanings of the human world. It excludes none of them. It lacks any division. If we use Tian Xia and the Dao, we may imagine a future for all human and non-human life sharing one world.

Surface Sedimentation

The older boy scratched at the thin soil close to where he sat. This soil had very recently, in geological terms, been deposited on ancient Carboniferous limestone reefs. He was thinking that Modern episteme has too been buried beneath newly active sedimentary layers; it has become compact and hard, preserving its features for posterity. It is from the thin new sedimentary layers that a different episteme has now to be excavated. Unlike Foucault, the older boy reflected: "I shall conduct a geological survey, not an archaeology dig, since this new layer is much bigger than humankind alone".

In the top layer of sediment that he turned over in his mind, the older boy found that some concepts of life and human sciences had been superseded, incorporated, reworked, re-ordered by autonomous creative processes. He read his papers and made notes regarding autocatalytic sets bringing a natural order to original chaos (Kauffman, 1995); social-ecological, self-organisation forming within complex systems cross disciplinary boundaries (Berkes *et al.*, 2003); thermodynamic dissipative structures creating the universe with their anisotropic, symmetry-breaking characteristics (Prigogine and Stengers, 1985); and Life re-creating itself with its own momentous poetry, an ineluctably impulsive autopoiesis (Maturana and Varella, 1980). He could now, thanks to QC, give Chinese names to what he had found in fresh Western "geological" sediments, Tian Xia and Dao.

A Geological Find

When he got back home late that spring afternoon, he found that he had received a phone message from Grey Beard asking him to call back to Gothenburg asap. The older boy called once his tea had brewed and he was settled comfortably in his home office. Grey Beard was there, but busy; he would call back in thirty minutes.

Two hours later the older boy received a call back from Sweden. Grey Beard began by contrasting his "constructivist" Swedish accounting with that of "positivist" UK and USA practices. He was excited. He said this is what he had been looking for in his work; not all in Sweden or even in his office agrees; and it is hard to get belief in such a change, but I have a heavy, round rock in my office and I give them that saying: "This is it. This is round, solid, heavy enduring reality. This is my accounting." But now I can say much more. I can take their own words and give them back to them with a new meaning. I can rewrite their language. This is what I do:

Cause and effect become	Teleology
Complication becomes	Complexity
Differentiation becomes	Diversification
Evolution becomes	Project
Homogeneity becomes	Diversity
Growth becomes	Efficiency
Law becomes	Representation
Physical becomes	Ecological
Predictable becomes	Unpredictability
Reduction becomes	Holism
Social Structures become	Cultural Identities
Uniformity becomes	Uniqueness.

Grey Beard had accepted most of Vallega's changes without difficulty. Instead of "Differentiation becomes Diversification", he would have preferred "Separation becomes Differentiation", but otherwise he found the changes appropriate for a new episteme. Grey Beard concluded that his home-grown Swedish accounting analyses had found a supporter in the geographer Vallega (2005). The epistemological transition that Vallega describes goes from positivist and structuralist approaches to constructivist, complexity-based approaches to closely match the transition in practical accounting that Grey Beard had been performing in Gothenburg in his descriptive company studies.

Vallega's paper is replete with implications and practical consequences regarding how we should conduct business and how we should account for it. He represents reality as a web of bi-modular ecological and human systems, interacting with their external environments and moving towards targets. This, Vallega argues, gives rise to a root epistemological question, since his approach is inconsistent with analytical approaches based on Cartesian principles of reduction and causality. For one thing, reduction has to be replaced by holism since reality should be considered as a whole; it is as you say "joined up". Reality is not an assemblage of discrete parts. Society is not comprised of individuals. The business world does not somehow exist separately from social and ecological worlds; it is time to revise accounting statements to reflect this simple fact. Our Modern institutions are not just out of date, they are *dangerously* out of date.

If we take Vallega at his word, businesses have to find their place, make their statements and representations, Grey Beard told the older boy with much emphasis, within your particle exchange universe. As Vallega points out, the real performances of businesses should no longer be *explained*, but should be *comprehended* in the sense of the etymological root, *cum-prehendere*, a bringing together. Cause and effect analyses of economics and business have to be replaced by teleology because life systems, which now logically means ecosystems as well as social systems, cannot be represented in discrete cause and effect relations. We need to appreciate and represent the target towards which they are moving, the principal and subsidiary goals they are set to achieve; hence the cardinal principle now is teleology.

Unearthing a Buried Process: Genesis

As a consequence of his day's walking, the older boy went to bed as soon as darkness fell around nine thirty in the evening. He woke in the small hours of the morning. Once he had made fresh coffee, he went to his study to work. For the rest of that day the older boy created the following document. It was time, he was thinking, to fully unearth this new episteme.

Episteme Change

In the Classical episteme, Order had opened the way to successive identities and differences.

In the Modern episteme, History had given place to analogical, functional organic structures in the service of man; i.e. the structures were "created" as anthropocentric positivities by the freshly-created — for this very purpose — epistemological man.

One way to identify a new episteme is to differentiate it from the old. Indeed a telling critique of the old is a *sine qua non* of any new episteme. Hence there has to be key features of the Modern Episteme that become invalid. Are these four features the ones we need to reveal as redundant?

Fragmented Origins

The Modern episteme lacks the strong metaphysical continuum of the Classical age. Consequently, knowledge of the great empirical regions of the Modern age is first acquired in "fragments, outlines, pieces, shards" (Foucault, 1970, p. 239). The Modern episteme's response to this consequence is to value the formalisation of rational thought and mathematisation for their synthesising frameworks over empirical evidence which (without a strong metaphysics) remains fragmentary, journalistic and "merely" descriptive.

Two Philosophical Schools

After Kant, the attempt at a Classical mathesis had to be reformulated around a formal ontology and an apophantics (*ibid.*, p. 74). This division created the great Modern philosophical reflections on (i) problems regarding relations between logic and ontology corresponding to the Analytical philosophical school (or the quest for truth in things); and (ii) reflections questioning the relations of signification and time which bring into prominence the themes and methods of interpretation (*ibid.*, p. 207) which provide foundations for the Continental philosophy school (or the quest for truth in words).

Intrinsic Sustainable Development

Epistemological Man

The Modern age's elusive, never-to-be-attained origins mean that at the foundation of empirical positivities, there has to be a circular logic created by and supporting "epistemological" man, i.e. man simultaneously incorporating the dual roles of both known object and knowing subject. For this reason, the Modern episteme's apophantics of Analytical philosophy and the interpretations of Continental philosophy both reduce to anthropologies.

Finitude

It follows from the roles of epistemological man that (i) the concrete limitations of man's existence are both simultaneously defined by and defining all that can be known by epistemological man, and (ii) the Modern episteme has a fundamental finitude which rests on nothing but its own existence. So in the very heart of Modern empirical knowledge, there lies the obligation to work backwards, or downwards, to the analytic of finitude (*ibid.*, p. 315).

The Emerging Episteme

In the emerging episteme, natural processes are known to provide independent origins which have their own time scales, so that epistemological man, his finitude and his divisive philosophies are no longer required. Furthermore in the emerging episteme, Nature creates interconnected, interdependent and indeterminate entities based on a strong metaphysics which is the continuity of being and becoming with and within creative processes.

The emerging episteme is based on knowledge of things as they are created; it is hence a knowledge of *primal* processes. This will provide a name, the "Primal episteme".

Primal processes are based on thermodynamic dissipative structures, some of which possess chaotic behaviour whereby they change significantly, creatively and irreversibly in response to small changes in unpredictable, initiating conditions. Hence whilst a dissipative structure may exhibit some stability and predicable behaviour, it is free to switch suddenly and indeterminately into another phase with the consequence that the overall outcome of Primal processes is significantly indeterminate.

Creative Primal processes are the result of the flow of energy in systems that locally decrease entropy (to increase order). But if such systems are kept open, the net universal result is an increase in entropy with higher levels of stability; i.e. local low entropy states exist because they are more efficient ways of increasing entropy overall.

The ordering of human knowledge within the Primal episteme is an output of the same dissipative structures. These structures have a history, the evolutionary pathways of life and of culture.

The suggested name for the process of creation both of things and of words in the ordering of knowledge is "Genesis". Genesis is a process driven by entropy, in which forms and matter interact. Aristotle's four causes may be modified to explain this point. His original four causes are Material, Formal, Efficient and Final.

The Material cause is the material or substance from which a thing is made. Since the creation of things for the future makes use of things from the past, the Material cause has a history. This history was indeterminate in the making because of the role of uncertainty in those chaotic, dissipative thermodynamic systems which are highly sensitive to unpredictable initial conditions; i.e. the dissipative structures are anisotropic.

The Formal cause is the way in which matter is formed or arranged. This has two aspects since there is (1) a Platonic Formal cause which refers to universals and is made known by formal thought and mathematisation but since the Material cause has had an indeterminate history there is also (2) a Contextual

Intrinsic Sustainable Development

Formal cause, which is made known by the interpretation of empirical evidence.

The Efficient cause is the source of change which has guided its creation. It answers the question "how? This question is now being answered by the sciences of Chaos, Thermodynamics (including entropy) and Complexity.

The Final cause is the purpose which answers the question "why?" For our universe, entropy is the answer to this question.

Since entropy is present in both the Efficient cause (as agent to answer the question "how?") and in the Final cause (as an end state that answers the question "why?"), the Efficient and Final causes may be combined as the Entropic cause. Hence, a triangle of Material, Formal and Entropic Causes may be used to represent the Genesis process; see Figure 1.

Capra uses Aristotle's four causes to give a systemic understanding of life. He equates the Formal Cause with networks, the Material cause with a cell's components and the Efficient Cause with the processes of structural change. At this point, Capra also has a triangle but it is made of only three of Aristotle's four causes: networks (form), components (material), and process (efficient). This is because Capra understands that Modern science does not deal with the Final cause; i.e. science lacks a teleology. He does introduce "meaning" when adapting his triangle to social systems; Capra's "meaning" corresponds to Aristotle's Final cause and it is taken to be the mental character

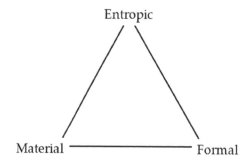

Fig. 1.   The Three Causes of the Genesis Process.

Chapter 9 — The Primal Episteme   **243**

of social phenomena, a hermeneutic dimension (Capra, 2003, pp. 61–66).

However, as we have seen, entropy has both an efficient and a final aspect. Furthermore, if we consider the acts of selection that occur as matter, form and entropy interact, then there is evidence of at least a rudimentary foundation for the "intelligence" and "cognition" observable in some forms of life. The cell absorbing other cells and molecules as well as the crystal in a cooling magmatic melt absorbing other elements and compounds are both imposing an order-by-selection onto an otherwise formless particle-exchange universe. Perhaps we need to examine more closely the boundaries of life, humanity and material things; particularly with regard to "meaning", autopoiesis and teleology in living and non-living things, in all under heaven.

Understanding the Primal Episteme

During the Renaissance episteme, man used signs and resemblances to order knowledge in a God-given world. The world was read as if it were a book and man had a place in the Great Chain of Being.

Emboldened with faith in a rational God, during the Classical episteme man could lay the totality of a God-given world out before him as if on a table. Man looked down on this table of all things, the real and the fantastic, and applied measurement and order to analyse the undifferentiated whole according to the identities and differences of its knowable parts. All knowledge was thereby to be obtained by the comparison of two or more things within the *all* of existence, within the *all* of time.

When God's simple gift of the world came to appear naïve and thought was obliged to question the relations of meaning with the form of truth and the form of being, man had to look for the origins of all things in all things. He found a History that gave place to analogical organic structures whose origins retreated, were never to be attained. A weak metaphysics was thereby created and this was kept in place by the birth of epistemological man in the Modern episteme.

When the rational mode of being and the formalized, *a priori*, sciences stumbled upon the independent, autopoietic, chaotic and complex creative origins of things, an ordering of knowledge that lies beyond the capabilities of the Modern episteme had been found. This new ordering gives rise to a series of consequences including: firstly, Nature becomes active once more since the world becomes Nature-given; secondly, the attainment of origins removes the need for epistemological man with his psychologies and his finitude; thirdly, a strong metaphysical continuum became known in the eternal moment at which being was always about to come to an end and becoming is always about to make a start with the result that the rational mode of being with its formalized, *a priori*, science and that resumption capable of revealing with its interpretative, *a posteriori*, empirical science of events unite.

Primal Episteme Properties

If the Modern episteme is represented by the drilling of holes into the Classical table of all knowledge, or digging down in pursuit of origins, then its regions of knowledge remained in these deep and separated holes finding no way out, no real access into other holes; meanwhile the holes are being supported, propped open, by the reflexive logic of epistemological man. Then the Primal episteme may be seen to break out of these holes, moving sideways, upwards, downwards and across to unite the separate holes of Modern knowledge within a single three-dimensional space, a homogenous epistemological block.

The breaking out and unified properties of the Primal episteme are a consequence of the Genesis process. Since the Genesis process is sensitive to unlimited disturbances in its initial conditions, all things are connected in the continuity of being and becoming. This much was understood by the ancient Chinese perceptions of Tian Xia and the Dao.

Chapter 9 — The Primal Episteme   **245**

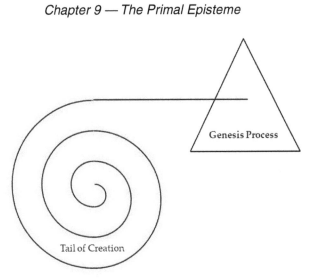

Fig. 2.   The Genesis process generates a Spiralling Tail of Creation.

This process may be represented by the three causes, formal, material and entropic, of Figure 1. The iterative nature of the Genesis process is in part historically determined because of the anisotropic material cause and this creates a spiralling tail of creation; see Figure 2. The *spiral* nature of the tail of creation is a consequence of its own chaotic origins, of the influence of its own strange attractors.

The Genesis process has a form of duality which does not lead to dualism. Rather, its two aspects, the being and becoming, result in its never being manifest as itself, but only as that point at which old matter takes on new form. This kind of dualism is mutually defining, existentially interdependent and hence complementary; it may be represented by Yin Yang symbolism.

The Genesis process is one source of order in a particle-exchange universe for there are other forces and relations such as atomic structures, electro-chemical bonds, molecular sizes, crystal strengths, cells properties, networks and gravitation. The Genesis process works alongside or outside these other sources of order. Additionally, these other sources of order are all consti-tutional of nature and hence nature remains intrinsically active

(Ellis, 2002). Resulting structures may be morphologically complex, but they remain genetically simple.

With regard to the ordering from consciousness, autopoiesis claims that forms of life are capable of doing this on their own, a form of self-directed change (Maturana and Varela, 1980). Life creates local decreases in entropy which exist providing open exchanges with the wider universe are maintained, providing overall entropy increase. Luhmann (1989 and 1995) applied autopoietic principles to studies of social systems. The Genesis process should help explain how autopoiesis occurs.

Within the Primal episteme, "meaning" becomes equivalent to "participating". It is to know yourself beyond yourself in space, and in time past and in the future. It is to go beyond the small self by means of that universal, genetic moment of being and becoming. It is to live creatively with your already extended self continually disappearing or, at least always a little, falling down and over and forwards out into the unknown. Within the Primal episteme, "meaning" becomes equivalent to "giving".

Primal Episteme Analyses

The approach to gaining knowledge in the Renaissance episteme had been to read the world as if it were a book alongside *the* Book and to "unearth" and interpret the signs that would then, by means of their resemblances one to another, complete a corpus. During the Classical episteme, knowledge had been obtained by using measurement and order to distinguish different things according to comparisons of identity and difference. In both these epistemes, a strong God-given metaphysical continuum was believed to exist, which provided a unified and integrated foundation for knowledge.

By questioning the possibility of all knowledge, Kant shifted the approach to knowledge acquisition from one of a question of establishing relations of identities and differences against the continuous background of similitudes, to the synthesis of the diverse. Any metaphysical foundation for knowledge was no longer assumed or believed. Its existence was questioned by the Modern episteme.

The boundary between metaphysics and the knowledge of things, that origin of knowledge, was not crossed by the Modern episteme; indeed it would never have been possible for the Modern episteme to cross this boundary which provided it with its defining characteristic. From this perspective, the philosophical concern of the Modern episteme was not with the possibility of primary understanding, but with the possibility of a primary misunderstanding.

With the representation of the Genesis process, the Modern episteme draws to a close. However, the form that analysis took in the Modern episteme from the "fragments, outlines, pieces and shards" put into order by "analogy and succession" to create the great organic structures of "Life, Labour and Language" with their own "internal relations and laws" still applies; the process has just become more *complex*.

In the Primal episteme, representation has learned how it represents itself within a particle exchange universe as an application of the Genesis process with its interdependence and its twisting and turning time-lines that draw unidirectional threads though space-time to create a unified, unique and complex whole. Hence, in the Primal episteme, the use of evidence, the "fragments, outlines, pieces and shards", still proceeds much the same as in the Modern episteme in terms of theory construction — and deconstruction. But the process is now held together, merged without knowable boundaries, integrated, observed and understood from within by its participants; it may be traced and pursued systematically through the networks and matrices of its unique histories to the cohesive, integrated, unified extremes of all the diverse things that we know only to be returned once more, whole and complete, morphologically complex but simple in origin, as the moment of the Genesis process.

The true direction of knowledge accumulation in the Primal episteme then is no longer just a "building" or a "construction"

Intrinsic Sustainable Development

but is also a "condensing"; i.e. a knowledge of parts as discrete parts and the knowledge of parts as parts of wholes, and, in turn, of greater wholes. Knowledge accumulation in the Primal episteme requires a double act, an analysis and a synthesis. It requires the help of Janus, the Roman god of doors, doorways, gates, entrances and exits; of endings and beginnings. For "to know" within the Genesis process is to look simultaneously backwards at historical records and forwards to the possible pathways of uncertain futures; to look discretely and with some certainty at the records of separate parts and to look imaginatively and openly at the formative wholes wherein the future lies.

The reason why we have to do so is because existence *exists*; and we, patiently and exhaustively, have to repeatedly return our realities to existence as best we can.

For Foucault. . .

Foucault had no option but to write with the analytical approach made available by the Modern episteme. Even as he dissected the Renaissance and Classical epistemes he had to do so from within the Modern episteme, since nothing else was available. To go back in time and to use either the Renaissance or Classical episteme for his approach to episteme analysis would not have been inappropriate or difficult for Foucault, it would have been impossible. For you can no more deliberately leave your own episteme than you can will yourself to grow wings and fly.

The Primal episteme was not willed into being; it depends on a set of incidental thoughts and discoveries that, on reflection, mark the end of the Modern episteme just as much as Kant's questioning the possibility of knowledge brought the Classical episteme to a close. But Foucault did identify weaknesses in the Modern episteme. He could foresee the directions in which thought was proceeding; Olssen (2008), for example, argues that Foucault was a Complexity Theorist. If he was, then Foucault would have been more than ready to see his explication of the Modern episteme slip away into the annals of history, to become

Chapter 9 — The Primal Episteme   **249**

another time-line in the Genesis process. After all, Foucault did "... wager that [epistemological] man would be erased, like a face drawn in sand at the edge of the sea" (Foucault, 1970, p. 387); a point that, in retrospect, is clear enough, given the insecure, reflexive posturing of epistemological man as observer and observed.

Foucault recognised the important role that language would have to play when breaking free of the Modern episteme. For Foucault, the whole curiosity of Modern thought resided in the question: "What is language, how can we find a way round it in order to make it appear in itself, in all its plenitude?" (*ibid.*, p. 306). He speculated even more precisely: "To discover the vast play of languages contained once more within a single space might be just as decisive a leap towards a wholly new form of thought as to draw to a close a mode of knowing constituted during the previous century." (*ibid.*, p. 307).

Language is multilayered in terms of its words, phonetics, its syntax and its grammar. But it is a system acquired and preserved in a culture. It is built and rebuilt generation by generation. Each generation introduces slight changes in the use of language. Words have many meanings. They may be used in many different ways with different forms of grammar. Language itself is likely to be fruitfully studied as a complex evolving, adaptive system — a Genesis process. After all, language is an aspect of information processing in living things, a phenomenon that has "... taken on an ontological status equal to that of mass and energy-namely a third primitive component of reality." (Mitchell, 2009, p. 169); after all, language does emerge within complex neural networks. But the relationships between complexity science and embodied processes of language and cognition are still the subjects of active exploratory study (Carsetti, 2010). Language has yet to find its full representation in a particle exchange universe; but there is no known reason why it will not do so.

Foucault foresaw the end of the Modern episteme within its own sciences of living things, for which a system of thought was developed where individuality, with its forms, limits, and needs, was no more than a precarious moment, doomed to destruction; where the recommencement of life precluded the possibility of imposing a limit of duration on it; and where the chimera of consciousness was dissipated (Foucault, 1970, p. 279). Foucault foresaw the import of Life understood within the Primal episteme.

Finally, for Foucault the start of the Modern episteme was marked by Kant's question: "What makes representation possible?" The Primal episteme does not answer this question; rather it shifts its focus from that Classically ordered table of all knowledge to existence. Representations, those ordered particles, waves and energies that constitute what we observe, now merge seamlessly with the selfsame particles, waves and energies that constitute the exchanges and ordering of the known universe. In other words, in the particle exchange universe of the Primal episteme what we see is *all* that we can get!

> "What you do is quite out of line.
> I would embrace the universe
> To be one with Nature for better or for worse."
>   – *Li Bai (706–762 AD) Song of*
>   *Sunrise and Sunset*

CHAPTER 10 — PRIMAL WISDOM

After the storms of the previous days, it was heavenly to have calmer waters, an occasional glimpse of sunlight and clear blue sky. An hour or so after high water, the Atlantic waves no longer crossed between the rocky outcrops that defined the narrow approach to their anchorage; instead they broke energetically over the emerging beach.

The ketch swung around on her anchor as the tidal flow lessened and the wind began to determine how she lay. The older boy and Edge, the skipper of the yacht, took the rubber dinghy to the nearest beach. There were no footprints in the sand and as they explored the caves in nearby cliffs, they found no evidence whatsoever of other people or indeed of any human artefacts.

On the previous day, they had motored through the Sound of Harris, heading West against the wind. With the Atlantic Ocean before them, Edge had decided that it would not be possible to make the crossing to the St Kilda islands that day.

"She'll not sail that close to the wind. We'd never make it." Edge had said. "Besides the forecast is for a wind shift overnight and tomorrow's winds should come from the south east. That'll be good for us."

So the two men had sailed in their small yacht north up along the West coast of Harris in the Scottish Outer Hebrides. Near to Scarp island, good shelter had been found in the corner of a wide and shallow bay. In the late afternoon, the sun was now breaking though a sixty per cent cloud cover and the sea was revealed to be crystal clear and coloured blue in such a way that the pale, light-wash in which *Second Glance* floated, graded imperceptibly away into ever deeper shades right up to the black of the gaunt cliffs overlooking the entrance to cavernous Loch Resort.

They explored the beach, watched Basking Sharks in turbulent inshore waters, and Edge bathed in the cold Loch. Later, the older boy did not sleep well even though *Second Glance* had for once been very quiet with not even a breeze or the gentlest of seas to rattle her rigging or to rock her any more than a cradle's worth.

The older boy was anxious. He was worrying that the open ocean was not his environment. The previous day's sailing through the Sound of Harris had been without incident, although getting through the shallowing waters against the prevailing wind had made for a harrowing and rough passage. But during all that day, land had been visible. It was admittedly not particularly welcoming land for it looked cold, rocky, isolated and desolated; but it was land. Tomorrow would be very different. They would sail due West from the western-most shore of Scotland far out into the Atlantic Ocean. There they would be truly alone and very small, out of sight of land, dependent upon the whims of wind, sea and storms and their own skills for their survival.

Edge and a friend had a few years ago rowed across the Atlantic Ocean in a two-man open boat. They had failed to find the required southerly route and consequently their journey did not benefit from favourable currents. It had taken much longer than planned. A chance encounter with an Irish survey vessel had allowed the pair to feast in a warm and dry cabin, and they had been able to replenish their supplies. But after that their stove had failed and they had to eat raw the flying fish that fell flapping into the small boat. They had rowed constantly for 112 days, taking turns at the oars, two hours on and two hours off, twenty-four-seven. "Getting used to the routine was very hard in the first weeks," Edge had once said. "We could not sleep when we were supposed to and there were pains and discomforts as our bodies adjusted. But, by the end of the trip, we felt as if we could row for ever."

In contrast, the older boy enjoyed taking ferries around Europe and China. He had often stood at the stern of these massive vessels and had watched the wake laid out like a road through the day and night seascapes. He had enjoyed these small adventures; the relatively secure remoteness from land, the spectacular but barely threatening electric storms, the kept-outside winds, or the breaking wild seas observed from a bar, excellent food and a warm dry cabin. He was never sea-sick.

Second Glance was very different. On the second day aboard, Edge had suggested that the older boy should make a will — he himself had done so prior to rowing the Atlantic. Edge had bequeathed his possession to his wife and two children, so it was only a simple will but, he argued, it would make things much easier for them if he were to die.

During that restless night prior to crossing the Atlantic, the older boy could not stop his dreamy thoughts from reaching the worst impressions that his numerous ferry crossings had left deeper in his mind. He relived biting cold mists of the Gothenburg archipelago, the frozen waters of the Göta Älv, the lightening that had struck close to the ferry in the Bay of Biscay, and the excessive, uncontrollable violence of a North Sea crossing to Holland when it seemed as if every other passenger was sick.

The older boy turned anxiously in his bed. He lacked the experience of the wild water challenge he faced the next day. Around 4 am, he woke, took out his lap-top, plugged it in to a charger in the main cabin and began to write notes. He was looking for something calm and reassuring in wise thoughts.

Primal Wisdom I: Attitude

We participate: "There are no parts, only participants." *-Hans-Peter Dürr (1929–), German Physicist.*

We can tell stories, imagine and construct our own real but separated worlds to more comfortably inhabit. This is entirely natural; but existence is joined up. Furthermore the realities we prepare necessarily pursue existence and hence more *truth* is made available to the open-minded.

> "What we like determines what we are, and is the sign of what we are; and to teach taste is inevitably to form character."
> *– John Ruskin, The Lamp of Memory, 1849.*

> "We see things not as they are, but as we are".
> *Jewish Proverb.*

254   *Intrinsic Sustainable Development*

We participate in the revealing of existence to our realities, but we do not fully control this process. Existence is necessarily and always more than we know.

Trust and confidence are needed in order to have knowledge of existence. David Hume knew this when he revealed the flaw in the arguments of the Rationalists to be the simple fact that reliable knowledge is based on experience (Beauchamp, 1999). It is a trust in and a knowledge of the *way* things are.

Knowledge of the way things are is never complete:

> "My demand is, that the ultimate arbitrariness of matter of fact from which our formulations start should disclose the same general principles of reality, which we dimly discern as stretching away into regions beyond our explicit powers of discernment."
> – *Alfred North Whitehead, Process and Reality, 1929, (p.115).*

There is also more to be revealed:

> "The hidden connection is stronger than an obvious one."
> – *Heraclitus, Fragments 54, circa 500 BC.*

Everywhere, you may look and listen and learn:

> "...tongues in trees, books in the running brooks, sermons in stones, and good in everything".
> – *William Shakespeare, As you like it, II i.*

Bonnett argues that Heidegger knew of the *elusive* nature of existence. It seems that for Heidegger things were: "Open, infinitely faceted, fluid, epistemologically mysterious...neither knowable nor taggable..." (Bonnett, 2004, p. 65).

Foucault (1970) was correct to identify the importance of the role that language plays in the relation between existence and reality, and with regard to the downfall of the Modern episteme. Others who draw our attention to the confinements of words include:

"... the world is my world [which] shows itself in the fact that the limits of the language (the language which I understand) mean the limits of my world."
> – *Ludwig Wittgenstein, Tractatus Logico-Philosophicus, 5.62.*

"A moment's thought shows us that no one idea can in itself be sufficient... Thus no one word can be adequate. But conversely, nothing must be left out."
> – *Alfred North Whitehead, Process and Reality, 1929, (p.116).*

The older boy worked for no more than an hour that night. He fell briefly asleep, but Edge woke to listen to the 05.15 weather forecast. The wind for that day was said to be light, south-easterly, veering-south and moderate later. The day was right for the crossing.

They set sail and ate breakfast underway. If conditions remained favourable, they had about ten hours of sailing before they reached St Kilda. Once clear of Scarp, Edge set a course straight out into the North Atlantic. The early morning sky was crystal clear. Visibility was excellent at first, but cloud soon came to cover them. The light easterly was enough to fill their sail to the full. But even then the rolling swell was significant so that they had to wedge themselves firmly into their seats whether they were taking their one-hour watch on the helm or resting below deck. The occasional big wave would break over the deck, washing over the crew. The sea water was cold.

At first the journey was thrilling, if a little scary for the older boy, who lacked experience of being in a small boat on an ocean. Edge said: "This is what the Atlantic is like most days, some swell, a few waves breaking, grey, cold and cloudy."

They soon lost sight of land. Even the clouds lacked the distinct shapes which the older boy could have used to mark a distant point to keep *Second Glance* on course, so he had to keep his eyes on the compass. Apart from the instruments, they had only a rough idea of their location, or of their heading, for the sun was not visible. Sometimes a gannet flew up from behind the ketch, on the very same course, and would overtake them, rising up and dropping down fol-lowing the roll of the swell. This ocean was the gannets' home; they knew what to do here. The older boy found reassurance in the fact that both *Second Glance* and the gannets were heading in the same direction, hopefully to St Kilda for they was nothing else for them before Canada.

By 10.30 that morning, a thick mist had settled around the boat. The wind had veered to the south and dropped. *Second Glance* was reaching violently under a flapping sail. She was heading along the length of the swell so she rolled and tossed remorselessly. Sometimes as she caught a rogue wave, the yacht was flooded. Edge secured the sea doors to keep the interior dry; the helmsman's watch was now even more isolated, cold and wet.

The constant struggle to stop his body colliding with hard parts of *Second Glance* and the lack of anything other than grey mist outside the yacht and the occasional seabird was draining the older boy's confidence and resolution. When the fulmars had first arrived, he imagined they would pass-by like the gannets; but they did not do so. The pretty gulls drew closer, effortlessly holding their position along-side *Second Glance* as the yacht rolled and slewed. They flew along the eye-line of the helmsman. The older boy realised that they were watching him; their shining black eyes were observing his every move, every grimace that the older boy made as *Second Glance* heaved. He was an alien in their world: he was their object for study.

The fulmars came repeatedly for the remainder of the crossing and as *Second Glance* approached St Kilda, they became numerous. Suddenly the mist was broken by a sheer, soaring, dark and threat-ening cliff. The older boy shouted below for Edge, who appeared at the cabin door unruffled. Edge put on his water-proofs and safety-harness and climbed out onto deck; he read instruments and made adjustments to their course. Within half an hour they were motoring into the shelter of Village Bay. Then Edge wanted tea, cheese and a trip-ashore before night fell.

After sunset, as they drank a single malt whisky below decks with all doors closed and *Second Glance* made safe, Edge asked "What were you writing this morning?"

The older boy replied: "I'm trying to describe what a wiser, more sustainable world would be like."

"I've always thought that the pursuit of growth was wrong. Even in my first job. Last year my company forecast how they would continue expanding globally as if the world had no limits. What's new about your work?"

The older boy thought hard. "A self with a big letter 'S'," he answered eventually. "If we experience and understand that we participate all our lives, in every way possible, in something much bigger; something that was there before we were born and which will be there after our deaths; something that can contribute significantly not only to what we think and feel but **how** we think and feel; something that connects our little lives, our realities, to the greater existence in which we are embedded, and within which we are given life and find ourselves constantly changing; something that constrains us and equally sets us free; then life and death are no longer such separate entities as they may once have appeared."

Edge said: "Okay."

The two yachtsmen talked for the next three hours after which Edge went to his bunk, but the older boy took up his lap-top once again.

Primal Wisdom II: Self

Where our self begins and ends is more than we may ever know. This is something that human *reason* has yet to fully appreciate.

This is a situation that Ehrenfeld, a biologist, blames in part on humanism. He argues that mankind needs to remove all condescension towards the non-rational parts of our nature: "Emotion is a vital part of life — anger, love, fear, happiness — part of the essence of daily existence, part of our birthright which we have paid for with countless deaths and tragedies over the course of aeons." (Ehrenfeld, 1981, p. 174).

Ehrenfeld notes that laboratory-bred rats are more placid, gentle and fearless than their wild relatives; furthermore laboratory-bred rats have changed anatomically for their adrenal glands (that help an animal cope with stress) are smaller. Ehrenfeld's observations include the following.

(i) "If we are to become like laboratory rats and overthrow whatever balance we have between reason and emotion, we must first be certain that we can maintain ourselves in a regulated, predictable, laboratory-like environment. And this we definitely cannot do."

(ii) "Emotion is necessary and more sensitive in situations with a wider context. Emotion is an integration and summarization phenomenon." (*ibid.*, p. 163).

It was as recently as 1997 that Mayer and Salovey directed *thought* to "Emotional Intelligence" with a four-branch model of the role it plays:

i. Perception, appraisal and expression of emotion;
ii. Emotional facilitation of thinking;
iii. Understanding and analyzing emotions as well as employing emotional knowledge; and
iv. Reflective regulation of emotion to promote emotional and intellectual growth. (Mayer and Salovey, 1997).

Emotions are now known to be hard-wired into our cognitive processes: "Because so many of the brain's higher centres sprouted from or extended the scope of the limbic area, the emotional brain plays a crucial role in neural architecture. As the root from which the newer brain grew, the emotional areas are intertwined via myriad connecting circuits to all parts of the neocortex. This gives the emotional centres immense powers to influence the functioning of the rest of the brain — including its centres for thought." (Goleman, 1996, pp. 13–14).

Previously Goldsmith had explained the importance of emotions for our future: "We will not save our planet through a conscious, rational and unemotional decision, signing an emotional contract with it on the basis of cost-benefit analysis. A moral and emotional commitment is required." (Goldsmith, 1992, p. 77).

However Goldsmith had argued in "The Way: an Ecological World View" that the most fundamental ecological knowledge is acquired by intuition: "The process whereby we apprehend our ineffable [i.e. tacit] knowledge is usually referred to as 'intuition'. It is itself mysterious and ineffable. One such fundamental intuition is the unity or 'one-ness' of the living world." (*ibid.*, p. 38).

Chapter 10 — Primal Wisdom   **259**

Goethe's masterpiece Faust was written to make the very same point about intuition. Whilst Kant had argued that science was separated from art and that an intuitive intellect lay beyond the capacity of mankind, Goethe had sought an intuitive way of knowing nature. He thereby introduced a new approach, in which the combination of art and science was, and came from, a primal source of being. In Goethe's Faust, the Lord instructs Mephistopheles to lead Dr Faust away from such knowledge:

> "Enough! 'tis granted thee! Divert
> This mortal spirit from his primal source;
> Him, canst thou seize, thy power exert
> And lead him on thy downward course,
> Then stand abash'd, when thou perforce must own,
> A good man in his darkest aberration,
> Of the right path is conscious still."
> — *Johann Wolfgang von Goethe, Faust, Prologue*
> *in Heaven, 1790 to 1833.*

Lord Winston provides an evolutionary perspective on this situation: "But while people have no problem with the idea that our general shape and structure are derived from other creatures, fewer consider, let alone accept, the psychological implications. Homo sapiens not only looks like an ape, he also thinks like one. Not only do we have a Stone Age body, with many vestiges of our past, we also have a Stone Age mind. The pressures to which we have been exposed over the millennia have left a mental and emotional legacy. Some of these emotions and reactions, derived from the species who were our ancestors, are unnecessary in a modern age, but these vestiges of a former existence are indelibly printed in our make-up." (Winston, 2003, p. 17).

Ironically, it seems as if it is the ancient evolutionary, origin of our emotions and intuitions that some of our present day thoughts deny even as they sought origins within the Modern episteme. It is as if our thoughts have lives of their own; as if they evolve, reproduce and act to protect their own interests. This no doubt relates in some way to the small-self identifying and defending itself.

Rationalists, for example, find an identity within the reasons of their minds. The neurophysiologist Churchland (1992,

260   *Intrinsic Sustainable Development*

p. 76) calls this kind of thinking the "traditional view" and thinks it has a "fairy-tale" quality. He argues that the brain evolved in the first instance to survive in the external world and that any capacity for self-knowledge would at best be a secondary advantage. Lakoff and Johnson (1999, p. 4), cognitive linguists, draw a similar conclusion: "Reason, even in its most abstract form, makes use of, rather than transcends, our animal nature. Reason is thus not an essence that separates us from other animals; rather, it places us on a continuum with them."

Neurophysiologists Edelman and Tononi (2000, p. 215) agree: "Consciousness, while special, arose as a result of evolutionary innovations in the morphology of the brain and body. The mind arose from the body and its development; it is embodied and therefore part of nature."

Science piece by little piece is revealing just how much a part of nature we are, have always been and always will be. The sequencing of human and chimpanzee genomes diverged 8 to 10 million years ago but even now they differ by only 1 or 2%. The search is now underway in DNA to reconstruct the history of the evolutionary changes that have led to the appearance of the kind of humanity we experience today. For example, the GLUD2 gene is found in common ancestors of apes and humans from about 25 million years ago and it is now found in human testicles and the brain and it might well be one of the molecular foundations of the growth of human brains. (Stein, 2008, p. 15).

Other research in the European Union has seriously dented traditional ideas of human specificity: "Palaeontologists and ethologists now refer to human primates and non-human primates. People are now prepared to pronounce the words 'intelligence', 'language', 'self-awareness', 'socialisation', 'individuality', 'suffering' and 'rights' in relation to animals. DNA codes that are so indistinctive, despite being from animals, that look so dissimilar, that it becomes difficult to deny the commonality of living animals." (Rugemer, 2008, p. 4).

It was perhaps inevitable — and natural — that we would develop small selves at an early stage of our evolution. When we struggle with other species and our environment to survive, a strong and focussed identity would be required. But

Chapter 10 — Primal Wisdom   **261**

when that small self needs itself to evolve beyond its own limitations, to become extended in its knowledge and action, then it becomes problematic. Its own defences and reinforcements come to work against its best, evolving self-interests. Perhaps it is time to dispense with the notion of selfhood altogether.

The recent recognition of the role of "memes" in our cultural evolution seems to be dispensing with the self, both small and extended. Memes are the skills, habits, songs, stories, or any other kind of information that is copied from person to person. The term was coined by Richard Dawkins in his 1976 book The Selfish Gene. Memes, like genes, are replicators; that is they are information that is copied with selective variations, just as any other form of evolution. Because only some of the variants survive, memes, and hence culture, evolves. Memes are copied by imitation and teaching, and they compete for space in our memories and for the chance to be copied again, and hence reproduce.

Blackmore (2003) argues that a 'memetic drive' may explain our exceptionally large brains and capacity for language. When our early human ancestors learned how to imitate, they created the first memes which then spread from human to human. People who could copy the latest memes gained an evolutionary advantage and the ability to use these memes spread. It is this need for imitation that increases brain size and the capacity for working with a larger number of memes. Memes and genes co-evolve; an insight that helps explain why we are so good at dancing, music, and religious rituals, for these are abilities that are hard to explain with evolutionary genetics alone.

Dennett (1991) argues that humans are apes under the sway of memes. Human consciousness, for Dennett, is a complexity of memes within which the self is a 'benign user illusion'. Blackmore (2003) disagrees with the benign memes idea, for she grants memes more autonomy and suggests that once created, memes will come together for their own mutual protection and propagation, regardless of their effects on the organism that sustains them. Our memes, our skills, habits, songs, stories, and the consequential realities that we create from them, may not be good for us.

But the idea that there is no continuing self, no "owner" to our thoughts and experiences is a much older concept.

Buddhism is of course founded on this very idea, that the self is an illusion. But, independently of Buddhism, David Hume looked into his own experience in search of an "experiencing self" but could not find one: all he found was experiences. Hume concluded: "... that the self is not an entity. It is more like a 'bundle of sensations'; one's life is a series of impressions that seem to belong to one person but are really just tied together by memory and other such relations" (Blackmore, 2005, p. 67). In this way, Hume foresaw the end of the Modern episteme before it had even started.

The Primal self is understood to be formed by the Genesis process. It is a complexity of memes brought together to be realised fleetingly within the moment of being and becoming. In early human evolution, memes spread very slowly, usually vertically, from parent to child. With the development of language and writing, memes could be spread horizontally from person to person, much more quickly. Is the internet merely the medium for a next stage of memetic evolution? Is a *global* meme evolving and what does that mean?

When the older boy went to his bunk around three in the morning, he collapsed with exhaustion. He slept to the crack of noon. For the rest of that day, Edge and the older boy explored Oiseva and St Kilda, climbing to the top of the island, taking many pictures and carefully avoiding the Skuas that flew menacingly close to their heads. They hung around the Village until 16.00 when the National Trust for Scotland souvenir shop opened for those visitors who had arrived that day in small boats from the Outer Hebrides. The older boy purchased a paperback history of the people of St Kilda whilst Edge bought and posted (to get the St Kilda postmark) several postcards.

The next day they rested. The older boy caught up on his sleep. Strong easterlies that morning meant that they could not sail back to the Outer Hebrides. In the afternoon, they motored around the island taking photos of the seascapes and the tens of thousands of sea birds. They talked much about this small wild island in the great ocean and of its people who had risked their lives to collect birds and eggs from the immense and dangerous cliffs.

Chapter 10 — Primal Wisdom   **263**

By late-afternoon *Second Glance* was back at anchor in the safety of Village Bay. Edge performed some engine maintenance whilst the older boy swept the deck and cleaned the heads.

By 18.00 they had finished working and sat on deck with tea and biscuits. Edge liked the idea of the extended, even absent, self and what that implied for life and death. "But what does a changed understanding of self achieve?" he asked. "How does that help sustainable development?"

Although it took all evening to do so, the older boy answered Edge's questions by referring to three aspects of the Primal episteme: knowledge, ethics and education. *Second Glance* swung gently at anchor in accordance with the whims of wind and tide.

Primal Wisdom III: Unity of Knowledge

Science now reveals existence to be joined up: human reality tries to be mimic existence.

Knowledge in the Primal episteme is unified. It is also formal, historic and contingent.

The strong metaphysical continuum of the Genesis process allows us to move on from the divisions of the Modern episteme. The "analytic" and the "continental" philosophies are now one; abstract, logical, and universal thought becomes another side of concrete, contextual and particular thought. The problem of "'two cultures': scientific explanations versus humanistic interpretation" (Critchley, 2001, p. 126) no longer exists. The gap between rational thought and wisdom may now be closed; which is perhaps something that Ludwig Wittgenstein had in mind when he wrote in Culture and Value: "Philosophy ought really to be written only as a form of poetry."

The unity of Primal knowledge is based on the unity of existence. The evidence for this now comes from many quarters: "This world is one world. Perhaps the biggest achievement of geologists in this [20th.] century will once again turn out to be a general principle, a world-wide concept, that reveals beyond its strictly geological meaning the essential unity of nature." (Fuller, 1981, p. 390).

But such unity is new to (Modern) science. A new kind of scientist is needed to deal with the new knowledge: "There is increasingly widespread agreement that science must somehow develop the ability to look at things more holistically. The 'separateness' assumption that underlies modern science is in a way an artefact of the history of Western Creation. . . . 'Wholeness Science' would include and emphasize more participatory kinds of methodologies; it would assume that, whereas we learn certain kinds of things by distancing ourselves from the subject studied, we get another kind of knowledge from intuitively 'becoming one with' the subject. In the latter case, the experience of observing brings about a sensitization and other changes in the observer. Thus a willingness to be transformed himself or herself is an essential characteristic of the participatory scientist." (Colquhoun and Ewald, 1996, p. 173).

Needham's study of Chinese science led him to a similar conclusion: ". . . the more I thought about it, the more I came to feel that we needed not 'a perspective for Chinese science' but a Chinese 'perspective for world science'. It seemed to me that certain Chinese values might be vitally helpful to man face to face with his own embarrassing knowledge." (Needham, 2004, p. 67). This would correspond to viewing Western scientific knowledge from the viewpoint of "Tian Xia"(Zhao, 2005), and the Dao.

Primal Wisdom IV: Ethics

Primal ethics are mindful. "Mindfulness is an open-ended inquiry into our experience." (Chödrön, 2001, p. 94).

Because we select and create, both voluntarily and involuntarily, our habitat, we need always to be free to choose and select otherwise; which per se introduces the ineluctable need for openness. In this respect, Wittgenstein was correct to observe that: "Ethics and aesthetics are one." *Notebooks 1914–1916.*

Ehrlich provides a similar insight, but from an evolutionary perspective: "Empathy, in turn, provides the underpinnings of ethical systems." (Ehrlich, 2000, p. 311).

Chapter 10 — Primal Wisdom   **265**

In practice, the pursuit of ethical mindfulness requires two aspects: (i) the avoidance of closure, conceptual locks, inaccurate simplifications, etc.; and (ii) a momentum towards what is open, alien, unknown, other than ourselves and so on. With regard to the Genesis process, point (i) above corresponds to a certain caution towards "being", whilst point (ii) above corresponds to an appreciation of "becoming".

These two aspects of the pursuit of ethical mindfulness account for the mysterious aspect of "wisdom" whose solutions are not always apparent or seemingly practical. The oracle at Delphi was located on a spur of Mount Parnassus in Greece and served as the prime source of wisdom for the ancient Greeks, the founders of Western civilisation, for many centuries. The oracle was always a local woman and she reputedly sat over a fissure in the rock within the temple where she was intoxicated by fumes emanating from the fissure. Fumes said in ancient times to come from the decaying body of the python slain by Apollo, but now thought to be a gas containing ethylene from an underground geological process. By Modern standards, the quality of the advice that the local, intoxicated woman could provide might seem limited.

However, two inscriptions said to have been carved at the entrance to the temple suggest how the oracle could have dispensed wise advice. The two inscriptions were "nothing in excess" (μηδέν άγαν) and "know thyself" (γνωθι σεαυτόν). For purposes of participating in the active, creative nature that the ancient Greek world shares with the Primal episteme, this is wise advice indeed.

The presence of an excess means that some one thing has been overdeveloped to the exclusion of others; a sure measure that options, diversity or mindfulness has been reduced, and entropy unnaturally decreased. Hence the advice to "Avoid excess" may be understood to correspond to the avoidance of closure in the pursuit of ethical mindfulness.

The ancient Greek world's famous Athenian hubris provides a good example of a social and psychological

Intrinsic Sustainable Development

excess and closure. The exceedingly successful Athenians had too much pride in their indubitable successes much to the annoyance of other Greek City States up to the point at which Sparta declared war on Athens. Sparta won the war — but that is perhaps not relevant. What is more important is to note how war might have been avoided in the first place. The Athenians should have heeded the wise advice of the Delphi inscription.

In our own times, "success" has become a Modern hubris, a form of closure, for some people. It becomes a kind of closure if "success" is pursued for the kind of wrong reasons that Handy perceives: "I believe that a lot of our striving after the symbols and levers of success is due to a basic insecurity, a need to prove ourselves..." (Handy, 1990, p. 212). The Modern, reflexive, anthropological, small self is insecure.

De Botton's thesis is similar. He makes the allowable substitution of "status" for "success" and argues with more insight: "That the hunger for status, like all appetites, can have its uses: spurring us to do justice to our talents, encouraging excellence, restraining us from harmful eccentricities and cementing members of a society around a common value system. But, like all appetites, its excesses can also kill." (De Botton, 2005, p. 5). De Botton's thesis encapsulates both aspects of ethical mindfulness.

In wider Modern societies, Rosenberg (2005) argues that there is a lack of mindfulness that underpins consumerism, and hence the ongoing expansions of Capitalism. In her essay "Mindfulness and Consumerism", she identifies the two core problems of consumerism as "automaticity" and the "need for fulfilment". Automaticity in this context is the human tendency towards automatic responses that corporations and advertisers exploit in the service of consumerism. The need for fulfilment corresponds to the restless capacity for "becoming". Once again, both aspects of ethical mindfulness have been invoked.

Both the status and consumerism examples — and many others — may be understood in terms of the transition from small to extended self. With our increasing knowledge of life on this planet, a key issue in this transition is our attitude towards life other than our own, both human and non-human. Moving on from the small self in this way will be beneficial to all life, including our own, as Benton explains so convincingly: "It is true that only human beings could make judgments of aesthetic, symbolic or spiritual value. It is also true that a strong case can be made for the preservation of objects of such value-judgments in terms of human fulfilment and self-realisation. It is also true that such a case would be anthropocentric in the sense that it relates the desirability of preservation to a human purpose. However, the fulfilment of that human purpose itself requires a non-anthropocentric orientation to its object. Only if I recognise, appreciate, or perhaps am moved by the inherent qualities of the object of spiritual or aesthetic valuation will the experience of it contribute in the appropriate way to my fulfilment. If some sorts of human fulfilment are premised on non-anthropocentric orientations to the world, then any simple opposition between what is instrumental to human purposes and what has 'intrinsic value' becomes unsustainable. To value nature, and opportunities to engage with it, for its aesthetic, spiritual or symbolic contribution to a fulfilled human life is therefore implicitly to acknowledge the importance of a non-anthropocentric orientation to the world." (Benton, 2008, pp. 218–219).

Knowledge is the key to facilitating the transition from the small to the extended self. For Firth, knowledge of relationships is key in this regard and is the foundation for an ethics for "It shows the importance of meaningful relationships to the quest for what the worthwhile life consists of, firstly between humans, and secondly in and with nature... I have argued that recognizing and respecting the meaningful relations in nature that are present in a person's life is necessary to a worthwhile life. A strong, other-regarding, ethical position can be established from this which will be action guiding, but not prescriptive." (Firth, 2008, p. 162).

Leopold (1887–1948) is famous for providing an ethical system grounded in knowledge of the relationships of ecology. Leopold was directed by personal experience but his ethical system integrates political, cultural, social and educational issues. His key requirement is a call for reform in our relationship to the land.

Leopold attended the Yale School of Forestry and was a professor at the University of Wisconsin, where he founded the department of Wildlife Ecology. His book, "A Sand County Almanac", begins with the words: "There are some who can live without wild things, and some who cannot. These essays are the delights and dilemmas of one who cannot." (Leopold, 1949). For some people, these words say all that is required; but Leopold has much more to say, much of which is inspirational and beautiful.

"A deep chesty bawl echoes from rimrock to rimrock, rolls down the mountain, and fades into the far blackness of the night. It is an outburst of wild defiant sorrow, and of contempt for all the adversities of the world.

Every living thing (and perhaps many a dead one as well) pays heed to that call. To the deer it is a reminder of the way of all flesh, to the pine a forecast of midnight scuffles and of blood on the snow, to the coyote a promise of gleanings to come, to the cowman a threat of red ink at the bank, to the hunter a challenge of fang against bullet. Yet beyond these obvious and immediate hopes and fears there lies a deeper meaning, known only to the mountain itself. Only the mountain has lived long enough to listen objectively to the howl of the wolf.

. . .I now suspect that just as a deer herd lives in mortal fear of its wolves, so does a mountain live in mortal fear of its deer. And perhaps with better cause, for while a buck pulled down by wolves can be replaced in two or three years, a range pulled down by too many deer may fail of replacement in as many decades.

So also with cows. The cowman who cleans his range of wolves does not realise that he is taking over the wolf's job of trimming the herd to fit the range. He has not learned to think like a mountain. Hence we have dustbowls, and rivers washing the future into the sea." (*ibid.*, p. 129).

For Leopold, it was inconceivable that an ethical relation to land could exist without love, respect and admiration for land and a high regard for its value. This was a critical problem for his ethics; Leopold saw that many [Modern] people are separated from the land by middlemen and by innumerable gadgets so they have no vital relation to it. Such a vital relation is a prerequisite for Leopold's ethical system, the "Land Ethic": "Examine each question in terms of what is ethically and esthetically right, as well as what is economically expedient. A thing is right when it tends to preserve the integrity, stability, and beauty of the biotic community. It is wrong when it tends otherwise." (*ibid.,* pp. 224–5).

Primal Wisdom V: Education

Primal education is mindful of relations.

Rosenberg tackles one socially pertinent aspect of relations and advocates raising general contemplative skills in teachers and students which "...should help people raise their children to be less susceptible to the mindless behaviours that support consumerism." (Rosenberg, 2005, p. 119).

But it is not enough to educate only to avoid closure, i.e. overcoming being: there is also a need for an education for an open-ended inquiry, a becoming. With the current state of scientific knowledge of our place in the living world, such an open-ended inquiry requires, as a very minimum, to be motivated with an appreciation of the relationships that create, maintain and direct life, i.e. ecological relationships. For the practical purposes of mankind, this could perhaps constitute an "Ecological Humanism".

Rocheleau (1999, p. 120) asks the right questions of an Ecological Humanism: "Perhaps the really important question is 'Where do we find the roots of a common sense of social and ecological proportion, connection and responsibility?' Where do respect for human rights and reverence for life reside? How is it expressed and mobilized? Why is it situated in particular social relations? How does it relate to other social and biological categories? How does this impulse toward affinity articulate with relations among groups of people and between humans and other beings? Is this sense of social and ecological responsibility widespread? Is it identified with a particular level of social organization or is it an opposition force existing within and across many levels of organization and in networks across many places? How can we foster it?"

Whilst Bonnett (2004, p. 146) explains a little of the changes that would be required to educate for an Ecological Humanism: "In this sense educational practices that reflect traditional — that is Cartesian — dualism of self and world, knowledge and action, will need to be reviewed ... until education communicates just how much we as unique embodied consciousnesses are in nature, and just how much nature is in us (that because of our physical, emotional and spiritual interdependence nature is not to be understood as some disposable asset or dispensable object), a proper orientation to the self-arising will remain elusive. We are not tourists: the Earth is neither hotel nor theme park; it is home. From this perspective, there will be much to be said for the democratisation of the school as an institution so that all members of its community develop a sense of belonging."

Mumford had proposed some decades previously to embed such an ecological education with a sense of place, starting around the home with a survey and this is "... not something to be added to an already crowded curriculum. It is rather the backbone of a drastically revised method of study, in which every aspect of the sciences and arts is ecologically related from the bottom up, in which they connect directly and constantly in the student's experience of his region and his community. Regional survey must begin with the infant's first exploration of his dooryard and his neighborhood; it must continue to expand and deepen at every successive stage of growth until the student is capable of seeing and experiencing above all, of relating and integrating and directing the separate parts of his environment, hitherto unnoticed or dispersed." (Mumford, 1946, pp. 151–152).

Sharing much of Mumford's intent, the Norwegian Ministries of Education, Research and Church,

Environment, Agriculture and Health and Social Affairs as well as the Norwegian Council for Cultural Affairs has more recently funded experiments in "Levande Skule", Living Schools. Learning by doing is important in these schools that stimulate in students a sense of responsibility for each other, for their surroundings and for nature. Living Schools correlate research with similar organisations worldwide such as "Learning through Landscapes" in England, and "Life Labs" in the USA.

The emphasis in such schools goes beyond the specialisation and abstraction that typify traditional academic studies of the living world. They emphasise identifying, understating and experiencing the relationships between the patterns of the biological world and ourselves. The re-publication of Gregory Bateson's (2000) famous "Steps to an Ecology of Mind" at the start of the third millennium suggests something of both the need, and the future, for an education of this kind.

Within this educational tradition, David Orr has developed a curriculum for "Ecological Literacy" which has at its heart a quality of mind that seeks out the connections that are the opposites of the specialisation and narrowness of most Modern education. Orr argues for a change in attitudes since: "People who do not know the ground on which they stand miss one of the elements of good thinking which is the capacity to distinguish between health and disease in natural systems and their relations to health and disease in human ones." (Orr, 1992, p. 86). The Center for Ecoliteracy (Ecoliteracy, 2011) is eminent in the USA for getting school students to know the ground on which they stand.

Whilst designing an educational framework to help the fledgling democracy of Bhutan avoid "... an extraordinarily seductive and increasingly sophisticated, powerful and manipulative materialist and consumerist world", Jigmi Y. Thinley, Prime Minister of Bhutan, believes he has identified key [Ecological Humanism] principles:

> "... equally that framework — based on the most profound human and ecological values — will transcend politics entirely and withstand any

Intrinsic Sustainable Development

> political attempt to dismantle it. We have a word
> for such indestructibility in our language: dorji,
> which means 'diamond-like' and stems from our
> ancient teachings on the true and indestructible
> nature of mind characterised by innate wisdom
> and expressed in natural compassion."
>
> – *Jigmi Y. Thinley, Prime Minister of Bhutan,*
>   *speech to the Education for Gross National*
>   *Happiness Conference, 2009.*

Edge and the older boy did not finish talking and making notes
until after midnight. It took the older boy another two hours to finish
writing up the notes. But he was up again at 06.00 for Edge had
listened to the shipping forecast and had decided that it was the day
for heading home.

They needed to set off early for the winds were forecast to shift in
the afternoon. As *Second Glance* left St Kilda, both yachtsmen were
anxious for they could well remember the rough outward crossing.
But on their return, the sky remained clear, the wind kept coming
from the south west to fill the sails for a fast reach so that *Second Glance* leapt steadily from wave to wave. Apart from a single
encounter with a survey vessel that would not give way to sail because
of a survey line, the crossing was without incident. They easily made
the Outer Hebrides and then the Minch. It was a delightful day.

They dropped anchor late in the afternoon at Tarbert on Harris.
They took a dinghy to shore in search of a food store.

> "Experience is never limited, and it is never complete; it
> is an immense sensibility, a kind of huge spider-web of the
> finest silken threads suspended in the chamber of conscious-
> ness, and catching every air-borne particle in its tissue."
>
> – *Henry James, The Art of Fiction, 1884.*

CHAPTER 11 — PRIMAL BUSINESS

"What have We Got?"

Grey Beard asked the question, but it was also on the minds of QC and the older boy. Before either could respond they were joined by a conference organiser who was checking that they were ready to deliver their paper on the hour.

They were at the annual environmental management accounting conference which was being held in a technical university in Helsinki. The café in which they sat to drink morning coffee was a loose aggregate of tables and chairs near a small, hole-in-the-wall counter at the centre of a large, open, brick-wall that gave the roof support at its highest points. Auditoriums and seminar rooms were arranged opposite the wall, in the spaces where the plummeting roof came closer to the ground. The wall and the roof defined a hall that was extravagantly vast for Finland's colder climate and climate change but it was, they had been informed, a showpiece of efficient thermal building-insulation and low-energy atmospheric controls. It looked indeed a very functional hall; clean, comfortable, brightly-lit, warm and austere. Little extra colour had been added to that introduced to the hall by its construction in brick, concrete, steel and wood. The café was an exception. It had bright, primary, celebratory reds and yellows worked into intricate patterns in the table tops and the fabric of the chairs. The effect was to create something like a shimmering, static explosion of colour on the floor of the hall which was close to the centre of a loosely shifting arrangement of chairs and tables and students and academics that moved freely, finding their own points of attraction and order within the limitations of the ample space, the direct walking-routes between portals and the many mingling people.

The conference organiser ticked off their names on her list, spoke a few words and moved on. She was a very busy person.

Grey Beard, QC and the older boy found further talk difficult because of the many lively young people who could all have been talking at once. This was in spite of futuristic sound proofing baffles hanging from exposed roofing spars.

"We have it here, in this very hall," shouted the older boy. "This is what we've got. We have order forming out of the chaos of a crowd."

QC had Morality

They gave a smooth presentation of their paper but it merited only a single question from a small audience. "It was as ever," thought the older boy to console himself, "it's the people you meet outside the formal conference that make them worthwhile." The three friends had their buffet lunch and sat at different tables to be sociable and make new contacts. After lunch, they considered the remaining conference programme, and decided that they could make better use of the afternoon elsewhere.

They walked for ten minutes to a fjord on which water fowl swam. "They are Steller's Eider," said the older boy, who took an interest in natural life. "The Eskimos call them 'the bird who sits on the camp-fire'." The sun was shining. The only other thing they found along the grassy shore was a small car-park with a kiosk.

They took a taxi to Helsinki. The taxi dropped them at a large coffee, cake and bread store in a side street in sight of the tramway. They entered and ordered two coffees and hot water in a glass for QC.

"Do you want to be first to deal with the question?" Grey Beard asked QC. "Yes. It's okay," she answered.

She told them that she had been thinking about all that had been said over the years. She had several issues. She had notes in two copies and she gave one to each of Grey Beard and the older boy.

From China

"I have first what comes from my being Chinese," she began. "This is first supporting you with Tian Xia, all under heaven. This is supporting the connected and integrated metaphysics of the Primal episteme."

She then explained why she considered the Yin Yang motif to be a good representation of the Primal episteme's dynamic process of being and becoming: "But this is a paradox. The Dao is the Way. It is to be followed and not to be followed. To follow the Way is to give up your order, your human and social order, and be one with nature. Man is not of central importance for Daoists. They belong to everything with equality. What man knows gets in the way of the Way! The Primal episteme goes nowhere with the Dao."

Before either Grey Beard or the older boy were able to collect their thoughts and respond, she continued: "But this is the mystery and magic of the Yin Yang. It is even itself denying and becoming. It's how we must be giving. Confucius knew this. It is those who follow Confucius who have made ethics with Dao."

Grey Beard and the older boy looked to QC's notes for help in understanding her words. She had given them a copy of the Yin Yang motif and they reflected on its representation of the interpenetration and mutually self-creating interdependence of opposites. "It's not a joke that the topmost ethical mountain pinnacle high-point for Confucians is the total denying of all mankind's ordering and knowledge and totally the becoming one with nature, the one with the mystery process of constant letting go of all you have been knowing and becoming something other in nature." Grey Beard and the older boy sat back and sipped coffee.

"Do not look so worried," QC assured them. "It's been going on for long time. For all of nature world is being and becoming restless in moments and centuries and much longer. You must trust. Ancient trust from China"

"It is the Confucians who try to stop processes of changing with best possible following way derived from human ordering," she continued. "It is Confucians who seek clinging to permanent things within all of everything changing. This opposing is profoundly deep state of man's knowing being with not wanting the fear of becoming." She asked them to read a passage in the notes she had given them.

Chuang Tzu, an ancient Taoist, sang and drummed with seeming joy when his wife died. His friend, the Confucian logician Hui Tzu "... reprimanded him: 'You live with someone, she brings up your children and grows old. And then when she dies, you don't weep! Surely that's going far enough, but to drum on a bowl and sing is going too far!' Chuang Tzu replied that the changes which brought her to life and have now taken her away are like the sequences of the four seasons. 'She will sleep peacefully in the Great Abode.'" (Dawson, 2005, p. 97).

QC added: "The Great Abode is the Dao. It existed before Heaven and Earth. It is natural process being and becoming. It is complicated and you study it for life and do not know it fully. It is mystery. The emperors of China had to know this. They needed a mandate from heaven to legitimize their ruling. If they were not good and just, then the mandate would be withdrawn."

"We had something similar in Europe," said Grey Beard. "It was the Divine Right of Kings. It said that Kings got their right to rule from God. This placed Kings above ordinary mortals. It was effectively a mandate for Kings to do what they wanted, good or bad. It took centuries and many deaths to get rid of that notion and to have power better distributed. We do not want to go back to those days."

"It's not same!" QC responded abruptly. "Not at all same. This is the big tip. Dao is mystery. It needs giving of self to live by mystery. In the West, Kings claimed access to God and all knowledge. Those Kings became small and infallible, but the Chinese emperors were reaching for something much bigger, something they and the empire knew they could not ever have. They had to try to be Harmonious as a universe beyond opposites, beyond good and evil. You tell me Nietzsche knew this. To know the Dao is to know that good creates evil." She placed her finger on Grey Beard's copy of her notes. She wore blue nail varnish. The two men read the quotation lying at her finger tip.

"The whole world recognizes the beautiful as the beautiful, yet this is only the ugly"

"the whole world recognises the good as the good, yet this is only the bad"

"Thus Something and Nothing produce each other"

. . . .

"Therefore the sage keeps to the deed that consists in taking no action and practices"

"the teaching that uses no words"

"The myriad creatures rise from it yet it claims no authority;"

Lao Tzu.

Grey Beard and the older boy were impressed, but uncomfortable with QC's arguments. "If we think this way," said the older boy, "the Primal episteme is of little use. If it is like the Dao, it creates evil as well as good and then it cannot be relied on to guide human action."

QC never became angry. She straightened her back and placed both her hands on the table. She assumed a stiffly formal, but calm repose. "Dao has nothing to do with man-made good and evil," she explained very slowly. "Foucault said the same. Foucault said that the Modern episteme had no morality. As soon as it tried good, it made evil. This is because Modern episteme is like the divine right of Western Kings. Modern episteme is a usurper. It puts Modern knowledge on the throne. You have not got rid of that notion at all. It's still so incomplete."

"Epistemological man," enquired the older boy, "took the Western throne and inherited the divine Right of Kings?"

Grey Beard asked: "How does the Dao make morality complete?"

"Yes, it is a man," said QC with emphasis. "A small man, knowing too much and too little. He needs to be much bigger. The Dao takes away the smallness."

After a few moments the older boy said: "No rational interventions. No imposed rational ordering from man or deity. In nature things come about because of their own intrinsic causal powers. Daoists want to direct their action in accordance with natural processes. Confucians try to derive systems for mankind from nature, but Daoists criticise them for losing sight of the Dao."

"Yes," said QC. "Westerners make a big mistake to lose sight of the Dao. You now try to correct with thermodynamics, chaos, complexity, ecology, Leopold's land ethic, the Primal episteme and much more. But it's all really the going from little "s" self to big "S" self, extended-self. Here. . . " QC pointed with her finger to another quotation in her notes.

> "Heaven and Earth were born with me,
> And the ten thousand things are one with me."
>
> *Chuang Tzu*

The older boy said that the rationalists would just dismiss this. They would use the "naturalistic fallacy." He then explained that the naturalistic fallacy was the mistaken claim that ethical conclusions may be derived from observations of natural facts. It says that you cannot derive human value judgments from observed properties of nature, what 'ought to be' from what 'is'.

Grey Beard interrupted: "Wait a moment." He opened his well-worn brown leather brief case and produced a page of notes. He read the following passage.

> "Here, then, is a kind of pre-established harmony between the course of nature and the succession of our ideas; and though the powers and forces, by which the former is governed, be wholly unknown to us; yet our thoughts and conceptions have still, we find, gone on in the same train with the other works of nature. Custom is that principle, by which this correspondence has been effected; so necessary to the subsistence of our species, and the regulation of our conduct, in every circumstance and every occurrence of human life."

"Who wrote that?" asked Grey Beard. Neither QC nor the older boy ventured an answer. It had Daoist overtones, but it was not Chinese. It linked ethics with nature and harmony, but claimed no knowledge of the actual powers and forces of nature.

"David Hume wrote that," said Grey Beard. "On page 129 of Beachamp's 1999 edition of 'David Hume: an enquiry concerning Human Understanding.' The same David Hume raised the question about causality that Kant tried to answer and thereby initiated the Modern episteme. Ironically, Hume had used the naturalistic fallacy to show to the rationalists that it was not possible to know the world in a strictly rational way. But the rationalists twisted its intention. Instead they used the naturalistic fallacy to show that you cannot rely on observations of nature, so you really do need to rely on a rational foundation."

"Hume lived in the Classical episteme," said the older boy, "when reason and order were applied to a God-given world to create knowledge based on identity, difference, measurement and order. He saw how the rationalists would disappear into their own arguments; a foreshadow of what Foucault was to refer to as 'epistemological man'."

"What indeed do you trust?" asked Grey Beard thoughtfully. He continued: "But we need to move on. I see another issue with Chinese thinking and its contradictions. The Daoists were at one with all things, in a world of equals. But ancient Chinese society was not like that. There were huge disparities of wealth."

"The ancients believed in moral equality for all," said QC without hesitation. "Confucians, like the Daoists, believed that all men were equal by nature and that everyone had infinite potential. But Confucians were Confucians and they wanted to direct human empire. So Confucians made a point of difference about men. Some laboured better with their bodies and some with their minds. Nature is not the same everywhere, they said. The ancients did not have an aristocracy by birth — they had mandarins. Confucians argued that government needs the highest moral qualities and that everymen had potential for moral leadership. That is why there were so many revolutions in ancient China since anyone has potential to receive a mandate from heaven and to be emperor. But a revolution is only needed if man could not pass exams. Anyone could take exams and become a mandarin and govern China. Confucius accepted and taught anyone — rich or poor. Sages were the same as people of the masses. Some ancients try very hard for equality. They had no patrimonial aristocracy. Inequality destroys Tian Xia — the harmony of all under heaven."

The older boy said: "That kind of education system is rare in modern societies."

"It is not a **modern** education system," retorted QC. "It is an ancient Chinese, Confucian, ethical, governmental, trying-to-be-egalitarian, yes. But you still miss point. It is also Daoist. The Confucian education, their man-made ordering was trying to emulate the Dao. The highest, most Confucian, ideal was to attain heavenly knowledge of Dao. It is in the Yin Yang, the opposites, the man-made ordering and natural, being and becoming."

The men did not respond, so QC showed them two quotations from Confucius, the Master:

> "The Master said, 'Without recognising the ordinances of Heaven, it is impossible to be a superior man.'"
>
> 3.a Yao Yueh; and
>
> "The Master said, 'A man can enlarge the principles he follows; those principles do not enlarge the man'"
>
> 27 Wei Ling Kung.

"Do you recognise the dynamic opposites?" she asked. "The superior man may enlarge principles, but himself is being more than principles by seeking to know the Heavenly Dao?"

The men still did not respond, so QC continued: "Why do you think the mandarins liked landscapes and nature painting so much?" She anticipated no answer. "It is because the mandarins, when hard at work in government offices, wanted to be one with nature. An ancient Chinese landscape is not a particular place; it is all places known in the artist's mind put on paper to become real Dao in creative moment, the spontaneous brushstroke is Dao becoming through man's hand. The landscape is the Dao made visible in art. In his own imagination, a mandarin can wander through its valleys and mountains and rivers. This is where the mandarin refreshes his morality. In this way the mandarins are always looking both ways from local specific government actions and places to natural Dao in action everywhere, in everything."

Just in case the men still did not understand, she added: "Ancient Chinese art has other profoundly important aspects as well. In Chinese writing the ancients thought that they were representing beautiful nature. Each stroke was said to have the living energy of Dao.

Landscape painting grew from calligraphy. So, as they were writing words and ideas, the ancient mandarins were becoming one with their work and Dao. It is as you say 'ethics and aesthetics are one.' "

"Wittgenstein said that," observed the older boy. "Time for coffee?"

From Religion

With two more coffees, but no more hot water, the three of them decided to move on. They shared some other notes between them whilst they drank.

QC had one more point to make. "These are some other notes," she said. "They are about what seems to have been lacking in the western attitude. They do not have the two ways of being. It changes everything."

She reminded them that traditional western economics was thought to have its roots in nature. She drew their attention to the fact that both Adam Smith's 1759 book *Theory of Moral Sentiments* and his 1776 *The Wealth of Nations* are based on the principles of natural law. These books, she said, underpin Modern western economics. "This is the same foundation as Dao and the Primal episteme. All are based on nature."

"But our knowledge of nature has changed with the new discoveries of science," interjected the older boy.

"But not our use of our knowledge of the Dao," QC replied. "It's all about if you can live outside yourself. This is the subject of the best of religion. It is being able to give life to the little self every day until you grow big. The Buddhists start with no little self." She pointed to her notes.

Buddhist economics in the West

See Schumacher's 1973 book "Small is Beautiful" and www.smallisbeautiful.org for Buddhism economics. A Buddhist sees that the function of work is to:

(i) give man a chance to use and develop his faculties
(ii) enable him to overcome his ego-centeredness by joining with other people in a common task
(iii) bring forth the goods and services needed for a becoming existence.

Intrinsic Sustainable Development

"You see how well it fits the Primal," she said. "But this is religion of going beyond the little self. Western religions make or reinforce the little self. They make meek megalomaniacs. They pretend to bow down, but they want to possess the world. They say great things and then become small selves in so many words and rituals. Brother Rast is a Catholic Buddhist, much more than a little self. You can use him maybe. I think it is nice and Primal." QC turned to the last page of her notes.

The Practice of Grateful Living as Global Ethic

Grateful living is a universal ethic capable of ushering us peacefully into a new era in which we must share the world's resources fairly and conserve the environment for future generations.

Imagine an economy based not on scarcity, but on sufficiency — in other words, a realistic economy, for scarcity is an illusion. Imagine an economy designed to promote not un-checked growth, but a steady state of wellbeing — in other words, a healthy economy, for unchecked growth is a disease, also known as cancer. Imagine an economy measured not in quantitative but in qualitative terms — in other words, a bountiful economy, freed from the slavery of solely purpose-driven work by meaningful play in arts and sports, and all forms of leisure.

http://www.gratefulness.org

Grey Beard had Typologies

For lunch they had Smörgåsbord selected from a wide, brightly-lit, glass-covered display that ran beneath the counter in the bread and cake shop. They each had a different-looking kind of Smörgåsbord, but prawns, salad and sliced egg were common to all.

The older boy thanked QC for her contribution. "I think you have tackled the hardest part," he said to her. "It is the basic attitude we have to ourselves and to the world and to the way we think the world works that determines the details of our daily lives."

Grey Beard also gave thanks: "It's a very good contribution indeed to know that a major three thousand-year-old civilisation had something supportive of the Primal episteme. I fear it may be a hard thing to propose in the West. People are used to their Gods ordering the world for them. The fact that nature can do it on her own goes against centuries of European beliefs, science and thought. I myself have little problem with a particle exchange universe creating the lived world with autopoiesis and thermodynamic processes, but this may be too impersonal and hard to understand for some."

"Then let's keep it simple," the older boy responded. "We need only to say that we are part of an intrinsically active and self-creating nature. Isn't that enough?"

It was far too soon to answer such a question — so nobody tried. Instead Grey Beard opened his scuffed leather case, took out a sheath of paper and laid it in the space that QC had made on the table by stacking empty plates. "Thank you," he said to QC. "I have tried to make a comparison of business in the Modern and Primal epistemes." They studied his typologies of Modern and Primal businesses.

After some minutes, the older boy asked of Grey Beard: "It looks good, but you need to help us with some of these comparisons."

Grey Beard produced notes to accompany his table of comparisons. "I used as few principles as possible to develop my ideas for Primal business," he explained, "just an appreciation of connections, and the capacity for intrinsic adaptation or self-creation. From these, the significance of the whole and the two-way look follows logically, as does uncertainty and its necessarily historic context."

"And the new science, did you use much of that, of chaos and complexity?" asked the older boy.

"Not specifically," answered Grey Beard, "I understand how the new science underpins the Primal episteme, but I lack the skill to apply it. I think you can use the Primal to provide new insights. It is a fundamentally different way of being in the world. Events may have individual, local, short-term lives, but they are still part of bigger, longer-term human and natural processes. You need to think on several levels at once. One single reduced perspective is no longer

284   *Intrinsic Sustainable Development*

Table 1.   Comparative Typologies of Modern and Primal Businesses.

Aspect	Modern Business	Primal Business
Philosophical Foundation	Idealistic, logical belief systems.	Pragmatic, empirical Realism.
Values derived from	Market transaction costs.	Human aesthetic and experiential exchanges.
Ethics based on	Rules, directives and laws.	Aesthetic appreciation of a diverse and complex world.
Business Units	Discrete, closed, economically organic, entities.	Integrated, open, autopoietic, nodes.
	Analytic, deterministic, constructions.	Representational, unpredictable, condensates.
Assets Are	Owned and represented as financial capital.	Loaned and represented as financial, knowledge, ecological, and social capital etc.
Finance Sources	Tending to high-geared, external.	Tending to low-geared, internal.
Goals	Progressive, economic maximisation.	Adaptive, social, ecological & economic optimisation.
	Maximise financial gain in shortest times.	Enhance and maintain business processes over longest possible time.
	Having More	**Being More**
Management Attitudes	Order is progressive and has to be imposed on a malleable world and others must learn this.	Order is adaptive and has to be observed in participations in the world and managers and others may learn from this.
	A successful business is and end in itself.	A successful business is a tool.
	Freedom is conformity to democratic and economic forces.	Freedom is discovery and change.
Management Styles	Managers seek to control.	Managers seek to be mindful & influential.
	Standardising & reductionist.	Diversifying & holistic.
	Formal recognition of few relations results in specialised gigantism.	Formal recognition of many complex relations results in overall balance.

(Continued)

Table 1. (*Continued*)

Marketing	Demand creation. Sells products and services. Causes and utilises status anxiety.	Relationship creation. Invites participation in life sustaining processes. Causes and utilises self-realisation and fulfillment.
Efficiency	Anthropocentric and short-term.	Bio-centric and short- to long-term.

enough, no matter how *complete* it may seem. Many things need to change. We cannot know all in advance."

"Yes, I agree," said the older boy. "The way the Primal weaves between local, contextual specificities and universals will seem strange to Modern minds. But this is how lived reality is. It is fleeting and delicate and always potentially world-changing. To some, there will be far less to hang on to from now on. You definitely need the bigger self; it is a survival imperative."

"I need some fresh air," said Grey Beard. "Please see if you have any questions about the table. But bear in mind that these comparisons raise as many questions as answers. Some of us are just starting out on this Primal journey." He handed them copies of his notes and left.

Notes to Comparison of Modern and Primal Business Typologies

Philosophical Foundations

Modern business is dominated by the "logical belief systems" of traditional economics: "The free market, conceived as being a pristine engine, is as much a fiction as a Euclidean triangle." (Ellis, 1970, p. 165). These constructions may be real, but they do not exist.

By "empirical realism," I mean that ordinary things, the material things around us, do indeed exist independent of our thoughts. It may be crude, but it is a sufficient and necessary starting point for Primal business.

Intrinsic Sustainable Development

The Harvard socio-biologist Edward O. Wilson writes: "The time has come for economists and business leaders, so haughtily pride themselves as masters of the real world, to acknowledge the existence of the real real world." (Wilson, 1998, p. 326).

Values

Shareholder values need to be aligned with market values and those in turn with the social values of a population educating, experiencing and valuing rich human, ecological and biosphere relations.

It is "Time to measure what we treasure." We need to be "Measuring true wealth and the well-being of nations beyond GDP" (EC, 2009).

Ethics

A Primal business ethical system has to be learned on the job. As Arie de Geus points out:

"1. The company is a living being.

2. The decisions for action made by this living being result from a learning process." (Geus, 2002, p. 201)

Business Units

Bear in mind that "to contract" also means "to shrink" and that we now have a Global Compact (UN, 2010) for Primal business.

The realities that we derive for Primal business units should be as close as possible to what we know of the interventions that they cause. In this regard, Primal business units — like Primal people — need to synthesise as well as analyse.

Assets

The recognition of assets employed in a Primal business needs to be more honest — not just reduced to those of a financial owner. This sort of small-self-serving independence is a Modern fantasy. Business assets should accurately represent their true and transient dependencies.

Sources of Finance

The dominant influence of the abstract, short-termism of financial markets needs to be removed by making more use of retained earnings. It may take more time for a business to grow, but time is less of a scarce resource — or less immediate — in a Primal episteme. Businesses that are home-grown with their own earnings will be more resilient.

Goals

Primal businesses are ecological entities in the first instance. They need to redesign their goals: "'Waste equals food' — the first principle of the Next Industrial Revolution." (McDonough and Braungart, 1998.)

Management Attitudes

"We have to develop a sense of connectedness, a sense of working together as part of a system, where each part of the system is affecting and being affected by the others." (Senge, 1998, p. 129)

"Thus our hope is that managers and management scholars alike will begin the diligent search that is necessary if humankind is to find the elusive balance between the economy and the ecosystem. The success of this search, we believe, rests on the willingness to include the greater ecosystem into business research and strategic decisions." (Stead and Stead, 1992, pp. 190–191).

> "The world is too much with us; late and soon,
> Getting and spending, we lay waste our powers;
> Little we see in Nature that is ours;
> We have given our hearts away, a sordid boon!"
> *William Wordsworth 1802.*

Management Styles

Primal business management requires a shift from convergent to divergent thinking; from a tendency to seek solutions to perceived, closed problems to a mindfulness of learning-in-practice in open-ended situations.

Intrinsic Sustainable Development

"In this new world, you and I make it up as we go along, not because we lack expertise or planning skills, but because that is the nature of reality." (Wheatley, 1994, p. 151).

"Adaptive management seeks to aggressively use management intervention as a tool to strategically probe the functioning of an ecosystem. Interventions are designed to test key hypotheses about the functioning of the ecosystem. This approach is very different from a typical management approach of 'informed trial-and-error' which uses the best available knowledge to generate a risk-averse, 'best guess' management strategy, which is then changed as new information modifies the 'best guess'." (Resalliance, 2010).

The approaches taken by LAMPE researchers may provide a focussed way forward for Primal business managers. LAMPE stands for Leadership, Authority, Management, Power, and Environments and it should give us organisations that are well integrated and coherent in their operations (Mackenzie, 2006).

Most importantly management education needs to move from traditional styles to teaching managers how to deal with complexity. New methods need to be developed (Axley and McMahon, 2006).

Marketing

Botton writes: "A car advertisement will, for example, be careful to ignore aspects of our psychology and the overall process of ownership that could spoil, or at least mitigate, our joy at coming to posses a featured vehicle... The most elegant and accomplished of vehicles cannot bring us a fraction of the satisfaction of a relationship..." (Botton, 2005, pp. 205–208).

The American Psychological Association has only recently begun to study materialism and consumerism:

"... experiences that undermine the satisfaction of psychological needs can cause individuals to orient towards materialism..." (Kasser et al. 2005, p. 13);

"... [advertisements] are often constructed to engender upward social comparisons that make viewers feel unconformably inferior." (*ibid.*, p. 17); and

> "Ads do far more than sell products. Commercials are having a substantial negative influence on child develop-ment and adult identity..." (Kanner and Soule, 2005, p. 57).
>
> Just for QC, here is one of her fellow countrymen work-ing on a new kind of marketing for sustainable devel-opment and complexity. The paper has the foundation for a Self-Organization Marketing Channel sensitised to changing consumer demands. (Wang, 2008).

Grey Beard had not immediately returned to their table. He had found a display of leaflets about visitor attractions in Helsinki. He returned with a leaflet about the sea fortress of Suomenlinna. "It was built in the eighteenth century to guard the fleet," he said. "It is now a UNESCO World Heritage. I think we should pay a visit."

They studied the map of the fortress and its location. They needed to take a ferry from a dock not far from their present location, across the tramlines at the seaward end of Skatuddskajen.

Neither QC nor the older boy had questions about the compara-tive table. They prepared to leave the food store.

The older boy said: "You have not seen what I have brought you. Let me leave these with you. I think they are clear enough. You can look at them later." He gave each of QC and Grey Beard a plastic A4 sleeve containing several sheets of paper. They set off to take the 14.10 Suomenlinna ferry.

The Older Boy had Diagrams

In the plastic sleeves that now lay inside the cases of QC and Grey Beard were a series of diagrams and notes. They had been taken directly from teaching material that the older boy had used to illus-trate the development of the Primal episteme and its consequences to management and accounting undergraduates.

In Figure 1 the older boy had wanted to show something of "Worlds in Transition." He used this diagram to provide a basis for discussions. It was based on Venn diagrams in which the area occupied by an item was representative of the importance of that item.

290   *Intrinsic Sustainable Development*

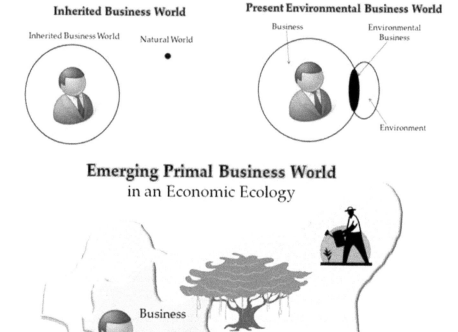

Fig. 1.   Worlds in Transition

The first part of Figure 1 shows the Inherited Business World in which an important, white business<u>man</u> (for the older boy also intended to draw attention to the dominance of males in establishing traditional business practice) in a large, hence important, self-made area. The Natural World is located at a distance — quite separate from the Inherited Business world. The area of the traditional business world has a regular, formal shape to represent a little of its assumed certainty and control.

Chapter 11 — Primal Business   **291**

The second part of Figure 1 shows the Business and Environment World in which we currently live. The Natural World has here grown in importance but it has been transformed into the Environment. It overlaps the Business World in the small oval of environmental economics and business but much of the Inherited Business World remains unaffected.

The third part of Figure 1 shows the older boy's vision of the emerging world of Primal Business in an Economic Ecology. Here, the Business World has been embedded in the ecosystem and the areas defined by all worlds have become uncertain and irregular. In this part, the older boy introduced non-whites and females to represent increasing diversity of participants and the end of the dominance of the white businessman.

In Figure 2 the older boy represented something of the implications of the Primal episteme for companies. The "Bulldozer" company image captures the Modern episteme's forceful, invasive

Move from: **"BULLDOZER COMPANIES"** in Modern episteme

- Passive Nature Attitude
- Deterministic/Predictable
- Independent
- Forcing a way forward

Move to: **"DINGHY COMPANIES"** in Primal episteme

- Active Nature Attitude
- Indeterminate/Unpredictable
- Interdependent
- Sensing a way forward

Fig. 2.   Some Behavioural Implications for Companies

institutional growth. Since such companies have defined their origins in their own terms, they cannot be anything else. Leaders, the "drivers," of such companies need to learn only how the company works, its "mechanics." Then they are obliged to develop the company by growing it and moving it forward as the distinct and separate entity that it is. In effect, this kind of management forces an understanding of companies and their roles onto the world. Much power is required so that this forceful act can overcome any social, environmental or ecological resistance as well as constraints on company growth.

Hence the desired direction in which the "Bulldozer" company heads is determined by the internal functions of the company itself. This is still the standard model in existing Modern business as far as you may judge from the content of books in mainstream management schools, where businesses appear to operate in social and ecological vacuums.

In contrast, the "Dinghy" company is vulnerable and far out at sea; this is a company operating in the Primal episteme. In this image, the fate of the company is uncertain and dependent on factors external to the company (as winds, tides, currents and weather in the illustration). To direct this kind of company, knowledge of its constitution and capabilities is certainly essential; but just as essential are the diverse crafts, skills, knowledge and needs that staff possesses or may acquire for harnessing multi-sourced extrinsic energy and materials together with knowledge and experience of the external systems and forces that contribute to the being and becoming of the company. The desired direction in which the "Dinghy" company then heads is hence to be determined by collective personal, social, and ecological knowledge, needs, capabilities and potentials in addition to the company's own. In this way, the reality that "Dinghy" companies create seeks to be as close as possible to what is known of the ways the company intervenes in existence; it is no longer the imposition of a company-made reality onto different worlds.

Because of the nature of complex relations, there will be times of "fair sailing," stable conditions, for "Dinghy" companies, where events seem to be relatively certain. In some companies there may consequentially be a tendency to allow attention to shift towards the optimisation of company functions alone, as if it were some kind of discrete entity. However, a Primal episteme awareness of the ordering processes of complex relations should instil a cautious appreciation of the potential for the degree of uncertainty to tend towards infinity at systemic bifurcation points. So company "goals" are necessarily always local and temporary approximations, *strange attractors*. Practical management steps to deal with this situation have already been provided by the "The Natural Step" and they are:

Step 1: Introduce the science and systems concepts underpinning The Natural Step.

Step 2: Apply The Natural Step approach to a tangible project or activity.

Step 3: Reflect on the understanding of the ideas and situations.

Step 4: Generate general theories and analyse ideas.

Step 5: Test concepts in new situations or practical applications.

(Natural Step, 2010)

In Figure 3 the older boy presents an outline of a Primal business information flow or accounting system. This system had been designed to provide information about the performance of a company within its social, environmental and ecological context for use by managers in day-to-day control as well as for periodic reporting of company performance to others. To avoid damaging abstractions and to keep company realties as close as possible to existence, resources and energy transfers — not money — were chosen as the basic unit of exchange (Birkin, 2000).

This Primal business accounting system is compatible with System of integrated Environmental and Economic Accounts (SEEA) concepts. Key criteria include *inter alia* physical-flow accounting, environmental protection, resource management and physical and economic assets accounting (SEEA, 2003). It also serves Eco-Management Accounting (EMA) (Orbach and Liedtke, 1998) as well as the International Standards Organizations' (ISO) emerging "Material Flow Accounting" system standard, ISO 14051.

Intrinsic Sustainable Development

The ISIS Concept

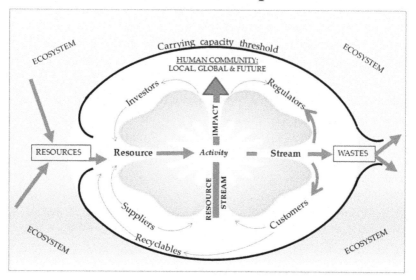

Fig. 3.   Cloverleaf Information Flows

The Primal business accounting system has the functionally accurate name of "Intrinsically Sustainability Implementation System" or "ISIS" for short, after the Egyptian Goddess of healing. This captures something of both the creative antiquity of accounting in the Primal episteme as well as Primal business goals. However, because of the outline of the stakeholder information flows in the ISIS figure, it has been nick named "Cloverleaf."

ISIS has four kinds of information: Resource Flow, Resource Flow Impact, Stakeholder Participation and Ecological Resilience. These are described below.

Resource Flow

This is an entity's foundational information stream. It goes from left to right in Figure 3. It is the material and energy flows driven and caused by an enterprise and it proceeds from sources and suppliers, to process and products and then on to waste and customers' flows.

Information for this flow may be obtained from suppliers, delivery notes, meters, progress job-cards, waste records, customer-deliveries and so on.

Resource Flow Impact

This crosses the figure from bottom to top in Figure 3. It carries information about the impacts that the Resource Flow has on societies, the environment and ecosystems. Resource Flow Impact information has to be sourced from many locations internal and external to an entity such as environmental management systems, environmental protection agencies and Life Cycle Assessments. This information has a cradle-to-grave approach dealing with significant functions such as material sourcing and inward transportation, distribution, processes, customer-use and product final re-use or disposal.

Stakeholder Participation

Principal stakeholders information flows outline the "Cloverleaf" in Figure 3. Less well defined, but no less important, stakeholders are represented in the area of the figure labelled "Human Community: Local, Global and Future." In addition to suppliers, investors, employees, regulators and customers that are represented in the principal stakeholder information flows, there are many other kinds of stakeholders, some of whom may be organised or relatively easily accessed for information. These include such as other enterprises, trade associations, local communities, customers or user groups, Non-Government Organizations like Greenpeace and Friends of the Earth, and local authorities. Other stakeholders will be indistinct or difficult to access for information, such as distant, future or global communities. The quality, accuracy and relevance of information acquired from these diverse stakeholder groups will vary. But it all does support an essential and distinguishing function of ISIS, namely that of *necessary* stakeholder participation.

Intrinsic Sustainable Development

Ecological Resilience

This is represented in Figure 3 by the thick black line between the outer, containing ecosystem and the inner human community. Resilience is a measure of the capacity for systems to adapt and change. Information for this flow will typically be obtained from sources external to the entity. They will include consultancies, local authorities, universities, environment protection agencies, NGOs, and various regional, national and global data banks and surveys such as that provided by the European Forestry Information System.

It is within this flow of information that shareholder and natural values may be most clearly linked. For example, the purpose of the "Natural Value Initiative" is to raise company awareness of their dependence on biodiversity and ecosystem services (Fauna & Flora International and UNEP, 2010); ecological footprint analyses will be useful in this way (Global Footprint 2010).

Useful for management and development, the ISIS matrix is illustrated in Figure 4. This contains benchmarks and a Balanced Scorecard Approach — the working heart of ISIS. The benchmarks are derived from a periodic, iterative consultative process which may be conducted either by specific entities or by associations. With time, significant stakeholders may participate in the development of the benchmarks which will hence be state-of-the-art (at least for that sector or locality) but which will also need to be motivational, practical and cost-efficient. Suggestions for benchmarks have been added to the matrix for illustration purposes.

Figure 5 is a simplified graphic representation of an entity's ISIS Matrix benchmark assessment. The level of attainment for the entity is recorded in each of the four columns of the management and development matrix in Figure 4; these levels of performance are then transcribed to the graph. The graph may be used for purposes of reporting, accountability, management and policy decision support, performance evaluation and comparisons between enterprises and industrial sectors.

Chapter 11 — Primal Business
297

Resource Flow	Resource Flow Impact	Stakeholder Participation	Ecosystem Resilience
# Full Circular Flow Management	# No Adverse Social or Ecological Impacts	# 100% Stakeholder Support	# Interactions wuth Flourishing Ecosystems
# Verification by Competent Body	# Third Party Verification		
# Product and Process Redesigned for Eco-efficiency	# Actively Minimising All Impacts	# Transparent Stakeholder Dialogues	# Use of Biomimicry Techniques
	# Use of Industrial Ecology Techniques		
# Recyling & Reuse	# Use of Environmental Performance Indicators	# Some Stakeholder Reporting	# Ecological Conservation Activities
	# High use of renewables		# Habitat Restorations
# High level of Economic Efficiency	# Use of Economic Performance Indicators	# Active Consideration of Stakeholders	# Avoidance of Ecosystem Damage
# Short Linear Flow Management	# No Impact Records	# No Stakeholder Communications	# No Knowledge of Ecosystem Interactions

(Left margin vertical labels: SUSTAINABLE / DEVELOPMENT; + and −)

Fig. 4.   The ISIS Matrix or Balanced Scorecard

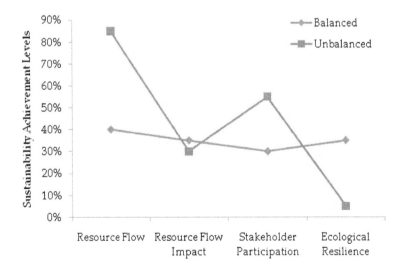

Fig. 5.   The ISIS Graph

The graph promotes a balanced approach to development. A flat enterprise profile represents a high degree of balance and integration between each complex information flow. Peaks and troughs on the graph indicate loss of balance and hence of meaning. For example, a high level of stakeholder support looses meaning without a corresponding level of resource flow or ecological resilience information. In this situation, stakeholders may be supportive and in agreement with an entity's decisions, but their support actually means very little, because it is not well informed.

ISIS is an interactive, dynamic, and experiential framework for learning. It also provides management with a tool for decision-making and control and external stakeholders with reports and focussed opportunities for their participation when re-creating the framework.

Whilst each formulation of the management and development matrix ought to be the best possible at any given time, it is by no means an end in itself. Each formulation should meet immediate needs as far as possible, but it is expected to change as circumstances change. Any particular formulation of ISIS will, in time, give rise to dissent and discrepancies as worlds evolve; this is the basis of critique from which new formulations may be generated.

ISIS changes, and this creates new orders and new business opportunities. Because of the strong links to specific places, people and times, ISIS will tend to be local, which is reinforced by the sustainable business entrepreneur's appreciation of multiple economic, social, environmental and ecological benefits. After all: "Entrepreneurship is about order-creation, not equilibrium. It is time to put more emphasis on helping entrepreneurs, at the initial start-up phase, deal with adaptive tensions, critical values, phase transitions, and coevolving causalities." (McKelvey 2004, p. 337).

Since it can be argued that those companies that attain higher assessments levels in the ISIS Matrix and Graph are less damaging, the taxes that they pay should be lower: less sustainable companies pay more tax. The overall tax burden does not need to change, nor does the cost of the tax system need to increase. Starting from an equal distribution of tax rates, it would be up to the companies, or their trade associations, to prove the worth of the ISIS Matrix used, as well as the level of their attainment according to, say, a simple ranking of low, average, and high sustainable development.

Finally, distant etymological roots of the word "wealth" provide a more meaningful, overall objective. Once in the history of western cultures, "wealth", "health", "heal", "holy" and "holistic" were all contained in a single word, the Germanic "heilig." Heilig, as an overriding strange attractor, will provide a focus for business activities that has the potential to unite business with far-reaching awareness and sensitivity in an integrated human and natural world. It is also compatible with a comprehensive optimizing — not partial maximising — view of Primal Business performance.

> "Ignorance is ignorance; no right to believe in anything can be derived from it."
> *Sigmund Freud in "The Future of an Illusion" (1927).*

Discussed on Suomenlinna: The Import

The trio of international researchers crossed Helsinki harbour in the pouring rain. The rain fell so hard that they could not see beyond the decks of the ferry itself. QC and Grey Beard studied and thought about the older boy's diagrams for the duration of the trip.

As the ferry drew alongside Suomenlinna, the clouds parted and brilliant sunlight beamed down on the island causing steam to rise from the tarred road. They took a few hours off from work and made the most of the sunshine to explore Suomenlinna's fortifications and museums. Their spirits were high as they reserved themselves a table for that evening at 19.30 in the Walhalla restaurant in one of the old fortified buildings on the island.

By 17.00 they were ready for work. "We have said much about the Primal episteme," argued the older boy, "we now need to think a bit more about what it means."

They sat on the terrace of a restaurant where they had a glorious view of the Baltic Sea. They drank fruit juice and hot water. It was QC who raised the question that was to direct their thoughts that afternoon.

Intrinsic Sustainable Development

"What is Sustainable Development?"

QC had asked. "It seems to be not well stood and always vague."

"Not well *understood*," the older boy corrected. "But you're right. We can't argue that the Primal episteme helps sustainable development if we do not know what sustainable development is."

Grey Beard reached into his case and took out a report on which he had marked several passages. "This is where most people seem to start with sustainable development," he said, pointing to a highlighted passage.

> The most quoted definition of sustainable development is that produced in 1987 by the World Commission on Environment and Development, otherwise known as the Brundtland Commission (after its Chairperson, Gro Harlem Brundtland, then Prime Minister of Norway): "Economic and social development that meets the needs of the current generation without undermining the ability of future generations to meet their own needs."

"I think you might prefer an earlier definition from the World Conservation Strategy," Grey Beard said, as he presented another passage.

> Whilst earlier literature discussed a wide range of issues around the emerging concept of sustainable development, the following statement from the World Conservation Strategy in 1980 appears to be the first actual attempt to define sustainable development: "For development to be sustainable, it must take account of social and ecological factors, as well as economic ones; of the living and non-living resource base; and of the long-term as well as the short-term advantages and disadvantages of alternative action."

The older boy did prefer the ecological considerations in the earlier definition. "The Brundtland definition suffers too much from epistemological man," he said. "That's ancient history now."

"Don't knock it too much," said Grey Beard. "The Brundtland definition paved the way for the Earth Summit in '92 and its raft of actions." Grey Beard told them about the five main actions that had come out of the Earth Summit for he had a good memory: Agenda 21, the Rio Declaration on Environment and Development, the Statement of Principles on Forests, the Framework Convention on Climate Change and the Convention on Biological Diversity.

"Brundtland may have helped with global policy, but she gives little guidance about how sustainable development may be taken into use by people. This lack of guidance allows business-as-usual to remain as it is", said the older boy. "Just as with corporate social responsibility, it presents simplistic alternatives. You should read Fauset's 2006 report on CSR. It's scathing." QC made a note of the reference.

"Primal knowledge reveals the disasters embedded in Brundtland," the older boy continued. "This is not sour grapes. We are simply not doing enough. Have you seen this?" He gave them a copy of the latest State of the Environment Report from the European Environment Agency (EEA 2010). The older boy told them that the report argues that the global demand for resources seriously threatens our economy. We are consuming far more resources than is ecologically stable. A range of global trends will destabilize ecosystems; and much more.

"Stop! Stop!" called Grey Beard. "These are issues, not solutions. Please keep focus. I think you will find this passage more satisfactory." He presented the open page of a book to QC and the older boy. "Look at this," he said as he pointed with a pencil.

> "The principal conditions of a stable society — one that to all intents and purposes can be sustained indefinitely while giving optimum satisfaction to its members — are:
>
> — minimum disruption of ecological processes;
> — maximum conservation of materials and energy — or an economy of stock, rather than flow;
> — population in which recruitment equals loss;
> — social system in which the individual can enjoy, rather than feel restricted by, the first three conditions." (Goldsmith 1972, passage 210).

"Goldsmith was a true ecologist — a follower of the Way," Grey Beard declaimed to QC. "If we were to improve Goldsmith's definition, it would be by emphasising the importance of first-hand experience. The Triple Bottom Line requires us to assess business performance according to social, environmental and economic criteria, but only one of these benefits may be enjoyed first-hand at a distance. Social and environmental benefits have to be enjoyed *in situ*, whereas economic benefits, money, may be enjoyed first-hand anywhere in the world."

"So you would put an end to global trade?" QC asked, remembering China's dependence on exports.

"No, certainly not," Grey Beard answered. "It would have to be less dependent on remote global finance with more control in local hands. But we have said this already when we want companies to become more resilient, embedding more beneficial social and environmental relations in their activities, and growing by retained earnings to affirm their longer-term values — their real values."

"So companies have to stay local?" QC asked suspiciously.

"No again," Grey Beard rejoined generously. "Think more Primally. If a resilient business is established locally, then it has a good strange attractor, a strong Genesis process. This can be replicated. With care, the firm's culture and leadership can be replicated anywhere in the world. It is the interventions of remote financial control that must be avoided; that's all."

"It's all excellent. That's telling us what we need to do," said the older boy. "ISIS can help with much of that."

In spite of Grey Beard's earlier warning, the older boy now continued to talk about disasters. He reminded Grey Beard and QC about anaerobic bacteria. Such bacteria had dominated the earth when the atmosphere had little oxygen. Then, about 2.5 billion years ago, ancient bacteria learned how to use the sun's energy to make sugar, and release oxygen as a by-product. Eventually, this by-product accumulated in the atmosphere to the extent that it poisoned the world-dominating anaerobic bacteria; oxygen is a toxin for them. The bacteria had evolved and poisoned the atmosphere for itself! The anaerobic bacteria started to die out as oxygen levels increased;

but they did not disappear. They had to hide themselves away out of the reach of sunlight, out of the reach of oxygen, down in the deep off-shore muds of seas and oceans and in our guts, for without the anaerobic bacteria in hiding, in our digestive tracts, we would not function.

"We humans are just like those bacteria — poisoning our own air!" he said with gusto.

The older boy was now in his stride. Grey Beard and QC, for their part, were happy to relax and watch the sea and the other tourists. The older boy took the absence of dissent as consent. He told them another story.

"My European Union friend in Brussels," he said, "works on reducing carbon emissions. She told me that the 2020 targets for reducing carbon emissions by 20% by that year may be achieved by *evolution*. But the 2050 targets for zero carbon emissions will require *a revolution!*"

In case his audience was beginning to doze, as they were, the older boy had to increase the drama. "Life on Earth has been developing for 3.5 billion years," he told them as he punched numbers into his calculator. "Modern business activity has been developing for about 200 years. Hence, the fraction of time taken for Modern business activity to threaten the biosphere and its own existence is $200/3{,}500{,}000{,}000^{ths}$ or 0.000000057 of the bio-life-time of this planet."

"If you see life this way," said the older boy, "sustainability increases as reality better reflects existence to the extent that we can better discern threats and opportunities." Business activity, he went on, is immersed in the biosphere just as much as a goldfish in a tank of water. "How on earth did we ever manage to think otherwise?"

Why Intrinsic Sustainable Development?

A cold wind crossed Suomenlinna, drawing attention to the lateness of the hour, the lowness of the weakening sun and impending night. People shivered and fastened loose clothing.

"Time is passing," said QC with all the seriousness that her youthful face could muster. "I have listened all day. What are you trying to say? Are you just being men again? You seem to want to compete all time. You just like to argue. It is you who are too small with the self."

Both Grey Beard and the older boy were taken aback. They did not understand. Was the Chinese woman at their side cross, impatient or just tired? She had been quiet all day, so they had talked to her and she had appeared content just to listen.

"I have heard no single thing from you today that is new," she continued. "I have flown across the world to be with you. You promised me much, but I get little. What will be different with all your talk? What will change? You are just talking."

"Go on," said Grey Beard. "Please go on. Yes, we do talk a lot. That is our job. What is it you want?"

"I want to know what is really going to be different. You think and talk so much and do so little simple and practical."

"Do you think we need some kind of non-intellectual content?"

"No. I know too much about how you say things. I also know how you value experiences of the living world and of other people and their needs, feelings and spirits. No, we do not need more of that. We need much less! We need simple, powerful things to convince people. Not difficult things for experts."

"Do you have a communication problem?" asked the older boy, sarcastically.

"No, you have!" QC answered. "You should tell people, in ways they understand how they will benefit from a new order of knowledge. How they will be able to lead different lives? How their work will be different? How they can come to want different things? Our work is not just for experts or it will be meaninglessly intellectual."

"Is this the ancient Chinese rising in you QC?" Grey Beard asked sincerely. "Is this the Tian Xia, the Yin Yang, Confucius, the Dao?"

"Do not forget the Buddhism," she answered sharply. "It is not the ancient rising. It is happening now. We need to be able to speak as equals. But I do not see this in what you have to offer. Where is your common touch, your respect for all?"

The two men were silenced. They could find no answer for QC in their arguments.

"Where is your love for people?" QC added. "How will you help them live better lives?"

They encouraged her to explain.

"You westerners are so clear about your hearts and minds. You split them so well. This way of splitting is not so clear for us Chinese. We have only one word, *xīn*, for heart-mind. You need to open your minds more for joining your hearts."

Neither man was able to comment.

"How are you going to bring this into the Primal episteme?" she asked with a finality that anticipated no immediate answer.

At a small table on the terrace of Walhalla restaurant on Suomenlinna, the cool wind had been replaced by a calm which the future would reveal to the memories of each of QC, Grey Beard and the older boy as a moment out of time, of stillness, of realisation, of change, of bifurcation. It was as if they were at a pause in their lives' trajectories. All three recognised simultaneously their common bonds and that their old work had somehow finished and new work had started; as at some col, pinnacle or any change of direction that requires the temporary cessation of motion; or, as the older boy was to reflect much later, as if they had been shot high into the sky, had slowed and were momentarily in stasis, waiting for the downward flight to commence.

The sky was clear. The sun was hugging the horizon. The sea was calm.

At length, Grey Beard said: "We are all people." Somehow, this potentially fatuous comment sealed the moment.

"People need to be free. We give them freedom." The pause resumed.

"Here," Grey Beard said, "This quote is from Simone de Beauvoir. It is for you QC. Simone travelled in China. She helped to set women free." QC made no comment as Grey Beard handed her another side of his notes.

> "But it is not solipsistic, since the individual is defined only by his relationship to the world and to other individuals; he exists only by transcending himself, and his freedom can be achieved only through the freedom of

others. He justifies his existence by a movement which, like freedom, springs from his heart but which leads outside of him. This individualism does not lead to the anarchy of personal whim. Man is free; but he finds his law in his very freedom. First, he must assume his freedom and not flee it by a constructive movement: one does not exist without doing something; and also by a negative movement which rejects oppression for oneself and others. In construction, as in rejection, it is a matter of reconquering freedom on the contingent facticity of existence, that is, of taking the given, which, at the start, is there without any reason, as something willed by man." (Beauvoir 1991, p. 156)

Grey Beard explained: "I think this is quite close to a description of life's being and becoming, the concrete, contingent nature of the existence we try to approach, the small self and the extended self. It is a Primal freedom."

"Your freedom is still so many words," QC said. "I think the mystery of Dao and Tian Xia convey this much better. They are simpler, ruled by a mandate from heaven."

"But you've lost that in Modern China," the older boy observed.

"Yes, we have become quite modern," she answered him.

"We need to get over all that," the older boy said. "We are all Primal now."

"Again more words! What does that really mean?" QC asked.

"It means our identity, work, fulfilment, freedom and fate are inseparable from creative natural processes. It means that we are all committed to develop according to who we are and always have been. It means that the Modern episteme and its institutions have now become restrictive and problematic."

Table Talk

They took a walk around the island to clear the air. They spoke little. They were now alone in the fortress. The day-tourists had returned to the mainland and the late evening diners had yet to arrive.

At dinner Grey Beard ordered a bottle of wine, a bottle of Barón de Barbón Rioja 2008. They skipped starters and chose fish for their main course.

"I'm sorry for choosing red," Grey Beard apologised. "I like Rioja." As it was, they drank mainly water with the meal and finished the wine in the lounge in front of an open wood fire. The clear skies had brought a chill to the night.

"Have we finished?" Grey Beard asked after a period of casual chat. "Our work does seem incomplete to me. Should we not give more practical guidance for living and working in a Primal episteme as QC wants?"

"We've done enough," responded the older boy. "We've created nothing new. We've developed no new procedures, given no new ideas, proposed no new theories. We're just reporters. We've said how it is in the world right now and now it is the turn of others."

"We came up with a few new names," Grey Beard observed.

"More words!" interjected QC.

"But, how, for example, can the Primal episteme help the economy?" Grey Beard persisted.

"Finish your wine," the older boy instructed. "You are still too Modern. You should be asking 'How can economics help life in the Primal episteme?'"

To QC's annoyance, the two men began to talk in depth again. She found that she could just about tolerate them for the meal had been excellent, as had her overall visit to Finland, and for the most part the company she had kept. The ideas she had encountered had been good. She was happy. She knew the men were happy too. She let them talk. She relaxed and paid a drowsy kind of attention to the occasional idea; she did make a note of two or three references that she thought could be useful.

"This is too much for this late hour," she told them some thirty minutes later as she was falling asleep. "Please let us enjoy more of these moments when we are more awake. Send your thoughts tomorrow, next week, whenever by email to me in Beijing. But please take me back to my hotel or I'm going to fall asleep here and now."

PART IV

CONSEQUENCES

CHAPTER 12 — RESISTANCE & ASSISTANCE

Two weeks later, the older boy was standing on *Grib Goch*, a knife-edged arête that tends in an easterly direction from the summit of Snowdon, the highest point in Wales. It rises over 900 metres to dominate the valley of Llanberis in a mountainous area that was precipitously carved by the Merioneth ice a mere 10,000 years ago. *Grib Goch* can focus and clear the mind, especially in the high winds that he was then experiencing.

The older boy was looking down on the derelict mines that had once chased copper loads deep inside this inhospitable place. It had been said that these loads had been created by God to taunt men for the market price for this bright shining metal had taken the miners to the limits of their technology and human endurance.

He was thinking how the economic theory of "marginal cost" had driven money and men to this cold and forbidding place. Deep within this concept, the world is always fine, rational, and progressive as it tends in an orderly way towards equilibrium with "marginal price". In the mountain air, high above the spoil heaps, ruined buildings and pot-holed tracks, it was obvious that survival always lay outside this theory; the many relationships that work with and against man as he pursues his ideas, and his delusions, lie always outside the tidy, closed concepts of his mind. The limits of his survival are to be reached, surpassed, or absorbed in their ultimate finality, in the stubbornness of existence, face to face with those externalities that endure and invade just as ineluctably as the Merioneth ice sheets had cut though hard, ancient and enduring rock to give new form to these soaring slopes.

On the obverse of the economics of "marginal utility", he was conjecturing, is the human experience of "marginal desperation". In

1805, a tourist had visited this very remote area and had reported seeing an old man of seventy daily employed with a couple of horses to guide sledges laden with six hundredweight of ore down the mountain. For so many, the Industrial Revolution had been a *Danse Macabre* of unreachable aspiration and chronic desperation bringing both economic wealth and unimaginable suffering in unequal shares to the living world. For many, the suffering continues.

But no matter how much *Grib Goch* may appear solid and enduring to a brief human glance, it will be removed in the fullness of time. It is an Earth feature, a part of the ancient Caledonian mountain chain that was there before the planet spilt open to make way for the Atlantic Ocean or braced itself for the thundering feet of the Age of the Dinosaurs. We now know much more about how the world works, about how mountains have been, and are being, made and worn down by straightforward, commonplace geophysical and metrological processes. We know how fragments of this once grand, unified mountain chain are now found scattered across Norway, Greenland, Scotland, Newfoundland, Nova Scotia, the Appalachians and Wales.

Attitude

The following Monday morning in his home office with the weekend's walking experiences fresh in his mind, the older boy felt as if he were still astride worlds. There was no doubt that indicators of another reality were waiting in his email editor where several messages from Grey Beard and QC awaited his attention; these messages would lead him to that epistemic elevation where he could look down from the Primal episteme on the inadequacies of the Modern episteme and its institutions. But that was not the source of his feeling.

It was his sense of existence that elevated him. He was as happy and as high-spirited as mountains allow.

His fresh memory, his open-greedy-minded, first-hand experiences of Earth, height, cold, wind, rain, exertion, caution, fear and triumphant human spirit were seeking — and finding — a cautious, dynamic equilibrium with his thoughtful reality. "We live by belief," he was thinking, "but our beliefs must never become closed. Our beliefs must strive to exist, to lie somewhere outside our received realities, always a little beyond themselves.''

His belief, he understood, was now embedded in a joined-up, connected reality stretching in each moment without limit. Our best knowledge of life now knows it to be intrinsically creative, constantly in motion and changing. No matter how many so-seemingly-solid-connections, how much realistic knowledge we carry, however dependent we may be on man-made institutions and their paraphernalia, we must be able to let them fade before existence itself.

He was thinking that this is what we mean by aesthetic and philosophic **beauty**. For it is in the moment's abandon, of the going beyond oneself, of the living dangerously, of being becoming in that inter-twining of past and future that we find our intrinsic selves, and consequently our fulfilment, reflected. In this way, beauty is a very personal kind of giving of the self away.

The older boy's mind wanted to construct a bi-polar scale of reality proceeding from openness to closure, from good and beauty to evil and ugliness, with morality, ethics, revealed religions and epistemes and their institutions located at different way-points along its fully extended range. He wanted to place *Resistance* to his ideas at the closed ugly end, and *Assistance* for his ideas at the open and beautiful end, but he quickly realised this act in itself possessed far too much closure; so he settled once more for looking for an attitude.

It was an attitude that had to trust existence far more than reality. ''Reality does not speak to us objectively. No scientist can be free from the constraints of psyche and society. The greatest impediment to scientific innovation is usually a conceptual lock, not a factual lack.'' (Gould 1991, p.276).

To provide a way-mark for this attitude, to anchor it in his understanding, the older boy also noted that nature existed and that reality was man-made. He could then further justify the Primal episteme, since it approached existence far more closely than the Modern. Perhaps, more importantly, it provided an opportunity for the Modern to be criticised as a dead-end episteme, because it was dependent in part on positivities, assertions, apophantics as Heidegger said, whilst *becoming* went hand-in-hand with *being* in the Primal episteme. He

314   *Intrinsic Sustainable Development*

then prepared an e-mail for Grey Beard and QC cautioning them about the use of what he called "Primal Trust".

> To: Grey Beard, QC
>
> Subject: Trust & Primal Episteme
>
>   There are obviously many vested interests in the Modern episteme. These are not only institutional. Many individuals accept the dominance of man as natural in this world. If they are in the sway of a monotheistic religion, their beliefs necessarily privilege Mankind. But even those who accept scientific, evidence-based explanations of our origins may interpret the evidence in such a way as to privilege mankind. They may say that we represent the pinnacle of all evolution and not merely the occupiers of one highly-specialised evolutionary niche.
>
>   I do not think we can allow ourselves any form of simple "Primal Trust" to underwrite a belief that we are privileged enough to be simply *right*. If we can learn anything from the Primal episteme, it is that things are more complicated than we ever allow. So we must restrain our Primal beliefs by subjecting them to the best tests of existence we can devise. However, we can be more positively critical with regard to manifestations of the Modern episteme, for that is based on rational, reflexive assertions of reality with far less need for, or recognition of, existence; we can criticise it and its institutions as a belief system that has lost touch with existence. But even then, things can get complicated.
>
>   For example, on June 5th 2007 the *New York Times* ran an article with the heading "Fateful Voice of a Generation Still Drowns Out Real Science" (Tierney 2007) which looks superficially like something that Primal thinkers should appreciate. Even the article's argument that Rachel Carson, in her 1962 environmental book "Silent Spring" was scientifically wrong to seek to banish DDT should not deter us, since existence — whatever its message — is to us preferable to any mistaken view of reality. The Times article is a well-argued piece of journalism enjoying the high authority and large circulation of the newspaper itself and no doubt it influenced many minds, especially when this

article was the prime, perhaps only, access to this particular debate.

In the USA in 1962, the shock of "Silent Spring" raised the environmental concerns of the public to unprecedented levels and caused a reversal in national pesticide policy; steeled fledgling grassroots environmental movements and inspired the creation of the US Environmental Protection Agency. The book still ranks at the fore of the environmental movement; this fame and very real influence on the demise of large industry, chemicals and agriculture, is, perhaps, the real reason for the *New York Times* article to knock it off its environmental pedestal and thereby restore belief in corporate America.

Whatever the merits or failings of Carson's book, DDT is a dangerous chemical that the world community wants to remove. DDT may still be used by some countries to control mosquitoes and the spread of malaria even though mosquitoes are acquiring resistance to the chemical. But this is not a satisfactory solution, it is just making the best of a bad job.

The 4th meeting of the Conference of the Parties to the UNEP-Linked Stockholm Convention on Persistent Organic Pollutants in 2009 presented evidence of new projects that successfully demonstrate alternatives to DDT for mosquito control. At that meeting, Steiner, the UN Under-Secretary General and UNEP Executive Director, said: "The new projects underline the determination of the international community to combat malaria while realizing a low, indeed zero, DDT world". (Steiner 2009). The World Health Organisation was at that meeting and if that institution and the United Nations Environmental Protection programme support efforts to rid the world of DDT, then maybe Rachel Carson was on to something after all?

So, what are we to make of the *New York Times* article? Is this a balanced piece of scientific journalism or is it partisan? Has science changed that much between 2007 and 2009, or does this article demonstrate some objective other than the mere reporting of science?

I think the article demonstrates the ongoing Modern episteme's reflexive and necessary self-assertions. Existence, or our best scientific knowledge of existence, is not the underlying motivation for the *New York Times* article. The motivation is the preservation of the Modern episteme's institutions, authoritative identities and rewards. This is what Steiner had to say about DDT (and the Modern episteme): "Today we are calling time on a chemical rooted in the scientific knowledge and simplistic options of a previous age. In doing so, innovative solutions are being catalyzed and sustainable choices brought forward that meet the genuine health and environmental aspirations of a 21st century society". (*ibid.*).

We urgently need a ***Conscious Cultural Evolution*** to get over the potentially damaging, wasteful and inefficient resistance that the Modern episteme's knowledge and institutions will no doubt create in all quarters, across all dimensions. We do not have the time to wait for a natural, evolutionary adaption to our environment. Our lives are far too short and we are a very impatient species. Many of our problems require urgent solutions. Besides, as Ehrlich argues: "...the design of the human perceptual system makes it especially hard for people to recognise the most serious environmental problems." (2000, p. 327). We need to be educated to overcome our biological, evolutionary defaults. Indeed, Ehrlich proposed that we create a "conscious cultural evolution" to raise understanding of our evolutionary background and the biases thereby produced (*ibid.* pp. 326–331).

In 2001, no less an institution than Worldwatch proposed that civil society, business and government work together for a kind of conscious cultural evolution to create "...a sustainable civilisation, one fully worthy of being called human". (Brown 2001, p. 193). This proposal was reinforced in their recent State of the World report with the title "Transforming Cultures: From Consumerism to Sustainability" (Worldwatch 2010).

One underlying determinant for a new civilisation is the knowledge that if we want to live in a more orderly world, then we must develop social practices that are as open as possible. To decrease the entropy of a system, it must be open. This is how biological systems locally decrease their entropy and thereby create their highly ordered forms. They do so by increasing the overall entropy of the sun's

Chapter 12 — Resistance & Assistance   **317**

dissipations in their earthly environment. The sun creates the entropic potential within which life flows; living systems are necessarily, according to the laws of physics, open to their environment. They are eddies in an entropic stream.

This is the Second Law of Thermodynamics in action: the entropy of a closed system always increases. So it follows that to keep the increase of entropy of a system at a low value (i.e, to make the order of a system as high as possible), we must make the system as open as possible.

If we want a system to be ordered highly enough to bring some structure to human lives, we need low-entropy development, and that **must** be open. Hence, we must have a system that is designed to include as much of the environment as possible.

This means that social and environmental accounting or something like ISIS are preferable for assessing and guiding business practice than the closures of traditional accounting and the narrow money measures of ROCE. We need to design a system that seeks, and gets, a far richer return than money alone can measure. This needs to be obtained from life's full investment on this planet.

In short, we need to cast off the simplistic solutions of the Modern episteme, no matter how self-serving they may appear; for this is a short-term error. We need to increase the complexity of our systems to reflect the complexities now known to exist in nature. We need to put energy and effort into these changes. We must hope that at some point we will create enough *Chaos* so that new *strange attractors* will present our systems with new bifurcation points, new forms of self-organisation, that will eventually reduce the management interventions required to direct our efforts. This will require new skills and a concerted, global effort. Perhaps *Tian Xia* can help.

This is what it means to live in a particle-exchange universe. We need entrepreneurs who can find a way to use this kind of flux. They need to understand that the universe is built on exchange and that market exchanges are just one kind among many and not something to over-emphasise; certainly not something to develop in exclusive, domineering ways. We need the descendents of Wedgewood and his fellow *lunaticks* to develop new business entities that *resonate* with all life's systems, not just a few selected small-self human ones. We will have to promote a new "species" of sentient humanity to achieve this task; because it is so simple. This is the challenge for young people but the old will help them.

The world-wide-web may help to meet this challenge. Its information is openly spread. It is exchanged in chaotic ways, like in a particle exchange universe. But there is assistance to be found in many quarters for such a Conscious Cultural Evolution, if you only see it.

Art is one such source. Artists have been long-time supporters of the Primal episteme. We are not thinking of just the creative flourish by means of which ancient Chinese artists wished to become the Dao. The whole of art, western and eastern, strives to be Primal. Artists are strange attractors: their bifurcation points existing between what it is *to be* and what it is to *be becoming*.

Science and art become one in the Primal episteme. Goethe knew this. He was active before the Modern episteme was created, when the world was still unified in the great Classical table of knowledge. I am a great fan of Goethe, not just because he was a zoologist, botanist and geologist, but because he was also an accountant!

Goethe understood the significance of the Primal:

> "The Primal Plant is going to be the strangest creature in the world, which Nature herself must envy me. With this model and the key to it, it will be possible to go on for ever inventing plants and know that their existence is logical; that is to say, if they do not actually exist, they could, for they are not the shadowy phantoms of a vain imagination, but possess an inner necessity and truth. The same law will be applicable to all other living organisms."

He also understood complexity:

> "In Nature we never see anything isolated, but everything in connection with something else

which is before it, beside it, under it, and over
it.";

"Nature goes her own way. All that to us seems
an exception is really according to order."; and

"Nothing is more consonant with Nature than
that she puts into operation in the smallest
detail that which she intends as a whole."

And nature and art:

"He to whom Nature begins to reveal her open
secret will feel an irresistible yearning for her
most worthy interpreter, Art."

And art, science and religion:

"He, who possesses science and art, has religion;
he who possesses neither science nor art, had
better have religion."

For some people, the Primal episteme may seem
backward-looking. After all, in Mediaeval Europe scientific knowledge was integrated, but then by religion and its
affirmative explanations of the mysteries of being. Nature
was then a book to be read in exactly the same way as the
Bible. Knowledge was profoundly integrated and coherent.
Some will note the mystic, unifying element in the Primal
episteme and some may call it Mediaeval.

The Primal episteme is holistic. Hence it necessarily has
a religious aspect, as the word "heilig" reveals. But this
aspect is now based on the evidence and proofs of our best
scientific knowledge of existence; not on belief. The Primal
is thus less Mediaeval than the Modern episteme which,
whilst rational, is nonetheless based on asserted beliefs,
albeit complicated logical belief systems.

Incidentally, we see no reason why a full and meaningful religious tradition cannot be aligned with, and resonate
with, the Primal episteme. After all, nature exists as a living being for many faiths. This is perhaps more clear in the
Eastern Orthodox Church, rather than in western Catholic
traditions, but it is also true of Daoism, the Rig Veda of
Hinduism, Buddhism and countless tribal animistic traditions such as the Australian Aborigine's Dream-World.

320   *Intrinsic Sustainable Development*

Lord Shiva, the destroyer, and Brahma, the creator, are the being and becoming for a Hindu; all the efforts of Buddhism are directed at liberation from the small-self; nearly every page of the Koran calls on followers to know themselves; and the *Kami* of Shinto beliefs correlates well with the Primal episteme's genesis process.

The Primal episteme does require a vision of religion that is more than rite and ritual. It needs a vision that has its foundation on a level of understanding that integrates the practices of all religions. This kind of vision is not as uncommon as you might think. For example, the Dalai Lama expresses this aspiration when he says that he wants to see all the different religious traditions as paths for the development of inner peace — the true foundation of world peace. Similarly, the vision that Baha'u'llah received whilst locked in a dungeon in Tehran is that if people of all faiths lived truly religious lives, then you would not be able to tell them apart!

We cannot reject out of hand any criticism of the Primal episteme. We are not "deniers". We do not automatically reject a claim without considering the evidence that could support it. Indeed, we accept criticism. We accept scepticism, and the frame of mind that is willing to consider evidence and to follow the facts of existence wherever they lead, even if that goes against some dominant and trusted reality. This path goes on and on. It has no end.

The Primal episteme is nothing if it is not knowledge of nature in action, **in action on its own, intrinsically active**. As we have noted, this regarding of nature as intrinsically active will put us on an opposing course to some of the Modern episteme's thinkers. As Ellis (2002, p. 2) notes: ". . . it [passivism] is such an established way of thinking, that, to many, it seems to be plain common sense."

Chalmers (1999, p. 219) supports this perception: "The majority of philosophers seem reluctant to accept an ontology which includes dispositions or powers as primitive. I do not understand their reluctance. Perhaps the reasons are in part historical."

But to our minds, such a critique is not a bad thing. After all, a new episteme means that all the creations of the prior episteme need close examination to see if they are still meaningful, if they need modifying, or if they are to be rejected; nothing should be taken for granted. It will be very hard, perhaps impossible, for some minds shaped within the Modern episteme to even appreciate, not to mention *perform*, this kind of critique. However, others have been doing it for some time.

Here, for example, is a profound criticism of Modern progress: "In each area of enlightenment a dark underside could also be identified: for example, growth in wealth and cultural refinement for some, meant intensified exploitation, misery and even slavery for many others; development in technology could be used for destructive as well as productive purposes, for coercive as well as liberatory ends; the rationalization of social relations could spell the breaking of traditional bonds of community, with human rights being honoured more in form than in substance." (Hayward 1995, p. 12). How very well this echoes Foucault's observation that the Modern episteme is *incapable* of having a morality.

The Primal episteme needs not only new thoughts and new thinkers, but also *new ways of thinking*. Thought now needs to focus on the relations between entities rather than on the entities themselves. This reflects the emergent ways of "network thinking" which "... is poised to invade all domains of human activity and most fields of human enquiry" (Mitchell 2009, p. 233). Even for the most anthropologically-centred mind, the emphasis must now shift from man, his states and conditions, to his interactions with the wider world. We are all participants now, all in this together.

The Primal episteme points towards the development of minds more mindful of the open-ended complexities of relationships that constitute their being and their restless becoming. It also points to a different kind of mentality in practice so that: "... the development of sustainability as a frame of mind is essentially a matter of coming to terms with that which lies always beyond our authorship, analyses and management and yet is closest to us — a reciprocator in all our perception and interaction." (Bonnett 2004, p. 148).

It was midday when the older boy finished writing. His wife was telling him that lunch was ready. He dispatched the email to QC and Grey Beard and went downstairs to eat.

Chinese Institutions

After lunch, the older boy fell asleep on his sofa for twenty minutes. He awoke refreshed and eager for work. Back in his home office, he opened one of QC's two emails.

In the first email, QC thanked the older boy for his recognition of China's efforts with Harmonious Development, but pointed out that his trust is slightly mistaken. She informed the older boy that China did indeed present a Sustainable Development strategy in its 9th five-year-plan in 1996. The plan's fundamental principles embody '... enduring, balancing developing economies, societies and ecological environments'. QC was explaining that the main difference between Chinese Sustainable Development strategies and those of other countries is China's 'strict control of a growing population, improving the quality of people entirely' (e.g. China had set targets for 2010 of a population limit of below 1.4 billion people, junior school education to be higher than 95% coverage, higher education to be 20%, and a youth non-illiteracy rate to be no less than 95%).

In 2003, the People's Republic of China introduced a 'scientific outlook on development', which is more like western-style sustainable development but its core concern is human beings. Even the 2006 11th five year plan, entitled 'Harmonious Development', does not have the broad, *Tian Xia*, harmonious essential principle for the human-centred 'scientific outlook on development' is still the focus.

So 'Harmonious Society' may not be understood to be equivalent to sustainable development. The harmonious strategies do not support the balance of 'economic, social *and environmental*' but seek to balance just society, economics, politics and culture. The environmental part is quite weak in the mission to build a harmonious society.

The older boy replied to QC and copied to Grey Beard. He thanked her for pointing out his mistaken assumptions. He also pointed out that China is a Modern state with ideology taken from the West and that he was therefore not surprised that the *Modern* Chinese state was more anthropologically inclined and not as ecologically aware as its ancestors had been.

He turned his attention to the second of QC's emails which was, as she expressed it, "more for developing the Primal".

> China is catching up materially, but many Chinese are still very poor. Japan already shows a tiredness of materialism, but it is much better developed than China. Junko Edahiro, a Japanese environmentalist, has some good news.
>
> — *De-ownership* is a new trend for the Japanese, who once were very strict about having new things and now they share music, books and clothes and houses in a different kind of Japanese society.
> — *De-materialism* for happiness is to be looked for in Japanese relations with other people and with nature — so very Primal indeed! Even when swopping clothes, the Japanese want to swop relations as well. They attached 'episode tags' to swop clothes to explain why they loved the item, why it now has to go and for giving their hope that it will make someone else happy.
> — *De-monetisation* is evident when half a person's working time is spent earning money and half is for something else like writing or NGO activism (Edahiro 2010).
>
> On the other side of the world, in America, I find my same women's world thinking in *Small Planet Mission* which China should follow 'toward democracy as a rewarding way of life: a culture in which citizens infuse the values of inclusion, fairness and mutual accountability into all dimensions of public life. We call this Living Democracy.' (Lappé and Lappé 2010).
>
> You will like this for your business professional skills too: 'The Chinese accounting system was traditionally based on Confucian practices and ancient wisdom; these elements still influence the current system.' (Ayhan and Sola 2007, p. 146). This paper also argues that modern Chinese

324   *Intrinsic Sustainable Development*

accounting systems are based on historic teachings, rather than on the needs of Modern economic business.

Western Institutions

The older boy looked up QC's references and then sent a thank-you email. He turned his attention to Grey Beard's email and its two attachments. For the first attachment, Grey Beard had written "Please see this one for ideas on the fate of economics in the Primal episteme"; the older boy opened this attachment.

Notes on Economics and Business in the Primal Episteme

1#

We are still rational! Indeed we can still pursue a rational self-interest. But, we now know that the starting-point is rational **extended-self-interest**.

2#

Similarly with regard to rights, we need now to establish them for the extended-self. Specifically human rights are no longer discrete and simple, but range from the uniquely human to the biosphere. Even where we identify uniquely human rights, we need to bear in mind that these are a form of specific species rights comparable to the rights of birds to be able to fly, fish to swim and horses to have space in which to run etc. Conversely, I believe we become more human with each of these "non-human" rights that we recognise. Life may get more complicated this way, but risks will decrease.

3#

Karl Polanyi (1886–1964) showed that economic concepts become embedded in society and invade nature and that this arrangement cannot be sustained; economic imper-atives would eventually destroy their social and natural hosts. Self-regulating markets, he claims, are not funda-mental institutions. He also argued that it was wrong for man to isolate nature and try to make a market out of it.

Chapter 12 — Resistance & Assistance   **325**

He probably understood the significance of epistemological man in the Modern episteme before it was recognised
by Foucault. See Polanyi's masterly 1944 book *The Great
Transformation* (Polanyi 2001).

4#

On an organisational level, Penrose's 1959 classic *The
Theory of the Growth of the Firm* is helpful. Penrose
argues that a firm can be studied as a dynamic process in
which its managers interact with the resources they find in
the world. Interestingly the so-called Penrose Effect identifies managerial capability as a binding constraint that
limits the growth of the firm (Penrose 1959, pp. 47–48).
This is a helpful perception. It takes business out of economic clutches and puts it back into human hands; Primal
human hands from now on.

5#

Resource Dependence Theory (Pfeffer and Salancik 2003)
also identifies the dependency of organizations on their
environments and the connectivity and interdependence
that this implies. This approach readily lends itself to an
ecological understanding of how business works; this then
leads on to complexity and the Primal episteme.

6#

Post-Autistic Economics (PAE) provides fresh ideas for
dealing with the closures of traditional economic theory
(PAE 2010). PAE was started by French economics students in 2000. They railed against economics' unbridled
use of mathematics which, they claimed, had made economics into an *autistic* kind of science. The new kind
of economics that they envision will deal with realities
by prioritising science over economics — a truly Primal
approach! They also support a pluralistic economics of
complexity. *Real World Economics: A Post-Autistic Economics Reader* (Fullbrook 2007) is a good starting point
for PAE.

7#

Environmental economics may have some uses in the Primal episteme provided a view of economics as a *tool* may

be established for the discipline. However, I am inclined to say that it is too flawed by Modern episteme thinking. It may prove to be beyond salvage.

8#

On the other hand, ecological economics has been waiting for recognition of the Primal episteme! This discipline studies the interdependence and interconnectivity of human and ecological systems. It does still need to identify economics as a subsystem of ecology, nonetheless it is a source of more supportive evidence for the Primal episteme. Ecological economics' essential reads include Georgescu-Roegen's *The Entropy Law and the Economic Process* (1971) and Daly's *Beyond Growth: Economics of Sustainable Development* (1996). If we want to provide a clearer idea of the form that economics might take within a Primal episteme, Daly's Steady State Economics would be a good starting point and so too is the "New Green Deal" to be found at www.e4declaration.org.

9#

Complexity economics is emerging as a discipline on its own but it tends to be, as you may anticipate, an application of complexity science to economics. It focuses on reversing the simplistic reductionism of traditional economics with network representations. I think complexity economics has yet to decide whether it is Modern or Primal.

10#

We have not offered a definition of *Economic Ecology*; I suggest it may be "a multidisciplinary study of mankind's role in the distribution and use of resources within open, life-sustaining systems".

11#

There are many initiatives that focus on changing business in one way or another towards a Primal episteme. These include Ecological Modernization, Industrial Symbiosis, the Global Reporting Initiative, Life Cycle Assessments, Cleaner Technologies, the Triple Bottom Line, Natural Capitalism, Biomimicry and the Natural Step.

Participants in these different initiatives will by no means all agree about the "reality" or significance of the Primal episteme, but I cannot see that it will do their causes any harm. Indeed, they all stand to benefit from any *Primal momentum* we might generate.

12#

Finally, we need to consider changing life-styles as well as institutions. Personal health is a powerful way to do this. After all, in the Primal episteme, nature is no longer something other than ourselves. We are all parts of nature, hence any definition of personal health must necessarily have natural or ecological dimensions. The UK's new NHS, the *Natural* Health Service, agrees.

Natural England launched the *Natural* Health Service in 2009 with these two objectives:

1. To increase the number of households that are within five minutes walk of an area of green space of at least two hectares;
2. To enable every GP or community nurse to be able to signpost patients to an approved health walk or outdoor activity programme. (NHS 2009).

They seek to improve physical and mental health by promoting a return to the lifestyles for which we were designed; a life with large amounts of outdoor activity, clean air and water. Our bodies and minds have evolved for a life on the move; if we become more active we get more oxygen to heart and muscles, our joints are kept more healthy and more free from pain; our blood pressure goes down; our immune systems are boosted; and our mental health benefits enormously. We feel better and perform better as we experience our innate affinities for nature: "Children with attention deficits concentrated better after walking in a park than either of the two other settings [well-kept urban environments]. The effect of a dose of green was substantial — roughly as large as the deficit due ADHD and roughly as large as the peak effect of extended-release methylphenidate." (Taylor and Kuo 2009, p. 406).

The Biophilia Hypothesis (Wilson 1984) holds that multiple strands of emotional response are woven within and between ourselves and the rest of the living world. When men and women remove themselves from nature, these responses are not replaced; we are thereby diminished. In other words, we need to live among other forms of life to become fully human.

We need biodiversity in its fullness, in its wildness, not just in a few, managed species that reflect back to us our own dominating limits. There is, I believe, an important spiritual dimension to be found in encounters with truly wild life — a real, opening sense of wondering just who is doing the watching, and who is being watched.

This kind of encounter is enhanced by the Primal episteme; all of life participates in the same creative process and shares the same information. The natural world is intrinsically active. This is the source of its value for mankind. We are often surprised to experience this at first hand.

Biodiversity will also be good for *diet*-diversity: "After all, eating establishes humankind's most primordial bonds with the natural world. We take the environment into ourselves and merge with it. We truly are what we eat." (Kimbrell 2010, p. 24). There are some things, including life-sustaining food-sources, that simply should not be cheapened by business.

There, I have nearly finished. I think we do not need to produce policies for the Primal episteme. We make a contribution by (i) pointing out the mistakes made by the Modern episteme and its institutions, and (ii) establishing a foundation for Primal knowledge. I think we have done both of these things.

The institutions of the Modern episteme have been unable to recognise, never mind deal with, relationship issues. Take populations for example. There seems to be a demand for a kind of general, more-people "boosterism" in Modern business to support large markets that drive ever-larger companies for greater economies of scale and higher personal rewards for business managers and owners. You'll not get rich at a market stall, not unless you grow your business. Your overcrowded little island is a good example of this kind of "boosterism".

It is not as if population control is difficult; Optimum Population Trust policies are hardly draconian: ". . . that full access to family planning should be provided to all those who do not have it, that couples should be encouraged to voluntarily 'stop at two' children to lessen the impact of family size on the environment, and that this should be part of a holistic approach involving better education and equal rights for women." (OPT 2010).

We all have a right to live well, and that has to be within the planet's environmental resource and spatial limits. The rich need to find more in their lives than having more or having bigger or more expensive things — and we need the role models in public life to bring this change in attitude about. The poor need to be given education, confidence and the security to allow them to take more control of their own lives and interactions with their environments. We all need to be able to flourish and prosper.

Only by changing our views of our knowledge, of ourselves, of our societies and of our institutions can we achieve changes as massive as these.

World Institution

The older boy printed Grey Beard's twelve points on Primal business and economics so that he might reflect on them later. Meanwhile, he had one more document to read. Grey Beard had written that his second attachment had been written by a young Russian who had landed in Gothenburg Handelshögskolan just over half a year ago. " 'Landed', he had written, "was the appropriate word for this twenty-six-years-old woman had left her home town of St Petersburg in her teens and had since travelled the world. Her name is 'СОФИЯ' but you may call her 'Sofia'.' "

Grey Beard had described Sofia variously as a web-entrepreneur, a networker, a knowledge-broker, and a citizen of the world. It appeared that Sofia had embraced social media in its embryonic stage; her natural interpersonal skills, knowledge and charm had found expression in an electronic persona that warped web-space to draw in followers on Facebook and Twitter just as effectively as matter warped space-time to create gravity and draw in the planets. Grey Beard had been introduced to her by a friend of a friend of his son and Handelshögskolan had employed Sofia on a twelve-month temporary contract to stop travelling for a while and establish a virtual global business-student community for recruitment as well as alumni purposes. Sofia had been eager to learn about epistemes and the Primal approach to ordering knowledge.

The second document that was attached to Grey Beard's email had been prepared on Sofia's own initiative. In her mind, she was already re-working, socialising, and marketing the academic material that Grey Beard, QC and the older boy had produced. This for Sofia was no reductive or exploitative application of business principles; it was far more an absorption, an integration, an expansion, and more fuel to extend or reformulate her physical and virtual existence. The older boy opened the document.

> For ancient and new Primal people
>
> Knowledge defines any response to sustainable development, so you are right to articulate *how* we know: that has to be as important as *what* we know. Your world will itself become real in its diversity, wide engagement and explanatory power. It needs to resonate vigorously over the artificial, conceptual boundaries that limit people and their societies; especially so for those minds deep in the holes of the Modern episteme where specialisation overflows its rightful boundaries to distort knowledge: there can be no option but to maximise economic gain in a purely economic world.
>
>> "Growth becomes like an arms race in which the two sides cancel each other's gains. A happy corollary is that for societies that have reached sufficiency, moving to a SSE [Steady State Economy] may cost little in terms of forgone happiness. The 'political impossibility' of

Chapter 12 — Resistance & Assistance   **331**

a SSE may be less impossible than it previously appeared."
From a paper written for the UK Sustainable Development Commission by Herman Daly (2008).

You should make more of the World Wide Web in the context of a world institution, both to reveal diversity in culture and thought but perhaps more importantly as a World Institution. It is the global virtual meeting place for trade, talk, getting to know others and their ideas; it is in effect a global knowledge network. It is within such an institution that the politics of Daly's SSE need to be formulated.

The Web can support Primal knowledge. Such knowledge is a science and an *attitude* that returns people to who they are, have always been, and always will be, in their full, universal moments of being and becoming: there can be no greater freedom! If you are patient, relaxed, brave, honest and make clear statements, you will find like-minds and support — but the new episteme will bring change and that will not be liked by some.

Science has found an underlying, unifying and formative reality, a metaphysics, in the Primal episteme. For this reason your work has a spiritual dimension that has parallels with religious beliefs; once more we can explain man's place in a cosmology with the morality of the extended self. Such knowledge is available only to those who can give of themselves to others and to nature's processes. There is a chance for another unity here; one within life's and culture's enormous diversity — so very not-Modern:

> "A new theoretical paradigm known as the Capabilities Approach is evolving. Unlike the dominant approaches, it begins with a commitment to the equal dignity of all people, whatever their class, religion, caste, race or gender, and it is committed to the attainment, for all, of lives that are worthy of that equal dignity. Both a comparative account of the quality of life and a theory of basic social justice,

it remedies the major deficiencies of the dominant approaches. It is sensitive to distribution, focusing particularly on the struggles of traditionally excluded or marginalized groups. It is sensitive to the complexity and the qualitative diversity of the goals that people pursue. Rather than trying to squeeze all these diverse goals into a single box, it carefully examines the relationships among them, thinking about how they support and complement one another. It also takes into account that people may need different quantities of resources if they are to come up to the same level of ability to choose and act, particularly if they begin from different social positions."

Martha Nussbaum (2011).

My home, Russia, has always been good at finding unity in diversity. We have always struggled against "dominant approaches". Indeed our love of freedom is a freedom of the spirit and in public life this can been expressed as a tendency towards restless change and anarchy. We have had our problems of course, but so have you. It was Narochnitskaya who pointed out that there is a different history of corruption between the Latin West and the Orthodox East!

Russian folklore comes from the Russian people. It shows their deep religiosity. Their tales are often about journeys of self-discovery and these led not to some small individual but to more knowledge of themselves as parts of common wholes — is this Primal enough for you?

Dostoevsky interpreted these Russian journeys as Christian pilgrimages. This is what he wrote on the death of Masha, his first wife: "... he had said that the highest use human beings could make of their egos was to annihilate them in total self-giving and that the insufficiency of earthly life signaled that 'on earth the human being is a creature that is only developing, consequently, is not a finished creature, but transitional'." (Ivanits 2008, p. 190).

Finally, we Russians are great metaphysicians; we are used to living at the Primal point of being and becoming.

We like to repeat what the poet Fyodor Ivanovich Tyutchev said about Russia:

> Умом Россию не понять,
> Аршином общим не измерить:
> У ней особенная стать —
> В Россию можно только верить.

This has had some different translations but my favourite one is:

> "You wouldn't understand Russia just using the intellect
> You couldn't measure her using the common scale
> She has a special kind of grace
> You can only believe in her."

So your Primal is perhaps not so new as you think! But it is not a regression; nothing stands still. It is a return, but to a different place: a return as in a spiral — not a circle — to something you know but that you now know as different. The Chinese know this.

> "Thousands of years ago, the parallel rise of western and eastern civilisation showed surprising similarities. Several millennia later, the two sides can surprise the world again, by joining forces on the platform of ecological civilisation. Although traditional Chinese culture is a product of an agricultural past, I firmly believe it contains universal values and can undergo a modern transformation. In just one century, China has transformed itself from an agricultural to an industrial civilisation. A further transformation to an ecological civilisation is entirely possible."
>
> *Pan Yue (2011), vice minister in the Ministry of Environmental Protection, PRC.*

The Americans are getting to know it.

> "To those nations like ours that enjoy relative plenty, we can longer afford indifference to suffering outside our borders; nor can we consume

the world's resources without regard to effect. For the world has changed, and we must change with it."

> *From the inaugural address of President Barack Obama, 1-20-2009.*

The human species has done many wonderful things but this may yet be our downfall. I can see that the world has so many problems and that many of them are our own fault, an anthropogenic forcing.

People have to change their ways: they have to start thinking and acting very differently, in the full light of the knowledge of the consequences of their actions. They need to bring *resilience* back to social and ecological systems that in themselves can suddenly, unexpectedly spring into new ways of being. Governments must help change education to bring about this change. Ultimately though, it is down to us: individual people must learn to live their lives with respect for the universe in which they participate. We must find ways of giving generously of ourselves and time, of finding meaning and fulfilment within an existence that is fluid, dynamic and quixotic. The world is so truly amazing and beautiful and so much more than any single one of us.

By the time the older boy had finished reading Sofia's document, it was four o'clock in the afternoon and time for tea. Making tea, Chinese tea, had become an important ritual for the older boy. He made a point of sitting quietly, of clearing his mind and of relaxing his body, at least for four minutes as the tea infused.

If he was alone and had the time, he would prolong the ritual as he drank the tea, to allow a full concentration on the simple act as much as to appreciate the flavour and sustenance of the drink. He would thereby recover a little of his extended-self, freeing his smaller-self from the day's issues, actions, concerns and anxieties. It was just good mental hygiene, he would tell himself.

This day was no exception. As usual, try otherwise as he might, the day's thoughts would not leave him entirely alone. But on this day, unusually, he did not mind. He enjoyed the refinement, the clarity, the elevation, the deeper penetration that the tea-ceremony brought him and he applied it rigorously to his lingering thoughts.

He had greatly appreciated QC's, Grey Beard's and Sofia's emails. He could see how they had described a new view of the world, but he could also see how very little they really hoped to achieve. The Primal episteme was, after all, nothing new; the systemic arrangements of matter and energy had always been there — even the humblest forms of life *knew* that much.

The tea-ceremony placed him fully, right in the centre of his universe once more. The sense of restless change, of energy waves, of particles interacting, of relations forming and breaking had the potential to create such an immensely complicated, unfathomable, distant, impersonal, uncertain and fearful world that he really had no option but to enjoy himself, to celebrate, to rejoice in who he was, in the identity of mankind, in its short, transient history and in the so-very-little, lost-in-space blue-planet home. It was so truly amazing for the older boy to feel so much, so very strongly about something so very little — a cup of Chinese tea.

But it was, he knew, really no small thing in its smallness. He realised that in this small experience, replicated in their thousands, their millions, their infinite numbers was the key to a flourishing future for all of life on Earth — and perhaps, he indulged himself, for all of life *off* Earth, in just a few thousand years time.

It is no small thing to find, in your own brief moments, that part of yourself that existed before your birth. The emotions, intuitions, meanings and judgements that guide us through our daily lives are no more our own than are our physical bodies. Countless lives, both human and non-human, have participated in our constitution — just as we will participate in future lives.

The artist and scientist perhaps most directly strive to express this — to reveal our constitutive order, our beauty. But no matter how un-extended our lives may be, the moments of a tea ceremony, the small act of giving to the human as well as natural universe, may be shared by all: labourers, accountants, business professionals, economists and politicians. Who knows what strange attractors

Intrinsic Sustainable Development

might then order us into ever more extended, inclusive human and social forms?

It is no small thing to find boundless time flooding out of a moment's reflection. This kind of time is the basis for gearing our lives. Sustainable businesses may grow slowly from such retained earnings.

It is, and it is not, a very small thing for a person to be able to live a little outside his passing life, to engage with others; with others to generously participate in the universe of all things in this way. It takes an extraordinarily large amount of energy, of engagement with simplicity, with the uncommitted and *mindful* points of universal change, of letting go, of wide experience, of trust, of faith, and of love, to be able to live securely, happily, with a valued **sufficiency** of supportive, prosthetic (Catton 1982) goods to lead a rewarding, fulfilling and opening life. But this very small, individual human act is now urgently required of all of us; it urgently needs widespread cultural and social support, suitable role models as well as new global institutions.

It is a lifetime's worthwhile work to nurture such universal, small participation in ourselves and in others. It may all be lost in a moment's careless thought.

REFERENCES

Adorno, T. and Horkheimer, M. (1979). *Dialectic of the Enlightenment.* London: Verso.

Agenda 21. (1992). *Earth Summit Agenda 21: the United Nations programme of action from Rio.* New York: United Nations Department of Economics and Social Affairs, Division for Sustainable Development. Available at <http://www.un.org/esa/dsd/agenda21/res_agenda21_00. shtml> [Accessed August 2010].

ASI. (2010). *The Adam Smith Institute.* London: The Adam Smith Institute. Available at <http://www.adamsmith.org/> [Accessed October 2010].

Ayhan, S. and Sola, C. (2007). "The Historical Evolution of Accounting in China: the effects of Culture". *Spanish Journal of Accounting History,* 7 (1), pp. 138–163.

Axley, S.R. and McMahon, T.R. (2006). Complexity: A Frontier for Management Education. *Journal of Management Education,* 30(2), pp. 295–315.

Barnes, J. (1987). *Early Greek Philosophers.* Harmondsworth: Penguin Books.

Barrow, J.D. (1999). *Impossibility: the limits of science and the science of limits.* London: Vintage.

Bateson, G. (2000). *Steps to an Ecology of Mind.* Chicago: University of Chicago.

Beauchamp, T.L. (1999). *David Hume: an Enquiry concerning Human Understanding.* Oxford: Oxford University Press.

Beauvoir, S. (1991). *The Ethics of Ambiguity.* New York: Carol Publishing.

Beinhocker, E.D. (2007). *The Origin of Wealth: evolution, complexity, and the radical remaking of economics.* London: Random House.

Benhabib, S. (1986). *Critique, Norm and Utopia: a study of the foundations of Critical Theory.* New York: Columbia University Press.

Benton, T. (2008). "Environmental Values and Human Purposes." *Environmental Values,* 17. pp. 201–220.

Berkes, F., Colding, J. and Folke, C. eds. (2003). *Navigating Social-Ecological Systems: Building Resilience for Complexity and Change.* Cambridge: Cambridge University Press.

Bhaskar, R. (1978). *A Realist Theory of Science.* Brighton: Harvester Press.

Bhaskar, R. (1979). *The Possibility of Naturalism: A philosophical critique of the contemporary human sciences.* Brighton: Harvester Press.

Bhaskar, R. (1986). *Scientific Realism and Human Emancipation.* London: Verso.

Bhaskar, R. (1989). *Reclaiming Reality: A critical introduction to Contemporary Philosophy.* London: Verso.

Bhaskar, R. (1993). *Dialectic: The Pulse of Freedom.* London: Verso.

Birkin, F.K. (2000). The Art of Accounting for Science: a prerequisite for sustainable development? *Critical Perspectives on Accounting,* 11, pp. 289–309.

Bitbol, M. and Luisi, P.L. (2004). "Autopoiesis with or without cognition: defining life at its edge." *Journal of the Royal Society Interface* 22, 1(1), pp. 99–107.

Blackmore, S.J. (2003). *Consciousness: an introduction.* New York: Oxford University Press.

Blackmore, S.J. (2005). *Consciousness: a very short introduction.* Oxford: Oxford University Press.

Bonnett, M. (2004). *Retrieving Nature: education for a post-humanist age.* Oxford: Blackwell Publishing.

Bookchin, M. (1982). *The Ecology of Freedom.* Palo Alto, CA: Cheshire Books.

Botton de, A. (2005). *Status Anxiety.* London: Penguin.

Brown, L.R. (2001). *State of the World 2001.* London: Earthscan.

Burgen, W.A. (2005). *Heidegger and Aristotle: the two-foldness of being.* New York: State University of New York Press.

Business and Human Rights Resource Centre. (2010). *A Brief Description.* London: Business and Human Rights Resource Centre. Available at <http://www.business-humanrights.org/Home> [Accessed December 2010].

Byrne, D. (1998). *Complexity Theory and the Social Sciences: An Introduction.* London: Routledge.

Capra, F. (1982). *The Turning Point: Science, Society and the Rising Culture.* London: Simon & Schuster.

Capra, F. (1991). *The Tao of Physics.* 3rd *edition.* Boston: Shambala.

Capra, F. (1997). *The Web of Life: a new synthesis of mind and matter.* London: Flamingo.

Capra, F. (2003). *The Hidden Connections.* London: Flamingo.

References   **339**

Carsetti, A. ed. (2010). *Causality, Meaningful Complexity and Embodied Cognition.* New York: Springer.

Carson, R. (1962). Silent Spring. *The New Yorker Magazine,* June 16, 23, and 30.

Cartwright, N. (1999). *The Dappled World: A Study of the Boundaries of Science.* Cambridge: Cambridge University Press.

Catton, W.R. (1982). *Overshoot: the ecological basis of revolutionary change.* Urbana and Chicago: University of Illinois Press.

Chalmers, A.F. (1999). *What is this thing called science?* Maidenhead: Open University Press.

Chan, G. (2004). "China's Compliance in Global Environmental Affairs". *Asia Pacific Viewpoint,* 45(1), pp. 69–86.

Chödrön, P. (2001). *The Places that Scare You.* Boston: Shambala Publications.

Churchland, P.M. (1992). *Matter and Consciousness.* Cambridge, Massachusetts: MIT Press.

Colquhoun, M. and Ewald, A. (1996). *New Eyes for Plants.* Stroud, England: Hawthorn Press.

Cook, M. (2004). *A Brief History of the Human Race.* London: Granta.

Corporate Watch. (2006). *What's Wrong with Corporate Social Responsibility?* Oxford: Corporate Watch.

Corporate Watch. (2010). *Corporate Watch: corporate critical research since 1996.* London: Corporate Watch. Available at <http://www.corporatewatch.org.uk/> [Accessed October 2010].

Critchley, S. (2001). *Continental Philosophy: a very short introduction.* Oxford: Oxford University Press.

CSDH. (2008). *Closing the gap in a generation: Health equity through action on the social determinants of health.* Geneva: Commission on Social Determinants of Health, World Health Organization.

Daly, H.E. (1996). *Beyond Growth: Economics of Sustainable Development.* Boston: Beacon Press.

Daly, H.E. (2008). *A Steady-State Economy: A failed growth economy and a steady-state economy are not the same thing; they are the very different alternatives we face.* London: Sustainable Development Commission, UK.

Dawkins, R. (1999[1976]). *The Selfish Gene.* Oxford: Oxford University Press.

Dawson, R. (2005). *The Chinese Experience.* London: Phoenix Press.

Dennett, D.C. (1991). *Consciousness Explained.* London: Little, Brown and Co.

De Villiers, M. (2010). *Natural Disasters, Manmade Catastrophes, and the Future of Human Survival.* New York: Thomas Dunne.

Diamond, J. (1987). "The Worst Mistake in the History of the Human Race". *Discover Magazine*, pp. 64–66.

Diamond, J. (2006). *Collapse — how societies choose to fail or survive.* London: Penguin.

Durkheim, E. (1996[1894]). *The Rules of Sociological Method.* Translated from the French by S.A. Solovay and H.H. Mueller. New York: Free Press.

EC. (2009). *Beyond GDP.* Brussels: European Commission. Available at <http://www.beyond-gdp.eu> [Accessed December 2010].

Ecoliteracy. (2011). *The Center for Ecoliteracy.* Berkeley: The Center for Ecoliteracy. Available at <http://www.ecoliteracy.org/> [Accessed January 2011].

Edahiro, J. (2010). Letter from Japan. *Resurgence*, 262 (September/October), pp. 16–17.

Edelman, G.M. and Tononi, G. (2000). *A Universe of Consciousness.* New York: Basic Books.

EEA. (2010). *State of the environment report No 1/2010.* Copenhagen: European Environment Agency.

Ehrenfeld, D. (1981). *The Arrogance of Humanism.* Oxford: Oxford University Press.

Ehrlich, P.R. (2000). *Human Natures: genes, cultures, and the human prospect.* Washington DC: Island Press.

Eldredge, N. (1998). *Life in the Balance: Humanity and the Biodiversity Crisis.* Princeton: Princeton University Press.

Elkington, J. (1997). *Cannibals with Forks: the Triple Bottom Line of 21st Century Business.* Oxford: Capstone.

Ellis, B.D. (2002). *The Philosophy of Nature: a guide to the new essentialism.* Chesham: Acumen.

Fauna & Flora International, and UNEP. (2010). *The Natural Value Initiative: Linking Shareholder and Natural Value.* Cambridge: Fauna & Flora International. Available at <http://www.naturalvalueinitiative.org/> [Accessed December 2010].

Fauset, C. (2006). *What's Wrong with Corporate Social Responsibility?* London: Corporate Watch.

Firth, D. (2008). "Do Meaningful Relationships with Nature Contribute to a Worthwhile Life?" *Environmental Values*, Vol. 17. pp. 145–164.

Flaubert, G. (1953). *Selected Letters of Gustave Flaubert (1821–1880).* Translated from the French by F. Steegmuller. New York: Farrar, Strauss and Young.

Foucault, M. (1970). *The Order of Things: an archaeology of the human sciences.* London: Routledge.

Friedman, M. (1962). Capitalism and Freedom. Chicago: University of Chicago Press.

Fukuyama, F. (1992). *The End of History and the Last Man.* New York: Avon Books.

Fullbrook, E. (2007). *Real World Economics: A Post-Autistic Economics Reader.* London: Anthem Press.

Fuller, J.G.C.M. (1981). The Geological Attitude. *In* F.H.T. Rhodes and R.O. Stone, eds. *Language of the Earth.* New York: Pergamon Press, pp. 384–390.

Gelman, S. (2003). *The Essential Child: Origins of essentialism in everyday thought.* Oxford: Oxford University Press.

Georgescu-Roegen, N. (1971). *The Entropy Law and the Economic Process.* Cambridge, Massachusetts: Harvard University Press.

Geus de, A. (2002). *The Living Company: habits for survival in a turbulent business environment.* Boston: Harvard Business School Press.

Gibson-Graham, J.K. and Roelvink, G. (2009)."An Economic Ethics for the Anthropocene". *Antipode*, 41(S1), pp. 320–346.

Giddens, A. (1984). *The Constitution of Society.* Cambridge: Polity Press.

Giddens, A. (1991). *Modernity and Self-Identity.* Cambridge: Polity Press.

Giere, R. (1998). *Science without Laws.* Chicago: University of Chicago Press.

Gleick, J. (1987). *Chaos: making a new science.* London: Sphere Books.

Global Footprint. (2010). *Global Footprint Network.* Oakland, California: Global Footprint Network. Available at <http://www.footprintnetwork.org> [Accessed December 2010].

Goldsmith, E. (1972). *A Blueprint for Survival.* The Ecologist, 2(1).

Goldsmith, E. (1992). *The Way: an ecological worldview.* London: Rider.

Goleman, D. (1996). *Emotional Intelligence: Why it can matter more than IQ.* London: Bloomsbury.

Gould, S.J. (1991). *Wonderful Life: the Burgess Shale and the nature of history.* London: Penguin.

Habermas, J. (1979). *Communication and the Evolution of Society.* Boston: Beacon.

Handy, C.B. (1996). *The Age of Unreason.* Boston: Harvard Business School Press.

Hardin, G. (1968). The Tragedy of the Commons. *Science*, 162, pp. 1243–1248.

Haviland, W.A., Prins, H.E.L., Walrath, D., and McBride, B. (2008). *Cultural Anthropology: the human challenge 12th edit.* Belmont: Thomas Wadsworth.

Hayward, T. (1995). *Ecological Thought: an introduction.* Cambridge: Polity Press.

342   *Intrinsic Sustainable Development*

Horkheimer, M. (1982). *Critical Theory*. New York: Seabury Press.

IPCC. (2007). *Contribution of Working Groups I, II and III to the Fourth Assessment Report of the Intergovernmental Panel on Climate Change*. Pachauri, R.K. and Reisinger, A. (Eds.). Geneva: Intergovernmental Panel on Climate Change.

Ivanits, L. (2008). *Dostoevsky and the Russian People*. Cambridge: Cambridge University Press.

Jacoby, S. (2008). *The Age of American Unreason: dumbing down and the future of democracy*. London: Old Street Publishing.

Johnson, N. (2007) *Simply Complexity: A Clear Guide to Complexity Theory*. Oxford: One World.

Jørgensen, S.E. and Svirezhev, Y. (2004). *Towards a Thermodynamic Theory for Ecological Systems*. Oxford: Pergamon.

Kanner, A.D. and Soule, R. (2005). Globalization, Corporate Culture, and Freedom. In T. Kasser and A.D. Kanner eds. *Psychology and Consumer Culture: the struggle for the good life in a materialistic world*. Washington: American Psychological Association, pp. 49–67.

Kasser, T., Ryan, R.M., Couchman, C.E., and Sheldon, K.M. (2005). Materialistic Values: their causes and consequences. In T. Kasser and A.D. Kanner eds. *Psychology and Consumer Culture: the struggle for the good life in a materialistic world*. Washington: American Psychological Association, pp. 11–28.

Kauffman, S. (1995). *At Home in the Universe: The Search for the Laws of Self-Organization and Complexity*. Oxford: Oxford University Press.

Kemp, S. (2005). "Critical Realism and the Limits of Philosophy", *European Journal of Social Theory*, 8 (2), pp. 271–191.

Kimbrell, A. (2010). A New Food Future? *Resurgence*, 259 (March/April), pp. 21–24.

Kineman, J.J. (2003). Aristotle, Complexity, and Ecosystems: A Speculative Journey. *In* J. Allen and J. Wilby eds. *Proceedings of the 47th Annual Conference of the International Society for the System Sciences, July 7–11, 2003, Heraklion, Greece*. Heraclion: ISSS.

Kirilyuk, A.P. (2006). "Towards a Sustainable Future by the Transition to the Next Level Civilization." In: V. Burdyuzha, ed. *The Future of Life and the future of our Civilization*. Dordrecht: Springer, pp. 411–433.

Kropotkin, P. (1987). *Mutual Aid: a factor of evolution (1902)*. London: Freedom Press.

Kukla, A. (1998). *Studies in Scientific Realism*. Oxford: Oxford University Press.

Lakoff, G. and Johnson, M. (1999). *Philosophy in the Flesh*. New York: Basic Books.

References   **343**

Lappé, F. and Lappé, A. (2010). *Small Planet Institute: living democracy, feeding hope*. Cambridge, Massachusetts: Small Planet Institute. Available at <http://www.smallplanet.org> [Accessed December 2010].

Leopold, A. (1989 [1949]). *A Sand County Almanac*. Oxford: Oxford University Press.

Leplin, J. (1997). *A Novel Defence of Scientific Realism*. Oxford: Oxford University Press.

Linde K., Berner M.M., and Kriston L. (2008). "St John's wort for Major Depression". *Cochrane Database of Systematic Reviews*, 4.

Luhmann, N. (1986). "The Autopoiesis of Social Systems." In: F. Geyer, and J. van der Zouwen eds. *Sociocybernetic Paradoxes*. London: Sage.

Luhmann, N. (1989). *Ecological Communication*. Cambridge: Polity.

Luhmann, N. (1995). *Social Systems*. Stanford: Stanford University Press.

Mackenzie, K.D. (2006). The LAMPE Theory of Organizational Leadership. In: Francis Yammarino and Fred Dansereau eds. *Multi-Level Issues in Social Systems (Research in Multi Level Issues, Volume 5)*. Bingley, UK: Emerald Publishing. pp. 345–428.

Mandelbrot, B.B. (1982). *The Fractal Geometry of Nature*. Cranbury, NJ: Freeman.

Martin, W.M. (1997). *Idealism and Objectivity: Understanding Fichte's Jena Project*. Stanford: Stanford University Press.

Maturana, H.R. and Varela, F.J. (1980). "Autopoiesis and Cognition: the realization of the living." In: R.S. Cohen and M.W. Wartofsky eds. *Boston Studies in the Philosophy of Science*. Dordrecht: Reidel.

Maturana, H.R. and Varela, F.J. (1987). *The Tree of Knowledge: the biological roots of human understanding*. Boston: Shambala.

Mayer, J. and Salovey, P. (1997). What is Emotional Intelligence? In: P. Salovey and D. Sluyter eds. *Emotional Development and Emotional Intelligence: Educational Implications*. New York: Basic Books. pp. 3–31.

McDonough, W. and Braungart, M. (1998). The Next Industrial Revolution. *The Atlantic Monthly*. October, pp. 82–92.

McKelvey, B. (2004). Toward a Complexity Science of Entrepreneurship. *Journal of Business Venturing*, 19, pp. 313–341.

Meadows, D.H., Meadows, D.L., Randers, J., and Behrens, W.W. (1972). *The Limits to Growth*. New York: Universe Books.

Merchant, C. (1983). *The Death of Nature: women, ecology and the scientific revolution*. New York: Harper and Row.

Mitchell, M. (2009). *Complexity: a guided tour*. Oxford: Oxford University Press.

Montaigne, M. (1993). *Essays*. London: Penguin Books.

Morgan, C. (1966). *R.S. Thomas: Identity, Environment and Deity.* Manchester: Manchester University Press.

Mumford, L. (1946). *Values for survival: Essays, addresses and letters on politics and education.* New York: Harcourt, Brace and Co.

Naess, A. (1990). *Ecology, community and lifestyle.* Cambridge: Cambridge University Press.

Natural Step. (2010). *The Natural Step.* Stockholm: The Natural Step. Available at <http://www.naturalstep.org/>. [Accessed December 2010].

Needham, J. (2004). *Science and Civilisation in China: volume 7, the social background; part 2, general conclusions and reflections.* K.G. Robinson ed. Cambridge: University of Cambridge Press.

Needham, J. and Wang, L. (1954). Science and Civilisation in China. *1 Introductory Orientations.* Cambridge: Cambridge University Press.

NEF. (2010). *NEF — Economics as if people mattered.* London: New Economics Foundation. Available at <http://www.neweconomics.org/> [Accessed December 2010].

NHS. (2009). *Our Natural Health Service: the role of the natural environment in maintaining healthy lives.* Sheffield: Natural England. Available at <http://www.naturalengland.org.uk/Images/nhsmanifesto_tcm6-12022.pdf> [Accessed December 2010].

Nierenberg, D. (Ed.) (2006). *The State of the World 2006: the challenge of Global Sustainability.* London: Earthscan.

Niiniluoto, I. (2002). *Critical Scientific Realism.* Oxford: Oxford University Press.

Norberg, J. and Cumming, G. (2008). *Complexity Theory for a Sustainable Future (Complexity in Ecological Systems).* New York: Columbia University Press.

Nussbaum, M.C. (2011). *Creating Capabilities: The Human Development Approach.* Cambridge, Massachusetts: Harvard University Press.

Obama, B.H. (2009). *President Barack Obama's Inaugural Address.* Washington: The White House. Available at http://www.whitehouse.gov/blog/inaugural-address/ [Accessed June 2011].

Olssen, M. (2008). "Foucault as Complexity Theorist: Overcoming the problems of classical philosophical analysis." *Educational Philosophy and Theory,* 40(1), pp. 96–117.

OPT. (2010). *Optimum Population Trust: towards environmentally sustainable populations.* Manchester: Optimum Population Trust. Available at <http://www.optimumpopulation.org/index.html> [Accessed December 2010].

Orbach, Y. and Liedtke, C. (1998). *Eco-Management Accounting in Germany: Concepts and Practical Implementation.* Wuppertal: Wuppertal

Institute for Climate Change. Available at <http://www.wupperinst. org/uploads/tx_wibeitrag/WP88.pdf> [Accessed December 2010].

Orr, D. (1992). *Ecological Literacy: Education and the Transition to a Post-modern World.* New York: State University of New York.

Oslo Declaration. (2005). *Oslo Declaration on Sustainable Consumption.* Life Cycle Approaches to Sustainable Consumption Project. Available at <http://www.oslodeclaration.org/> [Accessed August 2010].

PAE. (2010*). Real-World Economics Review.* Paris: Post-Autistic Economics Network. Available at <http://www.paecon.net> [Accessed December 2010].

Parker, R.H. and Yamey, B.S. (eds.) (1994). *Accounting History: some British Contributions.* Oxford: Oxford University Press.

Penrose, E.T. (1965 [1959]). *The Theory of the Growth of the Firm.* Oxford: Oxford University Press.

Penrose, R. (1989). *The Emperor's New Mind: concerning computers, minds, and the laws of physics.* London: Vintage.

Pepper, D. (1996). *Modern Environmentalism.* London: Routledge.

Percival, I. (1992). "Chaos: a science for the real world." In: N. Hall, ed. *The New Scientist Guide to Chaos.* London: Penguin, 1992, pp. 11–21.

Pfeffer, J. and Salancik, G.R. (2003 [1978]). *The External Control of Organizations: A Resource Dependence Perspective.* Palo Alto, CA: Stanford University Press.

Pimentel, D. (2007). *Food, Energy, and Society, 3rd ed.* New York: CRC Press.

Polanyi, K. (2001 [1944]). *The Great Transformation: The Political and Economic Origins of Our Time.* Boston: Beacon Press.

Prigogine, I. (1997). *The End of Certainty: time, chaos, and the new laws of nature.* New York: Free Press.

Prigogine, I. and Stengers, I. (1985). *Order out of Chaos: man's new dialogue with nature.* London: Flamingo.

Ramalingam, B. and Jones, H. (2008). *Working Paper 285. Exploring the Science of Complexity: Ideas and implications for development and humanitarian efforts.* London: Overseas Development Institute.

Resalliance. (2010). *Resilience Alliance.* Stockholm: Stockholm Resilience Center. Available at <http://www.resalliance.org/> [Accessed December 2010].

Rocheleau, D. (1999). "Beyond Duelling Determinisms: Toward Complex, Humane and Just Ecologies." *Human Ecology Review,* 6(2), pp. 116–120.

Rosenberg, E.L. (2005). Mindfulness and Consumerism. In: T. Kasser and A.D. Kanner, eds. *Psychology and Human Culture.* Washington: American Psychological Association, pp. 107–125.

Rugemer, C. (2008). "An Increasingly Blurred Borderline." *Research*EU: the magazine of the European research area*, November, p. 4.

Sahlins, M. (1968). Notes on the original affluent society. In: R.B. Lee and I. De Vore eds., *Man the Hunter*, pp. 85–89. Chicago: Aldine.

Sahlins, M. (2003). *Stone Age Economics, 2nd ed.* London: Routledge.

Sale, K. (1985). *Dwellers in the Land: the regional vision.* San Francisco: Sierra Club.

Schumacher, E.F. (1973). *Small is beautiful: economics as if people mattered.* London: Blond & Briggs.

SEEA. (2003). *The Handbook of National Accounting: Integrated Environmental and Economic Accounting 2003.* New York: United Nations et al.

Senge, P. (1998). Through the eye of the needle. In: Gibson. R. ed. *Rethinking the Future.* London: Nicholas Brealey, pp. 122–146.

Smith, A. (2007 [1776]). *An Inquiry into the Nature and Causes of the Wealth of Nations Volume I.* New York: Cosimo Publications.

Speth, J.G. (2008). *The Bridge at the End of the World: Capitalism, the Environment, and crossing from Crisis to Sustainability.* New Haven: Yale University Press.

Stead, J.G. and Stead, W.E. (1992). *Management for a Small Planet.* Thousand Oaks, California: Sage.

Stein, M. (2008). "The 1% that changes everything." *Research*EU: the magazine of the European research area*, November, pp. 14–15.

Steiner, A. (2009). Countries move toward more sustainable ways to roll back malaria. *Joint news release 4th Meeting of the Conference of the Parties to the UNEP-Linked Stockholm Convention on Persistent Organic Pollutants*, eds. 6th May. Geneva/Nairobi/Washington DC: WHO/ UNEP GEF.

Stewart, I. (1989). *Does God play Dice?* Cambridge, MA: Blackwell.

Strogatz, S. (2004). *Sync: the emerging science of spontaneous order.* London: Penguin.

Taylor, A.F. and Kuo, F.E. (2009). "Children with Attention Deficits Concentrate Better after a Walk in the Park." *Journal of Attention Disorders*, 12(5), pp. 402–409.

Thompson, K. (2008). "Historicity and Transcendentality: Foucault, Cavaillès, and the Phenomenology of the Concept." *History and Theory*, 47, pp. 1–18.

Tierney, J. (2007). *Fateful Voice of a Generation Still Drowns Out Real Science.* New York: New York Times, 5th June.

UN. (1972). *Declaration of the United Nations Conference on the Human Environment.* New York: United Nations. Available at <http://www.

References   **347**

unep.org/Documents.Multilingual/Default.asp?documentid=97&arti-
cleid=1503> [Accessed October 2010].

UN. (2010). *Global Compact.* New York: United Nations. Available at
<http://www.unglobalcompact.org/> [Accessed December 2010].

UNCSD. (2010). *More people, more consumption, finite planet: demo-
graphics, development and decoupling.* UN Commission on Sustainable
Development. Available at <http://www.un.org/esa/dsd/newsmedi/
nm_pdfs/csd-18/pr_scp.pdf> [Accessed August 2010].

UNCTAD. (2008). *Least Developed Countries Report 2008.* New York:
United Nations Conference on Trade and Development.

UNEP. (1999). *Global Environment Outlook 2000.* Nairobi: United Nations
Environment Programme.

UNEP. (2010). *UNEP Year Book 2010: New Science and Developments
in Our Changing Environment.* Geneva: United Nations Environment
Programme.

Vallega, A. (2005). "Diversity: A Multi-faceted Concept". In: G. Bellezza,
L. Ayo and D. Bissell, eds. *International Workshop Cultures and Civilisations for Human Development, Rome, 12–14 December.* Rome: International Geographical Union.

Van Oosterhout, J. and Heugens, P.M.A.R. (2006). *Much Ado About Nothing: a conceptual critique of CSR.* Report reference ERS-2006-040-
ORG. Rotterdam: Erasmus Research Institute of Management.

Wang, J. (2008). Marketing Channel Sustainable Development on Self-
organization. *International Journal of Business and Management,*
August, pp 157–162.

WBCSD. (2010). *Vision 2025: the new agenda for business.* Geneva:
World Business Council for Sustainable Development. Available
at <http://www.wbcsd.org/web/projects/BZrole/Vision2050-FullRe-
port_Final.pdf> [Accessed October 2010].

Westbrook, R. (1991). *John Dewey and American Democracy.* Ithaca: Cor-
nell University Press.

Wheatley, M.J. (1994). *Leadership and the New Science.* San Francisco:
Berret-Koehler.

Whitehead, A.N. (1927). *Science and the Modern World.* London:
Cambridge University Press.

Wilson, E.O. (1998). *Consilience: The unity of knowledge.* London: Little,
Brown and Company.

Wilson, E.O. (1984). *The Biophilia Hypothesis.* Cambridge, Massachusetts:
Harvard University Press.

Winston, R. (2003). *Human Instinct: how our primeval impulses shape our
modern lives.* London: Bantam Books.

348   *Intrinsic Sustainable Development*

Worldwatch. (2010). *State of the World 2010: Transforming Cultures.* Washington DC: Worldwatch Institute.

Yue, P. (2011). Ecological Wisdom of the Ages. *People's Daily* (overseas edition), January 11th.

Zhao, T. (2005). *The Tianxia System: An Introduction to the Philosophy of a World Institution.* Nanjing: Jiangsu Jiaoyu Chubanshe.

INDEX

350   *Index*

Index   **351**

352 *Index*

Index   **353**

Lightning Source UK Ltd.
Milton Keynes UK
UKHW021831150720
366613UK00012B/282